INDEPENDENT MONTHLY LITERARY MAGAZINE

Adelaide

REVISTA LITERÁRIA INDEPENDENTE MENSAL

ADELAIDE

Independent Monthly Literary Magazine
Revista Literária Independente Mensal
Year III, Number 14, July 2018
Ano III, Número 14, julho de 2018

ISBN-13: 978-1-949180-15-2
ISBN-10: 1-949180-15-8

Adelaide Literary Magazine is an independent international monthly publication, based in New York and Lisbon. Founded by Stevan V. Nikolic and Adelaide Franco Nikolic in 2015, the magazine's aim is to publish quality poetry, fiction, nonfiction, artwork, and photography, as well as interviews, articles, and book reviews, written in English and Portuguese. We seek to publish outstanding literary fiction, nonfiction, and poetry, and to promote the writers we publish, helping both new, emerging, and established authors reach a wider literary audience.

A Revista Literária Adelaide é uma publicação mensal internacional e independente, localizada em Nova Iorque e Lisboa. Fundada por Stevan V. Nikolic e Adelaide Franco Nikolic em 2015, o objectivo da revista é publicar poesia, ficção, não-ficção, arte e fotografia de qualidade assim como entrevistas, artigos e críticas literárias, escritas em inglês e português. Pretendemos publicar ficção, não-ficção e poesia excepcionais assim como promover os escritores que publicamos, ajudando os autores novos e emergentes a atingir uma audiência literária mais vasta.

(http://adelaidemagazine.org)

Published by: Adelaide Books, New York
244 Fifth Avenue, Suite D27
New York NY, 10001
e-mail: info@adelaidemagazine.org
phone: (917) 727 8907
http://adelaidebooks.org

FOUNDERS / FUNDADORES
Stevan V. Nikolic & Adelaide Franco Nikolic

EDITOR IN CHIEF / EDITOR-CHEFE
Stevan V. Nikolic
editor@adelaidemagazine.org

ASSOCIATE EDITOR
Raymond Fenech

MANAGING DIRECTOR / DIRECTORA EXECUTIVA
Adelaide Franco Nikolic

GRAPHIC & WEB DESIGN
Adelaide Books DBA, New York

CONTRIBUTING AUTHORS IN THIS ISSUE

Brenna Carroll, Terry Sanville, Bhavika Sicka, Paul Bentham, Thomas Healy, Mackenzie Gasperson, D. Matt McGowan, Jeff Kulik, Ana Vidosavljevic, Matt Ingoldby, Edward D. Hunt, Maureen Grace, Elaine Rosenberg Miller, Keith Jenereaux, Richard Luftig, Dave Barrett, George Carlisle, Virginia Hoeck, Ruth Deming, Susan Stacy, David H. Miller, Henry Simpson, Thad Elmore, Don Thompson, Ross Hardy, Peter Leight, John Horvath, Jean-Mark Sens, Belinda Subraman, Edward Bonner, John Grey, George Korolog, David Ryan Palmer, Anthony Lawrence, Ralph Geeplay, Jan Napier, Boris Kokotov, Lauren Collins, Anna Evas, Robert René Galván, Riley Bounds, Emily Brummett, Robert Eastwood, Andrew Spence, Mathieu Cailler, Nancy Nau Sullivan, Dufflyn Lammers, John Walters, Jeffrey James Higgins, Judson Blake, Leslie Tucker, Beth Mead, Emily Peña Murphey, Mike Dillon, Leah Sindel, Debra Neumann, Serene Jansen .

CONTENTS / CONTEÚDOS

POETRY

NEW TITLES

Editor's Notes

Stevan V. Nikolic

NEW BEGINNING

"You know Pastor, baking is a real art. Especially bread baking. There is something so divine about it. It is a pure alchemy. And all alchemical elements are there: flour that comes from the earth and represents material, water that you mix with flour to make the dough, air released by the yeast fermentation that makes dough rise, fire that bakes the bread. It is fantastic. And the aroma of hot bread released during baking is the most pleasant fragrance for our senses. Think about that for a moment, Pastor. Any food aroma that we like, no matter how much we like it, gets overwhelming after a while, and we open the kitchen windows and close kitchen doors so the smell doesn't get into the living room. Any smell, but the smell of freshly baked bread. Did you ever hear anybody complain about the smell of baked bread? Nobody, Pastor! Nobody. You hear people complaining about their neighbors frying fish, roasting pork, barbecuing sausages, but nobody ever complains about the smell of baked bread. And you know why? Because it is divine. It is magic – the magic of the craft."
— **Stevan V. Nikolic, Truth According to Michael**

"I think that both our lives and the potential directions our lives may go are predestined. By using our free will in making our life choices, we do nothing else but picking up one of many already predestined options. To us, it seems like we were making the decision, while in reality, we just selected one of many possibilities that were already a part of our destiny." "Don't you think God is so powerful that he can make us believe that we made some choices, when in actuality, he had made a choice for us?"
— **Stevan V. Nikolic, Truth According to Michael**

"Strangely enough, he didn't feel any guilt for separating himself from his past. Five years ago, he clearly heard in his dream a message brought to him by Archangel Michael from the God Almighty, telling him he should get up and leave everything behind; that his place was not there; that it was time to go in search for his true self and for his true destiny. Now, five years after, he was sitting in the Bowery chapel, a broken and homeless man, still trying to find that which he was looking for. But he didn't regret anything he had done in those five years. In his mind, it wasn't his doing. He sincerely believed that he surrendered his own will to the will of God and that everything that happened to him, good or bad, had to happen for some reason. It was God's doing. It was his destiny. He just had to figure out why."
— **Stevan V. Nikolic, Truth According to Michael**

"I was going after a woman believing that the key is in being with her. But the key is in writing about her. The key is in words and words are in me. Longing for her is just an impulse for words to come out. And the whole purpose is for words to come out. Words are important. Words about love. About life." — **Stevan V. Nikolic, Truth According to Michael**

"How far we can go with our liberty of conscience, without offending God, and disturbing the natural order of things..." — **Stevan V. Nikolic, Truth According to Michael**

"Why do you want so much this new beginning? Do you think the new beginning will postpone the end? Are you afraid of the end? Are you afraid of death Michael?" **(Ch.35)"**
— **Stevan V. Nikolic, Truth According to Michael**

AFTER THE MARTYRS
by Brenna Carroll

Is this blood, or is it wine? Am I damned or am I divine?

The wild wind whistled through her nostrils, warming itself for her lungs, and followed the breath in front of it out by the same route. Sister Ida followed her own route, weakly cutting through the wind on her way to the garden. She prayed as she walked, steps keeping rhythm to the Hail Mary, counting the rosary beads in time to her breath. The sky frowned down upon the sister, mirroring her own expression of slight contempt and vague discontent, but its dismal countenance was given away when the wind changed direction as if to aid the sister along on her path.

The garden appeared unseasonably vibrant against the grim backdrop of the sky. Sister Ida's small frame could be seen meandering among the rows almost methodically, following a pattern known only to her. In closer quarters, one would find the glow on her bony cheeks contrasted with the gauntness of her face. She brushed the leaves of each plant with delicate fingers as she wandered past, debauched greenery feasting on her labors and that of others. The place smelled earthy, clean and alive all at the same time.

It was an age without martyrs. Persecution had passed and the time when one could seek salvation in the coliseum or on the cross had drifted away like smoke off a funeral pyre.

That is not to say the world looked any different than it had before; it had happened subtly and all at once. One day, the world woke up to the news that Emperor Constantine had declared Rome Christian⬛ there could be no more martyrs, as the persecutor had become the proselytizer. Eight centuries had gone on in this way. The world was the same, but the people had changed.

One would think that the world would rejoice after the martyrs, but this posed certain problems for religious folk. How could one purport to follow Christ's path if one could not follow it to the end? How could one prove one's absolute devotion to the faith if one could not die for it? Anything worth living for is also worth dying for.

Some tried to do it anyway. They would beg Roman soldiers to murder them in the street, commit crimes unscrupulously in order to suffer the punishment, jump in front of carriages and dance into lion cages. Then there were those who turned it inward. They starved themselves, beat themselves, stopped sleeping but never took fate into their own hands. They let nature do their work for them, proving to the world that they did not need the world. Martyrs for the church, perhaps not. Martyrs for themselves, absolutely.

Sister Ida worked in time to her hunger. That ever-present beast was both her pride and her thorn. It was her strength and her weakness. Strength, because she could deny herself such a basic need and defy her own humanity; weakness, because her mind was consumed with thoughts of food instead of thoughts of God. It occurred to her now, as it had so many times before when her will began to wane, that she needed to further purify herself.

Heroic hunger is how she liked to think of it. She was not entirely free of the touch of vanity, and for this she felt sinful, but it was minor in comparison to her larger goal. Sister Ida wanted to escape her own human nature. The world chased her through her nightmares, pursuing her ceaselessly and attempting to force its cares and wants and desires upon her, but Sister Ida was stronger than the world. She had long since forsaken it, declaring starvation her salvation.

The sister departed from the garden and thought of salvation as she walked. Salvation was always on her mind. Her hands trembled softly, clasped tight together. Salvation was present in the habit she wore, the words she spoke, the garden she tended and the paths she walked. Salvation was present in her mind and in her hunger, proving to the world that she did not need the world. Salvation is what kept her working every day to keep the devil at bay.

She soldiered down the path back to the convent, imagining herself as one of the old Athletes of Christ, heroically perishing in the coliseum in a crowd of beasts. Not just beasts of the animal kingdom, but of the Roman one as well. Pagan beasts, urging on the slaughter of the righteous and buying themselves a seat in Hell just as the martyrs earned themselves a seat in Heaven.

Ahead of her but on the same path, Sister Ida saw a raggedy dog. His ears shot up in alertness as she approached, and his tail began to wag. Sister Ida stretched out her hand to let him smell it, and the dog tentatively but amiably came forward to lick her hand.

"What a sweet creature of God you are!" she exclaimed, slightly shocked at the sound of her own voice. It was hoarse from disuse, as she often fell into long stretches of silence when contemplating salvation.

The sister offered a piece of bread to the dog, which he first looked at skeptically, but, driven by hunger, snatched from her hand and ran off. She felt a certain sense of pride that she was unaccustomed to: She had given another creature what he needed to live for another day. Then she mentally reprimanded herself for indulging in such hubris. Only God provides for his Creation. We are just His vessels. If He had

wanted that dog to die, He would not have made our paths cross.

Sister Ida hurried into the convent so as not to be late for evening Mass. Shuffling past the other habits she found her spot near the altar.

"Sister, have you been denying yourself food again? You look like it," said Sister Adelaide.

"I have, thank you," said Sister Ida, trying to hide her blush and banish prideful thoughts. Regardless of her defenses, a whisper of satisfaction drifted in.

"If only we could all strive for such purity as you. I shall give you a special place in my prayers today to aid you in your journey to salvation."

Sister Ida nodded.

The priest started Mass, the sisters bowing their heads, kneeling, standing, kneeling, standing, crossing themselves, bowing heads again, as if it were all some bizarre dance. The priest began his homily:

"Only the Lord can die on the cross. Only the Lord can forgive us our sins. Only the Lord can put Death in chains. That is the truth we hold in our hearts as Christians, that the Lord is our one true salvation. But oughtn't we to show Him we are worthy of His love? Oughtn't we do our part in pursuing salvation?"

Sister Ida, much to her chagrin, could not give her attention to the homily. Her thoughts were instead occupied with yearnings for food and the pangs of hunger. She focused her entire willpower on the homily, but it would falter as soon as her stomach growled.

"In the days of the persecution, we could follow Christ's path to the very end. We could give ourselves up for the Church, and it was a beautiful thing. But in our time, that is not an option. They looked Death in the face, but in a way, we face a more difficult battle. We look Life in the face.

"So what is there left for us to do? Are we living in an age without salvation? Are we all damned because we were born too late? No, we are not; do not doubt God like that. We face a bigger battle, like I said, one against ourselves. To show we are worthy of salvation, we must deny ourselves the sinful, base desires which afflict us as human beings▯ we must transcend our humanity. We must show we are ready for Heaven, ready to accept God by casting off all that could distract us from Him.

"Look at Sister Ida," the priest said, and this time she was unable to stop the flow of redness on her cheeks. Two thoughts snuck in through her barrier: one of pride, and one of food. She harshly reprimanded herself for allowing these unholy thoughts in when she was being praised for doing just the opposite.

"She is truly allowing herself to be a vessel of the Lord. She does not think of hunger, she does not think of pain. She resists herself to show the Savior that she is ready to go beyond herself."

Sister Ida could not follow the rest of the homily. Specters of hunger and pride whirled around her head, holding her captive and telling her she was a fraud. Images of bread, of milk, of the garden, of the dog, of the Eucharist, of crucifixes, of the grave floated in front of her eyes. The more harshly she judged herself the more unrelenting these specters became. She felt a dismal pang in her chest▯ how could she be a true vessel of the Lord if her thoughts were held captive by worldly desires?

That night, the Sister resolved to strengthen her devotion. She was going to eat less, pray more fervently and clean out her heart to make room for Jesus. No matter the cost, she would be saved.

The room is dark, lit by candles in each corner. A table sits stolidly in the middle of the room, wooden walls and a dirt floor, messy in a quaint kind of way, and a large man sits at the table. A young girl, with eyes and freckles like the man's and startlingly black hair, sits across from him, appearing to be in deep contemplation. She cannot be older than twelve. There is a plate of food in front of the man and the child. The man eats hastily while the child pushes food around on the plate with a spoon.

"Ida, you have got to eat. Why are you not eating?"

"Pa, the priest told me the devil hides in every bite. I will not eat. The priest told me that I would get to Heaven that way."

"That priest is full of horse shit, Ida. How are you supposed to have the energy to pray or do charity or do any of the things you say you want to do if you don't eat? Jesus ate. The apostles ate. You can't devote your life to God if you're dead. I can't bear to see you turn into a walking corpse. Please, just eat something, Ida."

The door opens and a shaggy gray dog patters in. Suddenly, the room disappears and the floor falls out from under them, and Ida is sent plummeting down, down, down to who knows where. Terror makes a fist in her chest as she realizes this is not real, but she does not know what it is, and her screams are ripped from her mouth by the wind, or maybe they are not and the wind just mirrors her fear. Objects enter her field of vision: the dog, the Eucharist, and a Bible.

Sister Ida started awake, feeling the phantom terror still clenched in her chest. She promptly arose, looked around to ensure that she had a solid grip on her surroundings, and went over to the sink to wash her face. The water felt alive against her dry skin. She dressed, and leaving the convent, traipsed through the early morning darkness like a thin, gray ghost. It was far too early for the others to be up, but she took satisfaction in going to pray while the others slept. She immediately felt guilty because of this self-satisfaction.

Coming to the chapel, she knelt and blessed herself before she took a seat in one of the pews. There were always candles illuminating the interior of the chapel, which flickered at this new presence. Dropping down to her knees, she started the rosary, but to her consternation, she was unable to focus. No matter the mental barriers she put up, thoughts of hunger crept in to plague her with images of gluttony and sin. This was especially distressing in light of last night's dream, which she tried and failed to erase from her psyche.

The body and blood of Christ. The body and blood of Christ! That is all my soul needs to live. To Hell with my body!

She finished her rosary and sat in silence for a moment. The world seemed to hold its breath at this time of day, and Sister Ida held hers with it.

The growing light alerted the Sister that it was time for breakfast, so she rose, blessed herself, and made her way back to the convent.

It was not unusual for Sister Ida to leave some food on her plate, but this morning she left over half of her bread loaf untouched. Sister Millicent noticed and came over to where Sister Ida was sitting listlessly.

She asked Sister Ida about her hunger, and went on about how she "could never be as devout as you." In response, Sister Ida got up from the table and, grabbing the remaining bread, left the convent again in the direction of the garden.

On the well-worn path, Sister Ida again encountered the gray, scruffy dog. She approached him and offered him her uneaten bread, which he graciously accepted and promptly ran off with. His appearance struck her as different somehow, and she could not put her finger on it exactly. It was noticeable yet discreet. The Sister realized that, like her, the dog was gaunter than at their last meeting. The both of them took up less space in the world.

The freshness of the garden was a welcome reprieve for Sister Ida's tired mind. She strolled through and paid special attention to the small details she usually would have ignored. This was the only break she felt justified in taking from thinking about salvation.

The flowers in the garden were spotted with tiny bugs⊠ the type of which Sister Ida could not identify⊠ that formed tiny societies in their tiny worlds. The Sister noticed the way certain plants clustered together and others stretched away from each other towards the sun, while still others used each other as support to reach towards the light. Dew reflected light off stalks of grass like a million tiny mirrors, and Sister Ida thought that this must be what the Kingdom of Heaven felt like.

What must a martyr feel like? she thought, and craved that unreachable distinction. It was an

age without martyrs, so the righteous could no more die righteously than common sinners. Sister Ida contemplated her own battle, herself against hunger and gluttony, and she shivered. She had a long way to go.

"I think of food constantly. I reprimand myself, and the feeling intensifies. I restrict more, and the feeling still intensifies. What am I doing wrong?"

"When you think of becoming gluttonous, do you follow that desire?" asked Sister Ida's confessor.

"No. But what if I did some day?"

"If you have faith in your heart, you will not give in."

"I do, but I think about food so much that I cannot even think about God. What kind of Sister am I, concerned more with my physical survival than my spirit?"

"Sister, if you do not follow these urges, then you are doing everything right. Confess your gluttonous thoughts regularly and Christ will forgive you. Follow your current path and you will be like Christ."

Sister Ida would have stormed off, but she was too tired, so she wandered away feebly instead. She made her way to her room and slammed it shut, bursting into tears on her bed. She could not understand why no one would help her. Maybe my Pa was right! she thought frantically, though she knew she could not make herself believe it. Starvation had become her path to salvation.

With a pang of guilt, she remembered that raggedy dog. Grabbing her leftover rations, she ran out of the convent to see if he was by the path to the garden. He was, and he looked worse than ever: his eyes had sunken in slightly, his ribs were visible through his fur and his coat looked dull and dirty. Guilt overcame Sister Ida and she collapsed on the ground next to the dog, heaving from both her exertion and her emotions, and remained there for a good while. Faceless shame flooded her mind, spread through her body and wrapped round her soul until she felt she was aflame. She leapt up to return to the convent and the dog was gone, along with the rations.

Sister Ida took the long way back to the convent both because she was tired and because she did not want the other Sisters to see her tear-sodden face. It was at this time that she detected a faint, smoky odor. She kept walking, and the odor grew stronger. She rounded the corner and the convent came into view. She gasped.

Flames were leaping out from the near side of the convent, and the air was filled with smoke and the frantic cries of Sisters and authoritative shouts from the priest and the awful sound of wood snapping in heat. Sister Ida was mesmerized for a moment at the terrible majesty of it all: the flares leapt and burst and twirled the way she and the other girls in the village had danced as children. The fire grew and shrank and consumed and flickered with abandon. She could not help but stare until another Sister came running up to her.

"Sister, grab a pail! Help us!"

Sister Ida grabbed a pail but was unable to carry it very far. She tried to help them fill the pails but she was too weak to operate the pump. For the first time in her life, Sister Ida felt powerless.

What caused it? Another Sister, frustrated at her inability to be as disciplined as Sister Ida, had tried to burn herself with a candle in her room, dropped it onto the bed by mistake, and the whole place had gone up in flames.

For the next several days, Sister Ida did not leave her room except for Mass and prayers. Guilt draped over her like a blanket, a heavy blanket that she could hardly move or breathe under, and smothered her resolve.

In this time, Sister Ida became weak, so weak she was unable to attend Mass or receive the Eucharist. Some good the body and blood of Christ is going to do for my soul if I cannot accept it. She was at the point of death, yet she still refused food, and the Abbess had no choice but to allow her to pursue her chosen path of salvation. A sense of unease had entered her mind.

Finally, the sun came out, and she arose from her cocoon. It was still cloudy and a little cold, but she could stand in her own skin again. With the return of the sun came the return of concerns and worries. Sister Ida fled the safety of her room to find the dog.

It took her some time to find him. She searched the well-worn path first, then the long way to the garden, and found him about halfway along the path. Revulsion rose in her throat as she realized he was limp and still, and the Sister fell to her knees in deference to this lost life. Guilt tried to overcome her again, but instead a primal terror sparked in her chest and travelled up her spine and filled her head with thoughts of her own death. Her own funeral rose before her eyes, and it was not far away. It was lonely and cold and morbid, like the poor dog's. No matter the cause she was living for, she was just as fragile as this dog, placed in the world so tenuously. The smallest wind could wipe her out. With this newfound sense of mortality, Sister Ida resolved to live her fragile, fleeting, ephemeral life for herself. She could not be a martyr for Christ, but did He really need any? Instead, she could be her own martyr.

Anything worth dying for is also worth living for.

Taking a thing worth dying for and turning it into a life worth living is a difficult exercise in meaningful existence. Sister Ida found herself caught between two sides of herself: the pious ascetic, who gives up everything she has and then still more, and the sensible sister, who respects the limits of the human body. Not being one for moderation, she tried to do both but found that her heady enthusiasm had left her and she could not do that.

Coming in from the garden one morning, she seated herself at the table, slightly away from the others, for breakfast. Tentatively, she began to eat, and tried to ignore the incredulous glances from the other sisters. Sister Ida, that paragon of self-control and virtue, giving in to hunger!

Sister Ida looked down at her half-eaten bread and thought to bring it to the dog, but, with a pang of guilt, remembered his lifeless body in the sun. She no longer took that path to the garden.

Suddenly, something changed in her: her spirit had rebelled. Her spirit wanted to be let free, and she had the urge to jump on the table and shriek, but she reined her soul in. For the first time in her life, she felt like she had a choice.

Only God can die on the cross.

"I do not feel like I have to starve myself anymore. I do not know why, but I do not even feel guilty. What is happening to me?"

"This is all a matter of willpower and faith," her confessor said. "Everyone is afflicted with irreverent thoughts. The holy can suppress them."

"Does that mean I am no longer holy? Because I simply do not even feel all that impressed with the mass anymore. It all seems pointless."

"Have you done anything to let the devil in lately?"

"I have been eating more. But not in a gluttonous way."

"Well, this is going to be a matter between you and Jesus. Pray to him and he will guide you back to the holy path."

It struck Sister Ida that no answers were to be found there. She had to search for them herself. Frustrated, she took her irreverent thoughts and left her confessor.

The Communion song rang out in the chapel, and the Sisters sang and swayed along with the familiar tune. Sister Ida sat in her usual pew, near the front, but she was deep in thought. Irreverent thoughts plagued her mind but she was not especially concerned; rather, she took them and ran with them in the empty spaces of her mind where personalities bloom and life begins.

Sister Ida's row stood and lined up to take the Eucharist. The sister was still somewhere else and scrambled to keep up with the rest. Still, a seed of discontent was growing in her heart.

The body and blood of Christ. That's all I'm supposed to need to live. But I am a human being! If that dog could not survive on what God provided alone, then how can I?

Sister Ida stood next in line for the Eucharist, and a thought suddenly struck her with such force she lost her breathe: she was free. She was her own master and she was free.

Is this blood, or is it wine? Am I damned or am I divine?

Ida looked the priest in the eye, turned around, and left the chapel.

About the Author:

Brenna Carroll is a senior studying history at the George Washington University, particularly medieval female hagiographies and the saints that inspired them. She is especially interested in the intersection of asceticism, sanctity and female rebellion.

THRIFT SHOP SWAN

by Terry Sanville

Eugene folded his umbrella, stomped on the welcome mat, then entered the Goodwill Store.

The floor manager, Mingo, motioned him over. "If I were you, I wouldn't go back there."

"Why? What's going on?

"The Zombie Lady's freakin' out."

Eugene looked to the rear of the shop. A crowd of women of all shades and ages surrounded several racks of clothing. Pants, blouses, jeans, dinner jackets, and even bras flew through the air. Animal grunts broke the silence.

"Cops?" Eugene asked.

"Yeah, I called 'em. Didn't want to, 'cause that lady's got enough troubles. She's quiet most of the time. I've never seen her this bad."

"Maybe she's off her meds."

Mingo grinned. "How the hell should I know? I don't check prescriptions."

A police cruiser pulled off the boulevard into the parking lot, its roof lights flashing but no siren. Two officers in rain slickers eased through the front door and Mingo pointed. They moved forward and ordered the women to clear out. In a few minutes they led Zombie Lady outside, guided her into the squad car's rear seat, then drove away.

Eugene saw her every week or so, along narrow streets that ran through the old neighborhoods south of the Downtown. The first time she had almost run him over, moving like a sleepwalker on crank. Her dark eyes stared at something over the horizon, her face as white as a geisha's. She seldom looked at him, which felt strange since most street people treated Eugene as one of their own, and surely not as a retired school administrator. He liked his long-haired and bearded disguise.

She wore a full white evening gown, its ragged hem filthy from dragging the ground. Built like a young boy, she kept her red hair wrapped in a tight bun, carried a little girl's purse and a lace-fringed parasol.

"She crazy, you know," Chuntao, the pretty Chinese woman at Rainbow Donuts told him. "She stand in rain. I give her donut, free...but she no come inside."

"What's her name?" Eugene asked.

"Natalia, I think. She speak with accent...so not sure."

"She's a strange one."

"She look like girl, but she old. I tell by her eyes."

"Where does she live?"

"I think at Shelter, or under bridge."

After the thrift store incident, on his daily walks around town Eugene made up a short speech to tell the Zombie Lady, once he got up the nerve. After being retired for ten years and widowed for seven, talking with women had become harder, except maybe with Chuntao. But he searched for Natalia anyway, at Goodwill, UVS Thrift, The Hope Chest, and Fred & Betty's Secondhand. She looked intelligent, even in her spaced-out condition. But her eyes never seemed to quite focus.

"Why you care about crazy lady?" Chuntao asked. She poured him a third cup of coffee and leaned against the counter in the empty donut shop. "You think you save her? Be big hero? Forget it. She lost."

Eugene smiled and stared unseeing at the front page of the Wall Street Journal. "She's no more lost than I am. I wanted to be my wife's hero. But she died anyway. Once was enough."

"Not your fault...and...I don't believe you." Chuntao shook her head and returned to wiping the counter and refilling the sugars.

On a cloudy Monday, Natalia charged toward him on Pacific Street. He stood his ground. She continued on a collision course. Just before she smashed into him, she slowed, the impact gentle, with more bone than flesh. Eugene figured she weighed less than a hundred pounds. Her high-pitched scream made him jump.

"You're real," she said, looking into his eyes for the first time.

"Yes, of course. Why would you think differently?"

"I sometimes see...see people...like the ones following me. The voices tell me I should keep moving, run."

Eugene stared past her along the street, the sidewalk empty for blocks. "Yes, that would be frightening. But I must have scared them off. Look."

She turned slowly and followed his gaze. "They are gone. A big man like you would be fearsome while I am nothing. Sometimes, I'm not sure I'm even here. Am I here?"

Eugene abandoned his plan for making a speech. He grinned, reached forward and took her hand. "Yes, you are here." He felt her stiffen. Her breaths came faster. But she wouldn't release his hand.

"You must stop them from forcing me to practice. They will destroy me."

"Practice? Practice what?"

"I can't quite remember. But I know they do not want me to tell anyone. They say I will

suffer if I do. There is always one of them... watching."

"Hey listen, Chuntao at Rainbow is a friend of mine. Let's go there and get some donuts."

"I won't go inside."

"Why not?"

"Rats and bugs crawling everywhere."

"They aren't there when I go inside. Come on, have coffee with me."

Eugene pulled her gently along the street. They threaded their way through the neighborhood of dilapidated warehouses, muffler shops, and trailer parks until reaching the donut shop, at the junction of two broad boulevards.

Chuntao's eyes widened when they pushed through the door. "I see you find Natalia."

"We're here for some of your fine donuts, and maybe a little coffee."

Natalia clutched his arm in a vise-like grip and edged inside. They sat at a corner table next to the plate-glass window with traffic noiselessly blasting by outside. Chuntao brought two mugs and a coffee pot.

"May I have tea, please?" Natalia asked. "Some Lapsang Souchong would be wonderful."

Chuntao rolled her eyes but brought a teabag and hot water with honey to sweeten.

Eugene and Natalia sat looking at each other, not speaking, not forcing conversation. She smelled of sweat and unwashed clothes that had been rained on and had never fully dried. Chuntao served fresh donuts. Natalia nibbled on a plain cake, finishing only half of it.

"I'm sorry. I don't eat much, can't afford to gain weight."

She sipped her tea and continued to stare until standing abruptly.

"I must go, it's time for practice, time for practice."

"Practice what?" Eugene asked.

"I can't tell you. They will know."

She hurried from the shop. He watched her open-mouthed as she disappeared into the distance, her white gown bouncing as she walked.

"You do good," Chuntao said. "I never get her inside. I think she like you."

"How can you tell? She didn't say much of anything."

"You kind man. She will talk. You still have chance."

"Chance? What are you talking about?"

"You know, you know." Chuntao let out a high giggle and returned to her spot behind the counter.

After that day, whenever they met on the street, Natalia offered Eugene her hand or clutched his arm and they'd walk to Rainbow Donuts, sit without speaking in the late afternoon sun until she bolted for the outdoors. One evening, he checked under the Marsh Street Bridge and found her on a mound of dirty bedding, the river roaring not more than ten feet from where she slept. Eugene backed away, thought about how he might help. On a particularly stormy night he paid for a room at the Motel 6. He left her there watching a badly adjusted TV and fingering the dry clothes he had bought for her at Fred & Betty's Secondhand.

Two weeks went by without an encounter. Eugene checked all the thrift shops but couldn't find her, phoned the hospitals without success. He couldn't stop worrying about her safety: being raped by some homeless troll; caught by a flash flood and swept away; or attacked for no other reason than she was small, seemed frail, and an easy target.

The spring rains had slacked off when he caught up to Natalia. Mingo stopped him as he entered the Goodwill Store.

"Hey look, you know the Zombie Lady better than anybody that comes in here. Maybe you can get her to stop."

"What's she doing now?"

"She's tossin' the shoe section. Got the kids and their mothers in an uproar. If you can get her outta here, I won't call the cops."

Eugene crept toward the rear of the shop. Shoes flew through the air. A black stiletto-healed number slammed into a mirror, shattering it. Little kids and women screamed. Natalia moved along the shelves full of shoes, yanking pairs from their perch, grunting, then slinging them over her shoulder. She had cleared most of the women's selection and was working on the top shelf filled with the weird stuff that didn't belong in any particular category. She grabbed a pair of pink slippers with squared-off toes and stopped, then kicked off her flats, exposing raw feet, calloused, blistered, bones and toes badly deformed, with dried blood under the nails. She pulled on the slippers and wrapped and tied their ribbons tightly around her ankles. Standing, Natalia reached up and drew her filthy gown over her head. The crowd gasped. A pink leotard covered her upper body, breasts flattened by its elastic pressure. White tights encased her slender legs.

Mingo joined Eugene. "After she broke that mirror, I called the cops. They'll be here any minute. If you can get her outta here, I'm cool with it."

Eugene smiled. "No, let her dance. I'll talk to the Police and pay for that mirror."

Natalia had pushed herself up onto her toes, arms extended in a perfect "V" above her tilted head. She raised one leg and joined it to the other at the knee, balanced with no shaking, then moved rapidly across the floor, spinning, arms extended. Little kids from the toy section sat on the floor and formed a gallery of gawkers. They stared wide-eyed, smiling, while their mothers called to them to be still and watch.

Natalia danced with eyes half closed, moving from one position to the next, gracefully, fluidly, face fixed in a state of bliss. She moved along the shoe section aisle, threatening to crash into display racks, but always in control, her jumps perfectly executed, never a stumble or waver on the landings.

The thrift shop's front doors opened and two beefy patrolmen entered. Mingo hurried to intercept them as Natalia continued to dance before her spellbound audience. In a flurry of leaps and turns, she slowed to a kneeling position, then slid to the floor, eyes closed, hands clasped as if praying, her slender body still, at peace. The women clapped and the children joined in. Natalia rose to her full height and, with great dignity, made a deep curtsy. The little girls surrounded her, giggling, trying to copy her dance moves.

A cop stepped forward. "Excuse me, miss, you'll have to come with us."

Natalia backed against a display rack. "Father, I said I would practice more. I will...you'll see."

"It's okay, officer," Mingo said. "I'm not going to press charges for the broken mirror. You can let her go."

"I'm afraid not. We've received other complaints. This woman needs help."

The officers retrieved Natalia's gown, purse and shoes, escorted her outside to their patrol car. Eugene followed them.

"What are you going to do with her?" he asked.

"Are you a relative?" the cop said.

"No, just...just a friend...a good friend."

"They'll probably put her on a 72-hour psychiatric hold. You can call County Mental Health if you have questions. She'll be taken care of."

Natalia stared at him from the back of the car, her eyes clear, focused. A quiet smile of what might have been satisfaction creased her face. As Eugene walked home, he thought about how they might live together, how she could put on special performances, at schools, community arts events, show off her talents to those who would appreciate their beauty and grace. He tried building a story of hope for both of them.

Two days later, Eugene phoned Mental Health. Natalia had already been released to the streets. He searched all the places that she might hole up. As the weeks passed he slowly surrendered any chance of finding her.

"She out there somewhere," Chuntao told him. "I know you want to save her. But you lucky you not find her."

"Why the hell is that?" Eugene shot back, scowling.

"I say before, she crazy. She make you crazy, crazy sad. I want you stay normal. You my friend first."

"I haven't felt normal for a long time. Maybe I should start. And...and thank you."

Chuntao smiled coyly and refilled his coffee cup. He returned to reading the Wall Street Journal and she to wiping down the counter and refilling the sugars.

Months passed. One hot summer day, Eugene sat reading the L.A. Times. He let out a yell. Chuntao almost dropped a tray of donuts and hurried to his side.

"What wrong? You sick? You hurt? I call 911."

"No, I'm fine, I'm fine. But look." He pointed to a short column tucked away in the newspaper's back pages. A grainy image of Natalia stared back at them.

"What it say, what it say?" Chuntao demanded.

"Natalia was killed in a homeless camp far from here."

"I'm sorry, so sorry. But why she in paper? Like me, she nobody important."

"You're wrong...on both counts. It says here that she was considered a Prima Ballerina by dance critics about ten years ago, worked out of New York City and London until she disappeared from the stage."

"What happen to her?"

"Schizophrenia."

Chuntao shrugged. "What's that?"

"It's not important."

She frowned and reached for her counter rag.

"Wait a minute...wait." Eugene gulped his coffee and stared at his age-spotted hands. "It's very important. It's a sickness that strikes some sensitive young people. It smashes their brains with a sledgehammer and breaks them. They stumble through life looking for their own scattered pieces."

Chuntao stared at him, wide-eyed. "How...how you know?"

"I had to tell parents that pushing their kids to be the best doesn't always work." He banged his coffee mug down. "Fathers and mothers can carry the dark seeds of schizophrenia in their genes, and we don't know why."

"So?" Chuntao shrugged again. "Like I say, Natalia real crazy."

"Maybe it is crazy...to try and build beauty out of what rags you've got left." Eugene shook his head. "I'm glad I got to see her dance, even for just that one time. The thrift shop will never feel the same."

About the Author:

Terry Sanville lives in San Luis Obispo, California with his artist-poet wife (his in-house editor) and two plump cats (his in-house critics). He writes full time, producing short stories, essays, poems, and novels. Since 2005, his short stories have been accepted by more than 270 literary and commercial journals, magazines, and anthologies including The Potomac Review, The Bitter Oleander, Shenandoah, and The Saturday Evening Post. He was nominated twice for Pushcart Prizes for his stories "The Sweeper" and "The Garage." Terry is a retired urban planner and an accomplished jazz and blues guitarist – who once played with a symphony orchestra backing up jazz legend George Shearing.

BETWEEN THE SHADOW AND THE SOUL
by Bhavika Sicka

Shafiq stood overlooking the sprawling concrete wilderness that was Old City. The day was closing, and the muezzin's call to prayer could be heard wafting across terraces and mingling with the sonorous clanging of temple bells. In the gathering dusk, tea sellers poured frothing chai into earthen cups, and haleem vendors scooped out bowlfuls of steaming stew from large aluminum pots. Soon, the sun dipped below the western horizon, spreading its vermilion streaks across the sky, against which the minarets of the Charminar danced and blinked in the muted, nebulous glow, as they had always twinkled on evenings such as these for as long as Shafiq could remember. One of his life's only constants. Like his mother. And like Mehnoor.

Below, the pavement was still smeared reddish black with the blood of the goat that he had sacrificed this morning, a crusting carmine stain that had imprinted itself upon his mind's eye. He felt a dull throbbing in his temples, a heaviness that seemed to sweep over his being and soak into his very marrow. Trimming the lengthening ash of his cigarette against the outer edge of the parapet, he allowed his gaze to wander over to the haveli across the street its yellow sandstone walls chipping; its tall, majestic colonnades crumbling in disrepair and come to rest on the lobed window of the Palladian mansion, on the silhouette of the courtesan draped in diaphanous chiffon. His eyes traced the languorous rise and swell of her hips, the sweep of her thick mane of hair that eddied and cascaded around her shoulders, and her face now that she had turned toward the light of a candelabra with its lantern eyes and dimpled chin and earrings that

dangled like chandeliers. A face that had always lingered at the edges of his sleep, had always conjured itself up in his waking dreams, that countenance ever so inscrutable. A body like an ocean undulating, waiting to unfurl.

The hum of traffic had subsided to a suspended lull, and the walled city was now curtained by darkness. In the distance, the domed mosques with their tapering finials stood like budding breasts against a naked sky. His gaze trailed as she stepped out of her spangled saree, as it unraveled into a serpentine heap on the floor, the contours of her bare muslin body familiar and yet ever so mysterious. The candles in her window flickered in the whiffling wind like a will-o'-the-wisp winking in the forest. He wondered whether she'd ever realized that he was watching her, as he'd watched her all these years for as long as he could remember, his eyes always searching for her in this sea of blackness. He didn't know her name, but to him she was Mehnoor she who is the light of the moon; every vision of her gliding gracefully, shrouded in silk, skimming the lake of his desire.

He felt his skin burning, the warmth building, spreading, an aching and yearning that seemed to fill him up every night only to claw at him and leave him hollowed-out the next morning; an overwhelming tide of strange pleasure and even stranger sadness. When he pressed his eyes shut, the carmine stain was growing, growing, like a damp patch on a rain-soaked wall. The animal had not flinched when he had brought the cold steel to its throat, and its eyes had expressed and he tried to grapple with this thought momentarily, trying to discern what it was that the animal had expressed⬜ not fear, but an absolute void of emotion; peaceful, placid, as though prepared. Just as his mother had looked when his stepfather had forced himself inside her every night, as Shafiq remembered her and remembered himself, a boy of nine standing in the dim doorway, shaking and confused, his feet rooted and his fingers numb.

Looking back on his childhood, Shafiq would remember the dust and din of Moghalpura, a densely-thronged suburb where he'd spent his early years. His memories were fragmented, and would come and go like waves lapping the shore of his consciousness, some soothing and others tempestuous. He would savor some, whereas others he pushed far, far away into the shadowy recesses of that very consciousness. His memories were of his mother, a reserved and deeply religious woman, her burqa veiling her sorrows and her solitude, rare glimpses exposed when she'd lift her eyes from her cupped hands after prayer; and then there was his stepfather, a stern-faced Hadrami man of Yamani descent who used to run a mobile repair shop in Barkas, and who had sauntered inebriated into Shafiq's life, trampling over his father's grave and his mother's dignity.

Fourteen years ago, his stepfather had walked out on his mother, had moved to Masqat and married a young Arab girl and, last Shafiq heard, died from cirrhosis. And yet Shafiq felt nothing, nothing at all, not even a sliver of grief, of loss. Because his stepfather was the same man who had turned away to pursue more important matters⬜ such as frequenting brothels in Jahanuma, or squandering his family's savings, or drowning himself in lurid shayaris and cheap rum⬜ every afternoon when Shafiq had come home from school bruised or beaten or bullied by the older boys. The same man who had thrust a knife in Shafiq's tremulous hands every Bakrid, forcing the boy to slice an unsuspecting animal's jugular, to empty out its insides, its guts spilling out like a clew of fattened red-worms. The same man whose shadow continued to follow Shafiq, to lurk in dim corners of deserted bylanes, to crouch in his cupboard or hover over his mother as she slept, even today.

When Shafiq pulled his eyes open, the light from the haveli's window was suddenly brighter, jarring, almost blinding. He squinted, pearls of sweat beading his burdened brow. He saw Mehnoor bent over a chest of drawers, enveloped by a man in a flowing, black ankle-length kaftan, the wood moaning, bottles clinking, tipping over, shattering one after another after another. Shafiq found his hands trembling, the veins of his temples bulging and pulsating. He watched as she flailed and thrashed, heard her whimpering like an animal as she was spun around and hurled across the floor, across broken shards and splattered flecks of glass that glimmered like mica against her bare thighs. He had witnessed this spectacle of savagery before, but tonight it all felt different, as though he were not observing from afar, but was in the haveli, in the very room with them, complicit, somehow. It had, all these years, felt like a disturbing dream, a fleeting glimpse through a door left ajar leading to someplace otherworldly, but tonight, it felt eviscerating real.

Fumbling, reeling, he gripped the edge of the parapet-wall to steady himself. The wind had stilled, and a calm now brooded between them. He watched as she brought herself to her unsteady feet and stood facing an oval mirror, rivulets of blood meandering their way down her parted thighs, tainting the pristine marble floor. The figure, almost shadowlike, was upon her again, like a dark cloud trying to snuff out the stars. In that moment, for the first time, Shafiq saw her eyes, reflected, and her eyes appeared to meet his and to say⬜ and he tried to grapple with this thought momentarily, trying to discern what it was that her eyes were trying to say⬜ that she no longer needed help, only deliverance. And then she stopped struggling, her face blank, her wild curls matted together like the vines of an untamed jungle.

Shafiq stubbed out his last cigarette and tossed it over the parapet. After years, after what felt like a lifetime, his legs seemed to be uprooting themselves, slowly and yet purposefully, and he found himself tumbling through his dark living room, past the paisley-printed sofa, past the framed holy sites and cursive Qur'anic verses hanging mum on the walls. He entered the kitchen and fumbled in the drawer, bowls of lentils and minced keema lying untouched on the granite counter above. He stopped by his mother's room, by her bedside as she slept soft-snoring, making sure her frayed quilt was tucked in on both sides of her, making sure her inhaler was within her reach on the mahogany bedside table beside the burning agarbatti, a ritual he carried out every night, hoping, like a weary pilgrim does, that performed conscientiously enough, it would absolve him of all that he had failed to do for her in the past.

He found his legs carrying him down the narrow staircase of his apartment, across the potholed street that separated him from Mehnoor. The silence outside hung heavy like a chador, made even more palpable by the diffused amber glow from streetlamps. Gravel turned to soil as the pavement opened out into the neighboring courtyard, godforsaken and overgrown with weeds and droves of thornapple, their white trumpet maws gaping at the heavens. A melancholy moon had risen in the east, as pale and porcelain as her. He stopped for a brief moment on the haveli's verandah, looking up at the scalloped stucco arches and delicately carved screens trellised by creepers, filling his lungs with the cool night air that was laced with the heady scent of nightshade. The turbid swirl of his emotions seemed to settle and still, and for the first time, this tranquility lent him clarity.

He knew what he had to do when he walked through the cusped gateway. Perhaps, a part of him had always known. The inner rangmahal loomed bare and austere, its large mirrors cloudy and speckled with age, and in them, he saw himself, really saw himself, for what felt like the first time in his life. The oak-wood staircase creaked with every step he took, and the door down the hallway upstairs splintered and gave way without a creak of protest when he kicked it in. She was lying outstretched on a divan, the shadow now covering her, smothering her, thrusting itself inside her limp body, its thick palms pressed against her lips, her legs with their belled anklets dangling loosely over its large shoulders. When the shadow spun around in rude surprise, Shafiq found himself slicing its jugular, feeling that, for the first time, his knife had found its purpose.

The shadow convulsed and tottered to the floor, collapsing in a slick and growing pool of red. A stream of garbled oaths was spewed, words mixing with blood, sputtered out like betel juice. Shafiq looked down at Mehnoor, at her face in the soft subdued glow of the candelabra, expecting to witness a raging storm, but gazing, instead, at the surface of a calm and pregnant sea, unseeing eyes turned ceilingward. Who could tell what brewed, gathering fury, below those burnished waters?

He wanted so desperately to reach out and run his fingers through her tangled hair, brush the back of his palm against her cheeks flushed like fire, drink from the silver stream of moonshine between her legs, from the fountain of her lips smudged sanguine, swallowing all her words unspoken as yet. But, instead, he turned and walked away, letting the knife drop, the carmine stain shrinking, shrinking, and then disappearing.

About the Author:

Bhavika Sicka is an emerging writer from Kolkata, India. She has been a finalist for the Write India contest, and her work has appeared in Arkana, Crab Fat Magazine, and Jabberwock (the literary journal of the Department of English, Lady Shri Ram College, Delhi University). She is currently pursuing her MFA at Old Dominion University in Norfolk, Virginia, and is a fiction reader for Barely South Review.

WE COULD SMOKE
by Mackenzie Gasperson

"Smoke?" Robert's voice was suddenly behind me. It made me jump, and sent a shiver down my spine that only made the cold air worse. Adding to my goosebumps, my heart rate had just increased, making me feel shaky and embarrassed. I turned my head to look at him, and there he was, standing beside me, holding out a cigarette. One was already in-between his lips, the bright glow of the cherry illuminating parts of his face. I only smoked if offered – everyone knew that. "Rita only smokes when she doesn't have to pay for it." Luckily, people weren't quick to deny me what I wanted. Which, at that moment was, yes, a smoke.

I reached out to take the cigarette and had Robert light it for me. I inhaled, feeling the heavy smoke travel down my throat, into my lungs. It made me feel slightly light-headed, which added to my shaky hands syndrome I was having. "Are you cold?" Robert asked, going to remove his jacket. I quickly held up my free hand, blew the smoke out of the corner of my mouth and shook my head, puling the sheer wrap I was wearing tighter around my shoulders. He shrugged, straightening his jacket and taking a drag from his cigarette. "Why are you out here anyway? Party's inside." I rolled my eyes, as if I didn't know that.

"Just needed some air," I said simply, putting the cigarette to my lips. My lipstick left a stain on the end of the filter, and for a minute I remembered that day in the coffee shop, drinking from a white ceramic mug, seeing my deep red lipstick imprinted on the rim of the cup; looking into Ben's eyes as he gripped his own coffee mug, as if leeching the warmth from it. It hadn't been a particularly cold day.

"How – how has it been lately?" Robert emphasized just slightly on it, because he liked to act like he knew what was going on without giving it all away. It didn't matter; Ben's absence showed through the lines on my face and the bags under my eyes. Robert frustrated me; he seemed to be good at putting himself where he didn't belong at the worst times. But I always took a cigarette if offered.

That was something that had bothered Ben. "You always take cigarettes," he had looked wounded – like taking a cigarette from someone was offering an ungodly amount of other things, sex, drugs, love. Whatever the worst case scenario was, Ben had already thought of it.

"I like to smoke," I'd always say. "There's nothing more to it than that," Unconvinced, Ben would pout, and still scowled whenever I took a proffered cigarette. It was like something he couldn't give me that everyone else in the world could. Maybe that's why he disliked it.

"I have no idea what you mean." I answered. Another drag on the cigarette, then I ashed it casually on the ground. The wind caught it and swirled it into the distance.

"You're unlike anyone I've ever known, Rita," Robert said. It was out of the blue. Unexpected. Not entirely discouraged by me. My mistake had been this: when it came to discouraging men, I hadn't.

I dropped the cigarette on the ground, stamped it with my shoe. I crossed my arms to keep the cold out, hoping he wouldn't offer me his jacket again. That's always where it began: a simple offer of the jacket. Whether I took it or not, that would be the deciding factor. All I had to do was deny it.

"What do you say we go back inside?" I asked, gesturing my head towards the glass double doors leading into the restaurant. Goosebumps covered my arms and legs.

"Or," Robert already had the pack of cigarettes in his hand. He took one out and put it between his teeth, then offered me the pack. "We could smoke."

My baby had been no bigger than a sesame seed. A tiny, tiny thing. But it had affected me deeply.

Ben told his parents the minute we found out. The at-home pregnancy test showed two lines; one was bright and bold, and the other was so faint I could barely see it. But it was there. And so was my sesame seed baby.

Like an idiot, I began thinking of names. I wrote them in pretty cursive on any surface that I could write on. My notebook, my hand; I typed them down in my phone, to remember and show Ben later. I told my parents when I was comfortable with the idea. The internet told me, 'some pregnancies don't survive past 6 weeks', but I was ignorant, and excited. I was naive. I hardly tried to think logically – to calm myself down. I convinced myself I felt the sesame seed baby inside of me. Until I couldn't.

One day, I sat down to go pee, and when I looked down, blood had colored the water a sickening, deep red. And that was it. There was no doctor to be seen, no explanation to be had. Some pregnancies don't survive past 6 weeks. That was all there was to it. Suddenly, my sesame seed baby was there no more.

Ben and I were never the same after that. He dove head first into his work, and I dove head first into self-sorrow, and alcohol. My job was meaningless, Ben was meaningless. We woke up next to each other and barely said a word. I tried to tell myself, miscarriage happens to every woman, every day, all over the place. You aren't special. But the faint pen marks of my future baby's name were still on my skin,

and they were all over my notebook. Permanent reminders of what was gone. So I couldn't make myself feel better. I chose not to. And in doing that, I ruined many things.

Ben took us to a coffee shop one Sunday, and he told me what he felt. That we weren't syncing anymore. That I had to be happy again. That he couldn't take it, being so apart from me. He didn't know who I was anymore. Although I'd been expecting it, I had never prepared a response. Why are we in such a public place? I felt like the baristas were staring at me, honing in on our conversation, thinking, wow, what a shitty girlfriend. The other people in the coffee shop stopped staring down at their laptop screens and gave me dirty looks, or smirked at me. The angel on my shoulder said, pull yourself together! But the devil convinced me Ben was seeing someone else; Ben was the enemy. Ben doesn't know what he's talking about. He's out to get you, Rita.

I stood up, pushed myself away from the table, making the chair scrape against the floor, grabbed my bag, and without a word, walked out of the coffee shop. Ben didn't call after me, or track me down. I got home, he wasn't there. I got up for work the next morning, and he hadn't shown up.

When I stumbled in the door at 3am after a night at the bar and collapsed into bed, the things that were normally on his bedside table – his book, a glass of water, his reading glasses, unopened mail, his earbuds – were gone. I went into the bathroom; his toothbrush was gone. I threw open the closet doors; every single piece of his clothing, every single shoe, was gone.

My sesame seed baby was gone. Ben was gone. What else did I have?

When I received the invitation to the Christmas party my job was having, needless to say it was unexpected. Nearly everyone had suffered the brunt of my feelings not only when I had the miscarriage, but when Ben left. I had excommunicated myself from friendships with my coworkers at the price of expressing myself. Something that, I think, should never be done at work. Keep yourself to yourself, and leave it at that.

However, when coworkers approached me with faux-concern laced in their voices, it was hard to convince myself they were just craving a new spread of drama. So I spilled and spilled. And spilled some more, until there was nothing left, and everyone knew everything. I couldn't pretend I was professional – my coworkers didn't respect me as their superior. All they saw was a helpless, blubbering mess.

So yes, when the thick off-white manila envelope came in the mail, containing a sparkly dark green invitation that even smelled nice, with my name on the front in fancy cursive, inviting me to a Christmas party with people that knew every tragedy of my life – I was taken aback. Is this going to be like Carrie? Are they going to crown me queen of the party and then dump pig's blood on me?

But of course, I went, and there I had been, in a dress that required a wrap, standing next to Robert and smoking his cigarettes. There was no pig blood that I could see, and to make myself feel extra safe, I spent most of the party outside. And as annoying as Robert could be, there probably wasn't anyone else that would give me as many cigarettes as he'd given me. We talked about books, and music, and how horrible the drivers in the city were. "Except for us!" we both agreed, because everyone is a horrible driver except for yourself. Robert didn't mention Ben or "it" again, and I went the entire conversation not having mentioned how many times daily I considered going to the top of my apartment building and jumping off. So, although Robert was annoying, and not very handsome, and a little arrogant, he was my friend that night in a place that I felt truly alone.

It should be universally known – that the thing about sadness is that some way or another, it always comes back for you. Even when you're least expecting it, you could suddenly be thinking about jumping off the top of your apartment building.

But the thing is, how do you smoke free cigarettes when you're dead?

About the Author:

Mackenzie Gasperson was born and raised in Tampa, Florida, where she currently resides with her family. Along with writing, she also enjoys baking, sewing, and practicing Tae Kwon Do. This is her first published piece.

FILADELPHIA

by D. Matt McGowan

The way people talk about it just makes it worse. Taboo but titillating. Cheap excitement at the expense of others. Voyeurism dressed up as outrage.

The husbands decided to go golfing. Even mine, who I know for fact hates golf. He just wanted to hang out with his buddies all day, drink beer and smoke cigars. And that's fine. But not me. The thought of riding around in one of those silly carts out here in the hot sun sounded like a little slice of hell.

So, fine. We spend enough time together anyway.

I felt guilty for a while, because I was the one who thought of an alternative excursion. But really, except for one small problem, just a minor blemish on an otherwise perfect day, everything worked out just fine. Ask my girlfriends; I think they'll agree.

I went online and found an inland area known for white-water rafting. The central highlands, equidistant from the coasts, a half-dozen rivers cascaded down the western slope of a fifty-mile-long range bookended by volcanoes, one still active. The only downside was distance. So we left the villa early, at 6:30, and drove eighty-five miles to Canas, a small town at the base of Volcan Rincon de la Vieja.

When we reached the outfitter at 8:45, they were loaded up and waiting for us. Twenty-five tourists and five guides packed into an old military transport vehicle. The guides stacked five white-water inflatables – the tough kind with thick rubber lining – on a trailer and piled a mountain of gear – paddles, life jackets and helmets – in the back of the vehicle. After two miles on the main highway, we turned onto an unpaved road, the beginning of a slow and rough trek up the side of the range. When the clouds separated and the trees thinned, we glimpsed wisps of smoke rising up out of Rincon.

Daniel, the lead guide, was young and outgoing and had a beautiful smile. Like the rest of the guides, he did not wear a shirt. With his lean frame, vivacious personality and competent English, Daniel was a one-man public-relations machine.

There is a picture of us at the launch. Daniel is buoyant, smiling from the Gulf to the Pacific, his arms spread out and resting on Jane and Maura's shoulders. I am standing on the other side of Jane. Raye and Gretchen are leaning against Maura. We are tall and good-looking. Thirty feet to our right, down a steep, rocky grade, El Rio Corobici is roaring so loud that we have to yell at each other to be heard.

Soon after this photo was taken, Daniel announced that we were his "friends," meaning we would go in his raft. We were happy about this, because Daniel was pretty and fun to be around.

But now I have mixed feelings about Daniel. From the moment we stepped into the raft, shooting through the rapids and ricocheting off boulders like a pinball, he provided an exhilarating experience without compromising our safety. And I'll be honest, the way his muscles flexed when he worked that paddle was also a thrill. I can still hear him, "Okay, my friends, paddle on the right!"

But his hot-dogging and flirting prevented us from seeing wildlife. (This is just a small thing, nothing I would ever put on an evaluation.) We were too busy trying to keep our balance and not get thrown off the raft. Later, when I heard people talking about seeing a nest of baby howler monkeys, I was more than a bit frustrated.

After lunch at the outfitter – grilled dorado, black beans and rice – we headed back to the coast. I felt good driving, physically tired but replenished, having moved my body and spent all morning outside. I wasn't keen on being trapped a metal box for the next two-and-half hours, but I looked forward to the comfort of our villa, a hot shower and then drinks by the pool with friends.

At Liberia, where our plane landed four days ago, we turned left and continued west, toward the coastal range. My friends talked, going over the highlights of the trip, but soon they grew tired. I assured them I was okay to drive.

While they napped, I enjoyed the peace and quiet. At one point, after they'd been asleep for twenty minutes, I worried I'd gotten off-track, that perhaps I'd taken a wrong turn. But then I recognized two things – a bright orange building and an enormous Banyan tree with its wavy, fibrous roots above the ground – and I knew we were on the correct road.

I turned right at the big Chevron south of Belen. Now the mountains. The road narrowed and there many curves. Poor conditions for car-sleeping. One by one, my girlfriends started to wake up. I heard a yawn from the back seat. It was a drawn-out, dramatic affair with lots of stretching and a lion's roar at the end. Then there was soft mumbling and laughter. These were sweet sounds, made by close friends, people who cared about each other.

Maura, slumped in the passenger seat next to me, held out. Her snoring made us laugh. It started out as labored breathing, rising up to something like mild choking before returning to the regular stuttered breathing. But it intensified again, and she gulped for air, peaking finally in a flurry of staccato snorts. We tried not let our giggling wake her. She took care of

that herself after yet another slow build-up and violent burst.

"Oh gawd," she said, wiping drool from the corner of her mouth.

The women roared.

When they calmed down, Gretchen announced that she needed coffee.

How spoiled we are. Starbucks on every corner. We settled for a place called Wendy's SuperO, a grocery store on the main road, one block off the square in Filadelphia. We were now forty-five miles from the coast.

There wasn't a market like this in Potrero, the town nearest our villa. My friends were excited about purchasing a few items.

Before we reached the store, there'd been a flurry of texts with the husbands. They had finished golfing and were planning dinner. They said they'd grill if we picked up steaks.

Inside Wendy's, I saw a short, stocky man standing at the end of a cashier station. He grinned as we walked past the lines and made our way deeper into the store. It was a strange smile, the mouth held open, almost gaping, as if he couldn't breathe through his nose and was struggling to get enough oxygen. He had no teeth and his faded, half-buttoned Hawaiian shirt barely covered a prodigious gut, big as a rubber exercise ball. Cutoffs and filthy flip-flops completed his ensemble.

Not your typical Walmart greeter, but that's exactly what I thought he was. Why not? I was in a foreign country with different customs and a much smaller economy. Why wouldn't a proprietor pay this poor soul minimum wage to say hola and buenos dias all day?

But he didn't.

I did. I was trying to be friendly, so I made eye contact and said hello in Spanish. I looked right at him and said it. But he didn't say anything. He just kept smiling.

I noticed something else. His eyes. They were glassy, like frog eggs.

Though poorly lit and less tidy than American supermarkets, Wendy's Super O (every time someone mentioned the name – and it would be mentioned many times that evening – I couldn't help thinking of Wendy O, the Plasmatics singer who wore Band-Aids over her nipples) catered to Yankee tourists going back and forth between the Pacific Coast and central highlands. Something about being marketed to as an affluent, never-hungry gringa in a poor, third-world country depressed me. I had to get out of there, and did, after giving Maura a twenty and making up an excuse.

While my friends were buying steaks, limes, mangoes, gin, rum, containers of sunscreen and refrigerated bottles of coffee, I waited in the car. I hadn't talked to my kids for two days, so I checked my phone to see if they had called. They hadn't. But I knew they were okay; I just missed them.

I complain about the rudeness of others – my children and students, staring at their phones when they should be participating real human behavior, like saying hello or cleaning up after dinner. Yet that's what I was doing, mired in brain-candy crumbs that did nothing to improve my life, when my friends returned to the car. Worse, just like my kids, I couldn't let go of the stupid device, even after my friends entered the car. This I remember: When I heard them coming, I thought I had plenty of time, at least three more minutes to read e-mails while they loaded groceries and got situated in the Land Cruiser.

They were talking about scheduling and the difficulties of managing kids' extra-curricular activities. This mundane conversation helped me rationalize the obsessive behavior, and I continued staring at the phone until long after they had latched their seatbelts.

They were patient. While waiting, they continued talking and didn't ask why we hadn't left the parking lot. Perhaps they had done this too and now accepted it as the new cultural norm.

But if I had been paying close attention, I would have noticed that their conversation ended. Abruptly, as if a tornado siren started blaring. There were none of the usual trimmings – a laugh or a kind word of affirmation.

Then Maura said my name. The way she uttered it, carefully enunciating each syllable and almost whispering, got my attention. But my brain didn't function properly. I was slow and tone deaf. Had I not been, I would have looked at her, which was exactly what she was trying to get me to do.

"Are we ready?" I said.

I turned the ignition key. The engine fired up and I switched on the air-conditioning.

Behind Maura, on the passenger side, Gretchen cleared her throat. "Can we go now?" She started rolling up her window. I could hear the whine of its electric motor.

She and the other two women in the back fidgeted. I heard grumbling as I fiddled with dashboard knobs. Then Maura said my name again. This time, her tone jarred me out of the fog.

I turned. We made eye contact. She raised her brow, holding it there, eyes opened wide. Then she jerked her head toward the window.

He was a short man, barely five-and-a-half-feet tall. His hair was greasy and starting to thin. Maverick wisps stood upright here and there and took off willy-nilly, like Kramer on Seinfeld. His splotchy skin hated the sunlight. Patches of it looked hot and angry with infection. He was looking at us, but his eyes were faraway. Glassy and crossed. His mouth was open, as it had been inside the store, but this time I detected a faint sneer, the slightest lift of his upper lip on the right side. The sunlight made his shirt looked even more faded.

He was six feet from the car.

For a second, I thought he was going to say something, maybe ask a question. But he didn't. Nor did he move.

I don't know why I waited. What kept me from leaving the parking lot? The spectacle, I guess.

He swayed forward and his head twitched. His chin and cheeks displayed random islands of gray mixed in with black stubble.

Did he need help? I almost asked, but before I could, he stepped forward, closer to the car. His chest seemed to hurl forward when he did this, like the arm of catapult. His legs dragged behind. I heard gravel crunching under his feet.

The man took another step toward the car. Now I could not see below his waist. He stopped there, only four feet from Maura's door. Swayed like he was drunk.

Until then, his arms had been at his side, resting on the flanks of his belly. Now he drew them in, closer to the center of his body. I saw his shoulders and arms moving, but I could not see his hands.

Gretchen could. "Oh shit…"

Behind me, Jane unlatched her seatbelt and leaned across Raye and Gretchen to look out the window. She started laughing. It was strangely loud, the hacking and fiendish bark of a teenager.

"What?" I said.

"Go!" commanded Maura.

"What is it?" I said. "What's he doing?"

Maura stiffened. She turned away from the window. She dug her heels into the floorboard and pinned her shoulders against the seat.

"He's… he's pulling it OUT, is what. Let's go!"

I slid my foot off the brake and the Land Cruiser rolled backwards. I hadn't looked behind us or used the mirrors. We were still rolling when I heard a car honk.

I stomped the brake. The Land Cruiser slammed to a stop. As it rocked back and forth, the women gasped and tried to catch their breath, and the man stood there holding his penis. Seeing this, Jane lost control, laughing and kicking the back of my seat. The others were quiet as a cairn.

I felt guilty. The excursion was my idea, and the juvenile addiction to my smartphone had put my friends in a vulnerable position. How could I be so careless? I apologized, and they assured me that everything was okay.

Eventually I forgave myself. When I did, I discovered a deeper sentiment: sadness. That guy was mentally disabled, and I doubt there were any social services to help him. Then I thought, what would that be like, for your brain to work that way, the wrong way, but to still want sex, like everyone else. Sometimes biology is cruel.

But I didn't experience this feeling, this sadness, until much later, days, in fact, after that night's drunken review of day. We were at the villa, gathered around a long, rectangular coffee table. We were playing a homemade version of Charades. It was late, and we'd been drinking for hours. The game held our attention, but the major event of the day just kept resurfacing.

Maybe Jane was right. On one level, it was kind of funny.

During a break in the game, she stood up to go to the kitchen, as her husband made a waggish comment about the man's romantic strategy and chances for success. Hearing this, Jane stopped. She turned and faced the group. I don't remember what she did to get our attention, but whatever it was, it worked.

"Yeah, you gotta wonder how that's workin' for him," she said. "I mean, what would he've done if I'd gotten out of the car and..." She wobbled, shifting her weight from hip to hip and then pointing her finger at the ceiling and twirling it. "...'All right, buddy,'" she said. "'you know what, let's just do this!'"

When we finished laughing, my husband asked, "Was anyone else outside?"

"No," said Gretchen.

Maura was shaking her head. "Nope. Nobody."

"Well, you were pretty lucky," said Hank, Gretchen's husband.

Everyone nodded in agreement. I knew what Hank meant, that it could have been worse, and that was true. But I didn't feel lucky. At that moment, I didn't feel anything. Not angry, not scared, certainly not violated. Mainly I just felt drunk.

I wondered about my girlfriends. Did they feel lucky? I checked. I looked at all of them, but they weren't looking back at me. They were staring at the table or gulping gin.

About the Author:

Matt McGowan grew up in southwest Missouri and attended the University of Missouri. He was a newspaper reporter, and for many years now he has worked as a science and research writer at the University of Arkansas. His stories have appeared in Deep South Magazine, Concho River Review, Hawaii Pacific Review, Arkansas Review and others. He lives with his wife and children in Fayetteville, Arkansas.

COLLEGE TOWN

by Jeffrey Kulik

It's hot today, and as I look up at the sun I feel a bead of sweat rolling down the back of my neck. It reminds me of the old times, and I close my eyes for a moment and remember working in the garden behind my house under the same old sun. But, that was a long time ago and things are different now.

I feel a few flakes land on my shoulder so I dust them off. It's snowing again. At least, that's what we've taken to calling it when the ash flakes come down. It happens a couple of times a week, so we've all gotten used to it by now. I pass by the store and see Dr. Maltese, sweeping up the ash in the front doorway.

"Just keeps coming down, huh?" I ask.

He stops sweeping and wipes some ash off his face with a gray handkerchief. "This is getting ridiculous," he says. "I wasn't put on Earth to run a corner store."

"Hey, I didn't sign up to clean out sewers, but that's what I've been assigned."

"When I was Director of Parking, I used to sit in a big office and look at spreadsheets on two big computer monitors. I led meetings, shook hands, made decisions, handed out business cards, all of it. I wore a different suit every day of the week!"

"I know. I was there. I wore a suit every day, too."

It stops snowing and Dr. Maltese looks up into the sky. "I know, I know. I just feel like if I don't keep saying it, I'll forget. And it'll be like I was always this shopkeeper and nothing else."

"Nobody will forget. We have the archives in

"The archives. The archives? What's the point?"

"I don't know," I say, shaking my head. "I don't know anymore."

A dark cloud moves slowly in front of the sun, briefly enveloping us in an ashy shadow.

"You going to the meeting tonight?"

"Of course. You?"

"What else do we have to do?"

And when the sun reappears, it provides us no comfort.

We meet, as always, in the old library. There are new posters on the walls of the main entranceway. Dave does an excellent job rotating the artwork, even though we are quickly running out of resources. We may one day starve to death, but Dave will always have new, unseen poster prints and big metal clips with which to affix them to the wall.

"Hey Dave," I say, adjusting my eyes to the dim light inside the old library. We meet by candlelight now. We had started out with enough natural gas to make our own electricity which kept the whole place illuminated at night, but now we are conserving it to use to run the baseboard heaters in our office homes when winter comes.

I had once begged for a corner office with windows on two sides. Now, I'm glad I have just the one cold glass pane when it gets cold out. The drafts can be real killers.

"How have you been?" Dave asks, genuinely concerned, as always.

"You remember how I used to say that nothing could be worse than working for this place? Well, turns out I was wrong."

I always use this line with everybody. It's become my signature. However, it has become less humorous with each passing day that we are locked up here. No one laughs anymore.

Dr. Lombard takes the podium. Once, he was our Chancellor. Since the attack, he more or less serves as our mayor. Perhaps the better word would be president. This is, after all, our whole world now.

He is surrounded by the crackling light of a score of candelabra. The lighting makes everything he says that much more ominous. "Colleagues," he begins, arms outstretched.

"Do you believe this guy?" Hank, the carpenter foreman says, poking me in the arm. "He's no better than you or me or anybody. Why does he get to be up there?"

"The Board of Trustees named him Chancellor," I answer, dumbly.

"The Board of Trustees abandoned us, Charlie," Hank whisper-shouts into my ear. "I don't know why we still listen to this guy. What's he done for us? Nothing. Give me the word and I'll rush the stage and take this whole thing over."

"Just what we need," I reply. "A dictator."

"You've already got one," Hank shoots back, pointing at the stage. "You just don't see it."

I turn my attention back to Dr. Lombard. He runs his stubby fingers through his gray broom-bristle crew cut. He speaks to us through chapped lips. His skin seems so delicate now, almost translucent in places. "We've been together through the best of times and the worst of times..."

"Don't remember the best," Hank posits. I shush him and continue listening.

"And, after the gas, when all seemed to be lost, we came together as a University family. I want you all to know how proud I was of all of you. What could have been chaos, what could have been an even greater tragedy, became a time of unity."

"Yeah, yeah," Miss Molloy, the head of our de facto nursing and medical care group, seated next to me, sneers.

"And, that is why, my friends and colleagues, that tomorrow, I will be making a journey outside of the fence."

The room hushes to silence.

I look over at Miss Molloy, but she is staring straight ahead, mouth agape.

The next day, it is cold. These strange shifts in temperature are common now, and I take this one with the usual grain of salt. Mr. Conroy, who was once a high-level business manager with Central Administration, pounds determinedly on a rusty spigot which emerges from a mossy brick wall at the bottom of a decrepit lecture hall building which is now used as a makeshift sanitarium. The sanitarium is filled with those of us who had children or other family outside the walls when we were sealed in. The mothers moan for their children, the men for their wives, the students for their mothers and fathers and sisters and brothers. Some of our ranks never did acclimate to our new world.

"Did you hear what he said last night?"

"I was there, Charlie. We all heard him."
"I know. I just can't get over it."

Mr. Conroy stands and wipes his hands on the lapels of what was once a very nice silk suit jacket. "Look. First of all, there's no guarantee he's even going to get through the wall.

Who is he, David Copperfield? Second of all, let's say he does get out. Then what? If what they tell us is even remotely true, he'll be shot dead by the police in no time. I still love the old goof, but he's a grown man and if he wants to get killed, I say let him. I'm waiting until they give us the all clear."

"If there was going to be an all clear, don't you think we'd have heard it by now?"

Mr. Conroy laughs. "You sound like those conspiracy nuts down by Fillmore Hall. Our alarm alert system didn't work before the gas. No, I'm waiting for a bunch of soldiers to come in here and let us know its safe out there."

The gas attack happened three years ago. In my mind, I'm sure they've already sealed our fates.

I take a walk to the police station. They have a deep supply of dried food that they were saving for an emergency preparedness demonstration before the gas. Luckily, we had a team of expert food chemists on staff that could attest to the safety of the dried food after the incident. We have had rationing, no doubt, but I still have enough coupons in my wallet to last me another two years. What comes after that, I try not to think about about.

Dr. Foreman is sitting in a squeaky metal office chair behind a desk stacked with papers, working by candlelight. "What do you want?" he snaps at me, as the front door shuts behind me.

"I'm here for my ration."

He leans out of the shadows. "You're going to run out of those ration tickets if you keep using them like this."

"Just give me a ration, please."

"You don't want to eat the turnips and eggplants they're growing in the greenhouse?"

"I'm sick of fresh vegetables all the time. I want something that tastes like meat. How about one of those dehydrated Salisbury steaks?"

"I don't know – let me think about it," he muses.

Marla Hernandez has been standing in the corner this whole time, unnoticed. She used to be a nutritionist with our Public Health school, but since the accident, she been volunteering as a member of our police force. Two out of the three shifts were home when the event occurred, so we were left with only one shift less those who were out on vacation or leave. Marla was one of the first to volunteer to fill the void. There weren't enough uniforms, so the one she was wearing was less than ideal. Meant for a man, and large man at that, her slender frame got lost in the billowy blue shirt. But her demeanor helped assert her authority.

"Give the man his dehydrated Salisbury steak, Dr. Foreman," she demands.

"I told you to call me Chief!" he shouts back.

"Who died and made you Chief?"

"Al Morris!"

"Oh, yeah." I add. "He was a hell of a guy."

"Just shut up and take your rations," Marla says, handing me an oddly-shaped lump covered with aluminum foil. She grabs one of my ration tickets and sends me on my way.

I take a long walk around the perimeter of the campus. I remember when we had students coming in and out of here at all hours of the day and night. I remember when I would go home each night to my empty apartment. I wonder if there's a part of me that likes it better this way, the new way.

I remember the day it happened. It was bright and clear, which are always the most ominous days to me. First, there was a horrible buzzing from all our phones. Everyone's pockets and briefcases were suddenly alive with dread. Then the sky turned black. We all turned to our phones and computers for guidance, but all we got were confusing reports. After a few minutes of panic, we all started walking out of our buildings, looking to each other to make some sense out of the situation. We moved as a group to the three main entrances. But, the soldiers had already sealed us in. The gates were closed.

Our phones worked for a couple of days after that, and we would meet in big groups in the quad to try to figure things out. For a while, we thought that maybe war had broken out, or that somebody had finally dropped the bomb. We didn't know. The news reports were vague and pointlessly incendiary. Then, we thought it might have been some kind of chemical leak. We were trapped inside here for our safety, until they could clean up the contamination. The news anchors were no help. The stories were jumbled and confused. The options, so it seemed, were limitless.

It was the College of Liberal Arts that figured it out. They did air tests, soil tests, all kinds of tests, and they determined that there had been some kind of poison gas cloud over our region. None of us seemed particularly affected health-wise, but they said the effects might be long-lasting. They were probably sealing us in until they could tell how sick we really were. They didn't want us causing an outbreak.

A few of us tried to test the gates and the fences, but the bright lights from the soldiers' trucks parked just outside deterred us. Eventually, we all got used to the new way. Well, most of us did anyway, and we began to forge on.

Mankind is resilient, especially public university employees. We had long been trained to do less with more, to expect the worst and to improvise with impunity. We were ready for this. When the electricity turned off, Dr. Friedberg, the head of Campus Utilities, found a way to make our own using our natural gas reserves. The ladies who ran the goth rock fan club had a huge stockpile of candles, and the Department of Chemistry had a huge supply of lighters and lighter fluid. We made do.

Still, the fence haunts us. It looks like any other fence, really. Sometimes, I like to look at it and imagine a big open gate with people walking freely in and out of campus. But, those days have long passed. I was always told that when they built the University, it was a primarily a commuter school, and so they would close the gates every night and lock the whole place down. I suppose somebody much higher up also knew that story and took full advantage after the gas.

I used to go to school here, before I graduated, and they hired me on full-time. I learned all about the unethical experiments that used to abound on human subjects. I feel like our lives behind the fence are being recorded in some kind of study log. I assume there is outrage as to all of our whereabouts and some kind of big cover up. In my heart, I know they've all written us off.

I walk through the open front doors of the campus greenhouse. The young men and women inside are digging up the latest crop of turnips. I overhear them talking as I approach.

"Do you think he's really going to do it?"

"He's a fool. He's an old fool."

"Well, if he's a fool, then so am I."

"I could have told you that."

I approach them, still holding the dehydrated Salisbury steak. "Excuse me. Are you talking about the Chancellor?"

They stop their work and look at me with sour faces. I have interrupted them. "Can we help you?"

"I need some turnips."

A young lady with taped-together black-framed glasses stands up and sighs, annoyed. "Do you have your turnip card?"

I produce it.

She sighs again and robotically states, "As you know, you are entitled to one turnip a week, and with each turnip, we will punch another hole in your card. You may not exceed one turnip a week and this is subject to change based on availability. Do you understand?"

I nod. This is boilerplate stuff.

She places a big, heavy turnip into a brown paper bag for me.

"So?" I ask.,

She grimaces. "So, what?

"So, do you think he's going to do it?"

"The Chancellor?"

"Yeah."

"Who cares? We all know there's nothing out there. He's just another smug, sanctimonious patrician doing whatever he wants. When the phone signals cut off, I made my peace with it. This is our home now. Here's your turnip. Have a nice day."

As I walk out, I see a crowd gathering by the fence. I know now that it is time. Time moves strangely here behind the walls. All of us spectators, we huddle together, scared and confused. I look up and see that old familiar face preparing himself. I am nervous for him. I clear my throat.

I watch now, with the rest, all of us, all different, all trapped here together, as he climbs the wall. He ascends the ladder slowly, tentatively, and for a moment we think maybe he's lost his nerve. But, in the moment when he throws his legs over the top parapet it becomes real. He stops there at the top, looking out at the outside world as if for the first time. As I hear him drop down onto the other side, I feel my heart sink in my chest. I remember all the years I spent jockeying for position, undermining my co-workers, vying for my boss' attention, all of it. I think about my life inside these walls in all its totality. And now the most alive I've ever felt is watching with envy as a middle-aged man in a suit scales a short brick wall.

About the Author:

Jeffrey Kulik is a lifelong Chicagoan and a career civil servant who has previously been published in Arcturus and Public Organization Review.

A RECURRING DREAM

by Ana Vidosavljevic

Mila woke up to the sound of Fajr prayer. It was still pitch-dark outside. She came close to the window and pulled back the curtain. The sky was overloaded with starts. Mila was gazing at the beautiful twinkling carpet above. It was stunning. It seemed so close, as though she could reach and touch it. As though she could hold the moon in her hand. She lowered her head and she saw man hurrying to the mosque. She loved listening the early morning prayer. It was full of sorrow, lament, mystery and artistic beauty at the same time. She couldn't wait the dawn and she was eager not only to walk the streets of Sanliurfa, but to visit Gobekli Tepe as well. For most of people, laymen, Gobekli Tepe was an archaeological site. For archaeologists, anthropologists and those who studied human life and human culture this was an exquisite place, a place which seemed to not only question certain religious beliefs but whose mysterious stones maybe marked the site of the Garden of Eden.

Mila was not an archaeologist or anthropologist and she had never before been to Gobekli Tepe. However, a year ago, she had met a young archaeologist who had told her the stories and legends about this mysterious place. And her interest for this place grew so much that she started dreaming it. Those dreams were so vivid and so puzzling that they colored her everyday life. Not a day passed without her thinking about this place. Often would she dream the Gobekli Tepe's hills, yellow dust and strange skulls that were half-human and half-animal. Those dreams didn't let her do anything else except read about Gobekli Tepe. And the more she read about it, the more intense her desire to visit it became.

One dream especially kept her anxious and restless. She was sleeping but she was tired. That recurring dream exhausted her. Mila dreamed that she was walking alone on a dusty road that led to Gobekli Tepe. The sun was at its zenith and the burning ground was throwing out the golden dust.

Those golden clouds blurred her vision. But still, she could anticipate something strange approaching her. It was not a man, nor a bird and it didn't seem like any animal either. And still, it seemed alive. Alive but not walking, flying or slithering. It was more floating through the hot air.

The closer it was, the stronger her heart was beating. When it was almost within arm's reach, she realized that it was a skull. It was not a completely human skull. It was long and narrow with a pointy chin and narrow Asian eyes. The skull was so close to her face that it seemed she could feel its sharp edges. And in that moment, when her face almost touched the skull, she would always wake up. This particular dream tortured her. Awake, she was aware that she would dream the same dream over and over again, but the very process of dreaming always brought anxiety, blurry images, uncertainty, fear, anticipation. She read a lot about the skulls found in Gobekli Tepe and it probably influenced her dreaming, but she couldn't understand why she often dreamed the same dream. Since it was almost dawn and she couldn't go back to sleep, she spent an hour reading. Later, she was the first one to have breakfast in a hotel restaurant.

The hotel was half empty but still people didn't hurry to go for breakfast since it was served until eleven in the morning. Mila was in a hurry. She was anxious to visit Gobekli Tepe. She ate and stayed in the hotel lobby to wait for a driver and guide who were supposed to take her to the famous archaeological site. The driver came at 7.30. The guide arrived at the same time. The guide was pleasant, talkative and obviously full of knowledge. His English was excellent.

Once they arrived to the site, he walked her around and explained to her a lot about this amazing place, considered to be the world's first temple and believed to be a burial site as well.

Gobekli Tepe, at least the part that was excavated, consisted of circular and oval-shaped structure set on the hill. It was an impressive archaeological site but even more impressive were the stories, legends, mysteries, beliefs around it. Mila listened to them and didn't want to interrupt the guide even though she had hundreds of questions to ask. Finally, after a couple of hours, the guide seemed tired of walking and talking. It was getting hot. Mila knew that her tour would be over soon. She asked the guide to bring her to this site few more times and answer her questions. He agreed to meet her again the next day and bring her to Gobekli Tepe.

Mila and the guide met three more times. She would wait every morning at 7.30 in front of the hotel and the guide and driver would take her to Gobekli Tepe every of those days. The guide showed her every corner of the site. He explained everything he knew about every part of this place and answer those Mila's questions he knew the answers to. And when he didn't know what else to talk about connected to this site, he told her that he couldn't help her any further. Mila was satisfied but not completely. She thanked the guide but decided to stay in Sanliurfa few more days. She spent the next two days walking the streets of Sanlirfa, eating baklava in local restaurants, sitting in the Balikli Gol park and watching and feeding the fish in the pool.

It was a late afternoon and Mila was sitting on one of the benches in the Balikli Gol park. A middle- aged woman with a child approached. The child was playing with its toys and seemed very focused on its imaginary castles with little rubber soldiers that were scattered around the ground.

His mother was smiling looking at him and decided to take a rest. She came close to the bench where Mila was sitting and asked in a very good English if Mila didn't mind her sitting on the bench as well. Mila didn't mind at all and what's more she even longed for company. First, the woman seemed reserved and not willing to talk but all of a sudden, she started asking questions – where from Mila was, if she liked Sanliurfa, what brought her here, if she was married and had children.

Mila politely answered all the questions but didn't talk more than what was asked by the woman.

The woman seemed satisfied with the answers. Since it was hot, she opened her bag to take the bottle of water. A small picture with a strange colorful peacock fell down. Mila took it from the ground and gazed at it. It seemed familiar.

"I've seen something similar but I can't remember where..." she said.

She forced her brain to work better trying to remember where and when she saw this image or the similar one.

"It is Melek Taus, or the Peacock Angel," the woman said. "The Yezidis believe that Melek Taus is the true creator and ruler of the universe. The Supreme God created him as the greatest of all. Our religion is the oldest religion on earth and all other religions came after and from our religion."

Mila was more than interested to hear more about Yezidis, Melek Taus and their religion.

"So, Melek Taus is not God?" asked Mila.

"No," the woman said, "he is God's most important angel, also known as Shaitan or Satan. He is a fallen angel. He rebelled against God and was cast into Hell. But God forgave him."

"And how is Melek Taus related to Adam and Eve?" Mila was curious.

"He taught Adam and Eve secrets of worship and human evolution. He is the one who asked

Adam to "eat of the grain" and that's how we got wheat today."

"That's interesting," said Mila, "so you don't believe that he brought an apple, the symbol of knowledge, but wheat?" she was surprised even shocked.

"Yes, he brought the wheat that was domesticated by humans. And they stopped hunting and gathering and took up farming."

Mila was amazed.

"And very close to Sanilurfa, in Gobekli Tepe, it all began. Gobekli Tepe was the Garden of Eden."

Mila didn't hide her bewilderment.

"Gobekli Tepe is the oldest place on earth," continued the woman persuasively.

Mila was still digesting everything she had heard from the woman for the last twenty minutes, when the woman stood up abruptly, said "nice to meet you", took the child's hand and walked away.

Mila finally stood up as well. She hurried up through the Balikli Gol park and through the busy Sanliurfa's streets and reached her hotel room. She took her laptop and the next 5 hours she spent Googling and reading the articles about Yezidis and Melek Taus and their connection to Gobekli Tepe. She learned about the Book of Enoch and its story of fallen angels or Watchers. And furthermore, she read about Yezidis and the commitment to their own community. She learned that they must marry within the Yezidi community, and a Yezidi who married a non-Yezidi risked the expulsion from the community. She was taking all the information and all of a sudden she remembered!

When she was a little girl, she saw a small picture of the Peacock Angel in her grandma's drawer. She also remembered that her grandma was not in the house at that moment so she asked her grandpa what it was. After seeing the picture in Mila's hand, grandpa got furious. He grabbed the picture and asked Mila where she had found it. Mila told him the truth. Half an hour later, when grandma came back from the shop, the moment she entered the house, grandpa faced her yelling and showing the Peacock Angel picture. Mila had never seen him so angry. Grandma looked ashamed for some reason and asked Mila to go and play outside. Even fifty meters from the house, Mila could hear grandpa's angry voice. However, she saw her friend and they went to the park to play.

This memory struck her. Why did her grandma have the Peacock Angel picture? She needed some answers. She grabbed her mobile phone and called her mother. It had been a long time since she talked to her mother. Her mother knew Mila was going for some trip to Asia, but Mila had never told her where exactly she would go. Anyway, her mother answered the phone immediately. After the usual small talk, Mila asked her:

"Mum, why did grandma have the Peacock Angel picture? I remember finding it in her drawer when I was little. Do you know anything about it?"

A moment of silence.

"Mum? Was grandma a Yezidi?"

"I don't want to talk about it on the phone," said Mila's mother indifferently.

"Please I need to know," begged Mila.

"Not on the phone, Mila! We'll talk when you come back. Stay safe and call me when you're back."

She hang up. Mila was confused. She didn't fail to notice irritation in her mother's voice and a certain kind of shame.

Mila sat on the bed with the phone in her hand more than ten more minutes thinking about her conversation with her mother. When she got herself together, she turned on her laptop and booked the flight back. She needed to go back home and find out the truth. And the first flight was the next day.

The next day, she woke up soaked in sweat. The same skull dream tortured her again. It was only 7 in the morning and the driver was supposed to pick her up at 9 am and take her to the airport.

She had enough time to eat delicious baklava and say good bye to Sanliurfa. The flight was long but pleasant. She read books and magazines she bought in Sanliurfa and time flied. She arrived home the next day in the evening. She couldn't wait any longer to talk to her mother and hear the whole story, so she decided to call her immediately. Luckily, her mother sounded calm and told Mila that she was welcome to come to her house and talk. Mila didn't want to lose time. She quickly took shower, grabbed one beautiful sarong she bought for her mother in Sanliurfa and called a taxi. Ten minutes later, her mother opened the door, hugged her, seated her on a couch in the living room and brought her a cup of tea. Then, she sat as well in a wing chair across from Mila. Her mother closed her eyes for a moment, then, she took a deep breath and began:

"I don't know if you remember but your grandfather was a vagabond. Always ready to travel, to move, to go somewhere. When I was a kid, he would, every second-third day, put me in his old car and take me to different places, sometimes not that far from our hometown but the other days, we would go miles and miles far from it. We visited all the lakes, rivers, cities, villages in our region and few other regions until I reached the age of nine years. When he was young he was worse. He would grab his back pack and travel the most remote places on earth. When he was 21, he went to the south-east Turkey. In that time, probably he was one of the rare Westerners to set his foot on the soil of that part of Turkey. Initially, he planned to spend just a couple of days there and to continue his trip to probably Iraq and Iran. But he got very sick. He couldn't eat, drink or move from bed. He was so weak and in pain that he was afraid he would die there. Luckily, he met a nice young man, Misha, almost his own age, who was Yezidi and this young man took him to his home where he lived with his parents and sister. First, the family was angry that their son brought a Westerner to their house who would "spoil the sacredness of their home with his Western impurity" but then they agreed to take care of him until he got better. Misha's sister was the one who was bringing food and water to your grandpa in a small room where the family put him. Even though, they couldn't communicate verbally since the young girl didn't speak English, your grandpa fell in love with her.

Anyway, the only one in the family who spoke English was Misha. Since your grandpa spent almost one month in their house lying in bed and hoping to recover, he and Misha talked a lot every day.

Misha told him a lot about Yezidis, their beliefs and tradition. He told him about their commitment to the Yezidi community and ostracism of those who decided to marry a non-Yezidi. Your grandpa learned that his feelings for Misha's sister couldn't be revealed otherwise, both she and he would be in trouble. Days were passing and he wondered if the girl felt the same for him. He took a piece of paper and drew a man who was holding a flower in his hand. The next time the girl came to his room he gave her the drawing. First, after seeing the drawing, the girl looked confused and scared, but then he recognized a trace of a smile on her beautiful face. She took the drawing, folded it and put it in her pocket. The following day, he drew a man with a bunch of flowers, and the day after, a man with a heart in his hand. While taking the last drawing, the girl finally showed a real smile. But then, as if she regretted it, she ran away from the room. The next day she didn't show up. Instead of her, Misha brought food and water.

"That what you are doing is very dangerous," said Misha calmly. Your grandpa was taken by surprise. "I mean, making a young Yezidi girl fall in love with you..." he was looking your grandpa straight into the eyes, "my sister showed me the drawings you had given her...you know that we Yezidis don't mix with the other religions, beliefs, groups. If we did, the worst curse would fall on us."

Your grandpa didn't say a word. But he also couldn't help himself from falling in love with the girl.

The girl didn't show up the following day either. Your grandpa was feeling better and better and he knew he would have to leave soon. He decided to risk and talk to Misha about his plan. Misha was the only one who could help him. He told Misha about his feelings for his sister and he told him that he was planning to talk to Misha's parents anyway and he needed Misha as an interpreter. Misha got angry.

"You are absolutely crazy! You really are! We are Yezidis! My parents would never let their daughter marry a Westerner! And it is not only them. But the whole Yezidi community will stand against you. And my sister will be excluded from our community and will not be allowed ever again to even come and visit any of us here."

Your grandpa was deeply disappointed and hurt. He was feeling much better physically though and he decided to leave in three days. Every next time Misha came to his room, he was quiet and seemed deep in thought.

In the evening before your grandpa's departure, Misha came to his room.

"Two days ago I spoke with my sister," he said. "She seems really likes you and is willing to run away with you."

The words "run away" struck your grandpa. He didn't plan to run away from anyone and with anyone.

"I decided to help you," Misha continued, "I made my sister a passport. Don't ask how! And she will be ready to leave with you before dawn. You have to leave before anyone is awake. So tell me, do you still want her to come with you?"

Your grandpa didn't hide surprise. He was shocked by the Misha's plan but he couldn't back out of the whole situation and honestly he didn't want to. He was young, in love, and ready for big risks.

He didn't let himself dwell on the whole idea of escape. Instead, he took the girl's passport, thanked Misha and checked if all his belongings were packed. He couldn't sleep that night at all. At 4 am, he took his backpack, jacket and hat, met the girl in the corridor and they left the house without making any noise and without waking up anyone. They walked until the end of city where they found a taxi which took them to the train station. Luckily, when they arrived, they had to wait only twenty minutes for the train to Istanbul. And even though people were staring at the Westerner and Turkish

girl, everything went well. However, once they arrived here I believe you can imagine the shock of your great grandparents when their son brought a Yezidi girl to their house. But he was their only child whom they loved and supported in everything so they accepted her as his wife-to- be. But they were afraid that any moment someone might come to look for the girl and kill all of them in the house. Your great grandfather even bought special locks for the front door and a German Shepherd that stayed in the garden all night and day long. However, law was on their side since both their son and the girl were mature. Both of them were 21 years old.

After a year when they realized that no one was looking for the girl, they relaxed. Your grandpa and the girl, your grandma, got married and first they got me and a year after they got your uncle Misha.

Your grandma was a very smart woman. She learned English fast and even though I remember her strange accent when I was very little, by the time you were born, her accent was perfect. No one was able to say that she had been born in Turkey. However, you have to understand and I am sure you do that her life was not easy, before or after leaving Turkey. Giving up the whole her family and Yezidi identity was heartbreaking even though it was her choice. She suffered a lot. I remember finding her crying in her bedroom while holding the picture of the Peacock Angel and asking for forgiveness. She never heard anything about her parents and brother. Once when I was ten, your grandpa suggested going to her hometown alone and finding her parents and brother and trying to talk to them and beg them to accept him as their son-in-law, and to accept their marriage. She forbade him to ever again mention something similar. She knew how dangerous it would be to go back there and useless as well. She knew that kind of attempt would have no desired effects and it would be more than disappointing. She accepted that she would never again see anyone from her family. And she lived with it. The only reminder of that old life was the picture of the Peacock Angel."

The mother stopped talking. She went to the bedroom and after a minute came back. She came to Mila and opened her hand asking her to take what was in her palm. It was a small picture of the Peacock Angel.

"When I was little I found that picture in the grandma's drawer...she and grandpa fought over it.

Grandpa was very angry that she kept this picture," Mila said.

"No," the mother said, "they didn't fight over the picture. When your grandpa suggested going to find your grandma's family because he couldn't bear her suffering so much, she not only refused but asked him not to mention them again or anything that connected her to Yezidis. Years later, when you found this picture, he realized that she had never stopped suffering and probably felt guilty because she abandoned them. He was angry because she refused his help. He wanted her to stop feeling guilty and to stop suffering."

Her mother finished the story. Mila sat quietly holding the picture of the Peacock Angel. It must have been so hard for grandma to live the life with guilt and ignorance. But she didn't have other options. At least, it seemed so. The great thing was she had had a wonderful husband who loved her, children and grandchildren. She had the family that supported her, loved her, and made her life easier than the one she had led when she had been young. Some decisions were not easy to make but Mila guessed when you were young everything seemed easy. The only remnant left from her old life was that picture. And it was not a religious token as Mila had initially believed. It was a painful reminder to the old life. Her grandma kept this picture maybe to remind herself that we all did good and bad things in life. And as Yezidis believed that good and evil both exist in humans, it all depended on humans which one they chose. And even if they thought at certain moment they chose good but it was perceived as bad, they would be forgiven, as God forgave Melek Taus, the fallen angel.

Mila was happy with her own interpretation of her grandma's decisions, life, beliefs. After finishing the cup of tea, Mila kissed her mother goodbye and went home.

That night she lied in her bed eyes wide open thinking about the story her mother had told her a couple of hours ago. For a long time she couldn't fall asleep. But once she did, she slept deeply and peacefully like a newborn baby after finishing a full bottle of milk. There was no skull dream and the morning sun rays woke her up. She got up, came to the window, opened it and let the sun sneak inside her room. She made herself a cup of black Turkish coffee, took the Black Book, sat in a wind chair next to the window, face toward the sun and started reading it:

"Wherefore, it is true that My knowledge compasses the very Truth of all that Is, And My wisdom is not separate from My heart..."

About the Author:

Ana Vidosavljevic was born in Serbia and currently living in Indonesia. She has her work published or forthcoming in Down in the Dirt (Scar Publications), Literary Yard, RYL (Refresh Your Life), The Caterpillar, The Curlew, Eskimo Pie, Coldnoon, Perspectives, Indiana Voice Journal, The Raven Chronicles, Setu Bilingual Journal, Foliate Oak Literary Magazine, Quail Bell Magazine, Madcap Review, The Bookends Review, Gimmick Press, (mac)ro(mic), Scarlet Leaf Review. She worked on a GIEE 2011 project: Gender and Interdisciplinary Education for Engineers 2011 as a member of the Institute Mihailo Pupin team. She alsoattended the International Conference "Bullying and Abuse of Power" in November, 2010, in Prague, Czech Republic, where she presented her paper: "Cultural intolerance".

THE NEVER-ENDING WINDOW

by Matt Ingoldby

It was sometime in April when I returned from the clinic for a period of rest. My uncle had agreed to pay rent in my absence, but not to look after the place, which was as dismal and chaotic as I'd left it. I made some dutiful attempts to tidy up, but only as much as was needed to sit down at a clear desk and begin the grand project I'd conceived while inside the clinic.

Beginning today, I intended to produce a uniquely exhaustive autobiography, quite unlike anything written before in terms of scope: A single life described so comprehensively, and in such rigorous detail, that no aspect of human experience would escape it. I set a blank stack of paper before me and wrote my title on the first: A Grain of Sand.

Such a task, I recognised, would take more than my lifetime to complete. That much would fall to my successors. I was merely to lay the groundwork for this vast undertaking, akin to the mapping of the human genome.

My research began well. I tracked down historical images of the hospital where I was born, and filled six pages with descriptions of its architecture, colour, and environment (though even this, I knew, was insufficient.) Just before midday a square of sun fell upon the desk and matched the edges almost perfectly; this seemed to me a good omen, and a cue to continue my research into the night.

June soon laid waste to the city outside, and my room took on the climate of a greenhouse. The window had warped in its frame, and would not open. Days became unbearable: I couldn't think, could barely move; I lay in a cool bath, moaning.

At last I resolved against type and sound medical advice to seek outside help. I found the number for a general household repairman. He arrived the next morning full of practical vigour, with a toolbox so bulky it required both of us to manoeuvre it upstairs. He strode through the clutter and tugged at the stuck frame, talking a mile a minute; I gathered he could feel my awkwardness.

At last he stood back and whistled. I knew it with dread: The whole casement would have to be replaced. The welfare I received for mental incapacity would not cover this; I thanked him and apologised for wasting his time.

Taking pity on me, the man proposed to fetch his team and carry out the work at once, and I would pay only what I could. I agreed with awed gratitude. I asked him then if I might continue to work in the room while they replaced the frame. He said he didn't mind and left, vowing to return within the hour.

I had just re-entered the trance of my research when a knock at the room door re-woke me. I welcomed a number of men to the room (how many I could only tell once they were inside) who requested tea with sugar. When I returned with the tray, I did not recognise a soul, and left the mugs quietly on the workframe. Coming in then was a man with a plank of wood, which he unfolded into two, then four, of equal size to the first, until I looked away. Meekly I sat at the desk and attempted to resume my work.

But the scale of my labour, once thrilling, now weighed almost physically upon me. Every word I wrote seemed depthless, every sentence lacking all that I had hoped to capture.

I raised my eyes from the page to an orgy of activity. There were, at first glance, far too many workmen to fit inside the room, and yet there was space for us all. I stood up unheeded, saw numerous helmeted heads descend from the ceiling and sway there, loudly chattering. A square of floor where the carpet was drawn back now swung open, and more men rose through it, marching to a military drum. A spanner turned and so, imperceptibly, did the room. A ladder scrolled across my vision and continued for a long time; longer, certainly, than would seem to fit in end to end. I looked for a window, but could see none, although the space was airier and lighter than before. A hail of infinite sparks hid the instrument that made them. I saw suddenly a room that was my own, and another beside it, and many more, as many as there were angles to observe it; and in one there was a window that was jammed, and in the last, (for it stood to what reason I had left there should be a last,) would be a window that was new and open. But this room, I realised, was impossible to reach.

A powerful dread possessed me. I reeled and closed the door, not knowing whose room lay behind. With the vaguest intention to return when work was over, I wandered downstairs and outside. At the road I risked a glance over my shoulder.

The same bricks held a new frame; and through it, gazing blankly at the sun, I glimpsed my successor. He opened the window.

I was found unconscious beneath it and returned to the clinic soon after. My notes were never recovered. I do not know what became of the room with the window, or how it would appear now. I expect it has changed.

About the Author:

Matt Ingoldby works as a copywriter in the UK. His stories have appeared in The Pennsylvania Literary Journal, The Next Review, the Lowestoft Chronicle, Existeré, Octavius, Crimson Streets, Story & Grit, and one or two anthologies, working his way up to a novel. He is an active member of the Waterloo Theatre Group, and a keen runner. He currently lives in London.

HIT MEN HAVE FEELINGS TOO

by Edward D. Hunt

Boston's North End

After dropping his boss, Albee, at home in Milton, Tony Gazzo returned to the North End. Albee Parillo after becoming more successful had moved to Milton away from this Italian conclave. He told Tony he wasn't needed tomorrow and that he would be spending time with his family. Tony's schedule was somewhat unpredictable, but for the most part he worked the hours Albee worked, picking him up in the morning and dropping him off at night. Tony was mostly a bodyguard, an enforcer and a driver but he was trusted with other assignments as well. He was often the one to give others in the crew assignments. If he said it, they knew it was coming from Albee.

Tony got along with the rest of the crew but really wasn't close to them. He really didn't make friends. He kept to himself. He did have one redeeming quality that Albee valued very highly, he was loyal to Albee, willing to die for loyal. Not something you come across every day.

On the way back in the car from Jamaica Plain, Albee talked about his concerns with some of their "business" partners and the possible exposure they might have if as rumored there may be a federal investigation underway. Albee wouldn't be sharing this unless he thought Tony was going to have to get involved. He didn't need to say that, Tony understood. Albee stressed how delicate the situation was and in how many areas they and their partners had and have some common interests. Hopefully they could clean up their own mess but Albee wasn't betting on it.

Tony was one of the few people Albee confided in. He knew anything said would never go any further and he knew he didn't have to explain it in too much detail; Tony would get it.

Driving in the North End was always challenging, but even more so when something was going on at the TD Garden. It was summer so no Celtics or Bruins but there was a full concert schedule. Tony remained calm, there was no place he had to be and no time he had to be there. Utilizing a narrow side street he finally got to the small parking lot behind the commercial building where he parked for free. Albee had arranged it and he wasn't sure of the exact ownership but somehow Albee was involved.

His apartment was three buildings down on the third floor above a small coffee shop that was open late. The apartment was small but expensively furnished. Typical male décor with leather furniture and dark woods and a seventy inch large screen television. It was always neat and extremely clean with gleaming hard wood floors and well maintained oriental carpets. No one was allowed to enter the apartment when he wasn't home. He cleaned it himself and had an elaborate alarm system. He really didn't have anything valuable and except for two hidden hand guns. There was nothing incriminating in the apartment. He had several safe deposit boxes in local banks under various names where he did have a lot of money and valuables stashed. He also owned a small cabin in New Hampshire under an alias that even Albee wasn't aware of. He had enough money stashed in multiple accounts that if he had to make a quick exit he was prepared.

Instead of going directly upstairs he decided to eat downstairs. He sat at the counter as was his habit. Gina always worked the counter and the other waitresses worked the floor. In addition to working the counter, she handled the cash register. The owner, Louie trusted her and no one else. They were related somehow. She was the only waitress tonight. The restaurant wasn't busy but she was. She was always in motion, finding something to clean or organize during down times.

Without being asked, Gina poured him a cup of black coffee and placed it in front of him. She nodded at him in response to his smile. She wasn't attractive. Tall, skinny, with pockmarked skin, she always kept her long wild hair tied back when she was working. She rarely said much and never smiled. He knew she was on some sort of medication and he knew when they were adjusting the dosage because she would mumble to herself. She would probably be unemployable anywhere else or at least anywhere where customer contact was required.

There wasn't much on the menu, a few sandwiches and a few daily specials scrawled on a blackboard. Most people just came in for the coffee and the Italian pastries.

"Still have some beef stew." She said this without looking up from under the counter where she was rearranging the condiments. She knew he liked the stew. She looked up long enough to see him nod which prompted her to set him up with a napkin and silverware.

He watched her walk away to go get his stew. Tony Gazzo wasn't attractive either. He was big and intimidating with very pronounced features. A large nose and big lips with a receding hairline. Close to forty he could easily pass for much older. He knew he scared people which was a plus in his work but he really didn't understand why he scared people when he was trying not to.

His personal life was pretty limited. To meet his sexual needs he had brief hookups with strippers and other professionals who were afraid to say no to him. He knew they were afraid but he had never forced them and if they truly acted reluctant he backed off. His needs were minimal so it wasn't that much of a hardship.

Most of his time not working was spent by himself watching Netflix and HBO. He liked the "Game of Thrones." He also liked to read westerns. Mostly Louis L'Amour.

The other waitresses pretty much ignored Gina; they talked with her about work related issues but never anything else. They didn't seem to be trying to be mean or hurtful, they just didn't have anything in common with her. Gina acted like she didn't take notice but Tony was sure that she did; he knew that she was intelligent. During slow times she sat on a stool near the register reading books.

Most people from the neighborhood who came into the restaurant gave Tony his space. Rarely did anyone sit on the stools right next to him, and even those he knew would only nod or briefly say hello.

Gina was different, she wasn't afraid of him. Whether it was because she didn't highly value the life she lived or she sensed a kindred spirit; she seemed comfortable around him and comfortable saying whatever came into her head. When it was raining she told him he should be wearing his raincoat and offered him her multicolored umbrella which he politely declined. She also would warn him on what to eat or not to eat. "Stay away from the meatloaf." No one else in his life talked to him like this or took any interest and he found himself looking forward to it.

He was almost finished with the beef stew and she had refilled his coffee cup without being asked. Tony thanked her and she smiled slightly in return.

Two young wannabe wise guys entered and sat down seven or eight stools away from Tony. Both had said, "Hi, Tony," on their way in. They lost their swagger when he stared back at them and nodded. They were kind of loud and had probably been drinking but Tony ignored them until they started making comments about Gina.

"Would you?" The shorter one challenged his friend.

"Not even with a bag over her head." The other one snorted his response spilling his coffee.

"Well, what about in the dark, and nobody else would ever find out?" The short one persisted, well in earshot of Gina.

"Shit no, not even with your dick!" They both laughed at that.

They were still laughing and didn't even notice Tony until he sat down beside them and took a knife out of his pocket. Snapping open the knife, he pressed the blade into the neck of the last one to speak. "Say something else and I will cut out your tongue before I slit your throat." Tony said this in a monotone which made it even more frightening. Neither one doubted he would do it.

"Jesus, Tony, we were only screwing around. We didn't know she was a friend of yours!" The wise guy without the knife pressed to his throat spoke up, the other one was blubbering and couldn't be understood.

"Leave and don't come back." He put the knife away and they both jumped up and headed toward the exit.

Gina had ignored them and continued to keep busy throughout all of this but now she stopped and looked at him. He nodded at her and she nodded back.

Two weeks later he stopped into the Coffee Shop right before closing and ordered coffee. She was the only waitress on again and she was busy restocking the shelves, and refilling salt and pepper shakers and napkin holders. When she was topping off his coffee she hesitated for a moment and then looking at him directly said:"I can come up for a while if you'd like."

Looking back at her, he considered it and what she possibly meant. "Okay," he nodded in response.

She brought up some left over pastries and he made a pot of coffee. She looked at all the books on his bookcase and his cd player and his music. She didn't sit down until he brought her coffee and then they sat together on his leather sofa side by side.

"Do you want to watch something on television?" She asked this picking up the remote not waiting for him to answer. "Is there anything you would like to watch?"

"Not really, you can pick something." Tony was trying to be agreeable. He was awkward at best in social situations.

She settled for a movie "Our Souls at Night" which wouldn't have been his first choice. It was a love story about an elderly couple. She explained that she had read the book it was based upon

by Kent Haruf and she had really liked it. He nodded, not really caring what they watched.

He was starting to dose off by the end of the movie. She turned off the television, picked up their coffee cups and plates and brought them to the kitchen.

She came back into the room and bent over and embraced him, saying she should go. He nodded in response and stood up as she picked up her oversized handbag and her sweater.

"Maybe we can do this again Saturday?" she looked at him expectantly.

"Yeah, sure...that'd be good." He was nodding again.

She kissed him on the cheek.

Providence, Rhode Island

Tony Gazzo hadn't been back to Providence since before he went to prison; more than seven years ago. Coming back from New York, he had been struggling with the urge to go by the house and see if she was still there. At Albee's request Tony had made a problem for their friends in New York disappear. It wasn't the first time and Tony had a reputation for being very good at what he did. Albee always gave him a bonus for this kind of work but Tony would have done it for nothing.

Tony stayed away from Providence, too much history. He had done a lot of damage here, on his own and on Albee's behalf. Providence had been his home. Tony really didn't have any emotional ties to Providence or to any other place. In actuality he didn't really have any emotional ties to anyone or anything. Something with this woman from his past that he couldn't explain. Maybe something with Gina, he didn't know yet. Probably the closest tie he had was his connection to Albee and that was forged years ago when Albee aligned with a faction that was battling a group that included the man that Tony held responsible for killing his father. His father was a small time bookie and while he wasn't able to articulate his feelings, he felt something when his father had been gunned down coming out of a Chinese restaurant. Tony was only fifteen and was on his own after that. His mother had died during childbirth and it had always been just his father and him with a hired housekeeper or two. He was always different but his father seemed somewhat oblivious to the fact and accepted him the way he was. His father got really angry whenever anyone suggested that there was anything wrong with him. At school some therapist diagnosed him as possibly having some form of highly functioning autism but his father wasn't having any part of that. Tony was always a big kid and strong and the few kids who made fun of him paid a price. At thirteen he beat a fifteen year old badly enough that he needed to be hospitalized and even his father couldn't keep him from being sent off to Sockanossett, the youth reform facility in Cranston. He was still there when his father got on the bad side of someone better connected and was shot down in the street. Tony showed no reaction when he was told, but immediately began planning his retribution.

He bided his time and at the age of eighteen started working for a friend of his father doing odds and ends. It didn't take long before he was given some additional responsibilities as an enforcer and driver for his boss who trusted him. Not long after that the same local crew that had encroached on his father's territory started leaning on his boss. Tony volunteered to eliminate his father's killer and make a statement while doing so. This was his first hit and it established his reputation, especially when the man's head turned up in a dumpster owned by his boss's rival.

They were still badly outnumbered and probably wouldn't have survived if his boss hadn't established an alliance with Albee. It was a violent couple of years, even for Providence, with killings taking place all over the city including Federal Hill, the Italian stronghold once

always thought to be a safe neighborhood. The violence became commonplace and somewhat accepted and a small Italian restaurant on Atwells Avenue became popular after a sanctioned hit took place in a booth near the front door. Customers would request that booth and be willing to wait. Providence was always a very tolerant city with corrupt politicians being forgiven for their crimes and sometimes reelected. Albee recognized Tony's potential and took him under his wing. Albee was smart enough to treat Tony as you would any explosive; useful in certain situations but needing to be handled with extreme care.

Providence wasn't the same city today, with tourists now visiting a much safer Federal Hill, eating at sidewalk cafes and purchasing traditional Italian pastries and other desserts.

Prostitution wasn't even legal anymore. For years it wasn't a priority due to the lack of specific laws and codes for prosecution. Street hookers were harassed and picked up occasionally in the neighborhoods but for the most part ignored when they lined up outside the old railroad station. A small hotel on Washington Street was once known for its large number of prostitutes hanging out in the bar. Rooms were let by the hour, not the day. Today it was now low income housing helping to provide homes for some of the city's homeless.

Tony didn't know what to expect when he pulled up in front of the large old Victorian. It badly needed a coat of paint. Just off Prairie Avenue in South Providence, the neighborhood had changed too, from a mostly black population when Tony was growing up to a mixed neighborhood including Asians and Hispanics. Always a poor and violent area, it still attracted immigrants as a place to get a start or a foothold but also street gangs fighting to protect their turf. Tony did feel a connection to the woman in the house, somewhat protective. If asked he wouldn't be able to explain his feelings.

He was just about to get out of the car when his phone began vibrating. Tony rarely got calls but had expected this one. He could tell by Albee's voice he was pleased.

"Our friends in New York were very appreciative of your assistance. Will you be back tonight?"

"Dunno, stopping in Providence."

"OK. Talked to our partners. They are in agreement that maybe we should get involved with that thing I've been worried about. Has to be handled very carefully. We'll talk in the morning."

"All right. I'll be back early." Albee had already briefed him on what he wanted him to do. Albee had had also stressed that he should minimize the violence. He would try but things happen.

He sat in the car for a few more minutes staring at the house. When he was a boy he had come here with his father at least once a week. Often they would stay overnight. The women here were kind to him and he would often bring some toys with him when he was small. He would wait in a room off the main parlor and they would check in on him and bring him snacks from time to time and marvel on how well behaved and quiet he was. If they weren't staying over his father would come out after a few hours and they would go home. If they were staying, she would come out and get him and bring him back to her room. His father would already be asleep on one side of her bed with the blankets and sheets in disarray. She would climb in beside him and pat the place next to her. Laying down next to her, she would cover him up. He remembered falling asleep smelling faint traces of her perfume with her arms wrapped tightly around him. This was the only woman he could remember his father ever being with.

Knocking on the door, it only took a few seconds before it opened, someone must have been watching the street. A young, pretty, dark skinned woman stood smiling at him, stepping back to let him enter. She led him into what used to be called the parlor. It was late and only a few women remained. The room hadn't changed much with its old fashioned furniture and floor length velvet drapes. The wingback sofa and chairs looked like they may have been reupholstered, he couldn't tell, but the furniture was in good condition. There were a few scratches on the end tables and the coffee table. The only significant change was now the women were of multiple races and not just black.

The woman who let him in turned and still smiling addressed him. She had one hand on her hip. "How can we help you, sweetie?"

"Vanessa."

"Nessie? Nessie don't do no business! She's what you call management." She was laughing when she said it.

An older woman who recognized him from before spoke up. "She'll see him, tell her Tony is here." The serious tone of her voice made it clear it wasn't up for discussion. The younger woman shrugged and left the room.

Tony stood patiently waiting and no one invited him to sit down. He was aware as always that he was scaring them, and again, without intending to. They were relieved when Vanessa entered the room. She smiled at him and he actually smiled back.

"Long time, Tony."

"Long time." Tony stood there looking her over. A tall attractive black woman, she had aged well. Her hair was all gray now and she seemed a little curvier but not really fat. She had to be at least sixty.

She knew better than to hug him in public so she took him by the hand and led him back to her room.

Her room was larger than the others and had a sitting area and a small kitchenette. Several prints depicting the ocean were on the wall. Edward Hunt

"Coffee?" He nodded in response and she poured him a cup from a half full coffee pot not having to ask him how he took it. She didn't bother to offer him something stronger; she knew he didn't drink.

They sat on the small sofa together and she talked while he listened, nodding from time to time and occasionally offering one or two word comments. She talked about people they both knew and about things from the past and about her life now.

"Do you need anything, are they treating you all right?" This was the first thing of any significance Tony had said and she smiled in response.

"No, honey, I'm fine. They leave me alone but how about you? Are you hungry? I could make you something."

"No, thanks. I stopped and ate on the highway."

"Are you staying over? You look tired." She looked genuinely concerned.

"I'd like to."

"Come on." She reached out and took his hand again and he followed her to her bed. She was already in a low cut nightgown and climbed in and patted the place beside her.

He slowly undressed putting his shoes under the bed and folding his clothes neatly and placing them on a nearby chair. Stripped down to just his boxer shorts he climbed in with his back towards her. She wrapped her arms around him tightly and within minutes he was fast asleep.

About the Author:

Edward Daniel Hunt has a B.S. from the University of New Haven and M.S. from Lesley University. He hopes to have his first novel "Penance" published soon. He has recently had short stories published in the Scarlett Leaf Review and Down in the Dirt Magazine. Much of his early work and social life was spent in restaurants and bars as evidenced in his writing. He is a member of the Maine Writers and Publishers Alliance and Mystery Writers of America.

DAGGER

by Maureen Grace

"Ohhh," he cried quietly, so as not to scare off the passers by; their handouts had allowed him to eek out the barest of succor for (could it really be?) twenty-seven years. He shifted position - the meager carpet he sat on did little to keep the cold from penetrating his body. Uncrossing his legs, he leaned back against the stone edifice - a commercial building in Camden Town - one of the old piano-making factories long gone to trendy shops and sidewalk cafes.

It was his corner. After all these years, no one challenged him. It was a decent spot; at a busy intersection -especially at rush hour - commuters came out of the Tube right into his path. A penny here, a pound there, it added up. You could tell a lot about a person from the knees down. How they walked, for example. Did they shuffle belaboredly, or sprint like gazelles? Footwear gave even more away. The shiny loafers; impeccable hose - rarely did they notice him. But the shufflers did. The weekends were always good - the kids with stiletto heels and high-top sneakers. He hated the Goth look (his neighborhood had become its mecca) - mutilating their smooth young skin with tattoos and piercings, and capping it all with purple or pink hair. It offended his aesthetics; still they would toss some coins his way as they hurried to their gathering spots. But it was the business folk who sustained him. Early morning handouts.

"How's it going, Alfie?" Another pound warmed his ungloved hand. Billy Anderson had taken a personal interest in him. Over the years they had become friends, sharing stories, always in generalities, about their young dreams - before life had had its way with them. They were complicit in their aversion to specifics, allowing a freedom of ideas without the Achilles heel of particulars, or emotional exposure. Billy was quite well off. Family money, Alfie surmised; but the bloke was quite enterprising in his own right. Hard to keep a shop going for a decade.

He shifted again. It didn't help. The Christmas lights bounced off the ice-slicked puddle just off the curb - a silent rebuke for a broken life. He was suddenly struck with an awful clarity - he was homesick.

"Too cold to beg today, come in and have a cuppa," Billy offered. Alfie rose slowly. He followed him into the cafe. It would take a few minutes for the heat to kick in; but it was already a relief.

"Sit in the leather chair, Alfie. Take a load off," said Billy motioning to the most comfortable seat in the shop.

"Can only spare a minute, Mate," said Alfie.

Still quite dark at seven, it was the beginning of his workday. The early morning rush.

"Why the long face these last weeks?" asked Billy with a hint of privileged guilt in his voice. Normally, Alfie would exploit it; but not today.

"I want to go home."

Alfie was surprised at the pleading in his own voice; so was Billy.

"And home is where?"

"Brooklyn, New York in the good old USA -and by the way, my name is Henry Wordsworth Blaylock. First person I've shared that with in over twenty years."

Alfie aka Henry removed his bright red stove-pipe hat - always a crowd pleaser - a way for busy commuters to spot him. It was damp and wet. He touched his gray-flecked beard with unpleasant discovery. What a wreck.

"I never took you for a Yank," said Billy.

"That was the idea. I came over in '87 - a graduate student in art. Believe it or not, on full scholarship. That's when I met Julie. An Aussie, on scholarship too. I fell so far in love I never found my way back."

"What happened to her?"

"I drank a lot. Julie couldn't handle it. She hung in till '89; finally gave an ultimatum - the booze or her. I chose the whisky; or maybe it chose me; I couldn't shake it. She went back to Melbourne. Heard from her once in '92 but that was it. I don't blame her. But honestly, I loved her; still do."

"And your family?"

"Couldn't face them; the cajoling and all, so I just got lost. I became Alfie. Remember the song, What's it all about, Alfie? Still don't know. I just want to go home."

Billy regarded him over his steaming cup. After a moment, he said,

"I'd like to help you with that, Alfie or should I call you Henry?"

"No, Alfie is fine. And how could you help?"

"My friend, I'm going to sort out your paperwork and buy you a first class ticket to New York City. I only ask one thing: write and let me know how you are. I'll make it round-trip - just in case."

"No can do, my friend. I'm a bum with no clothes and no money." It was true, but they both knew he had his game on again.

"In for a penny, in for a pound," smiled Billy. "Meet me here tomorrow at two. And take a shower. We're going shopping."

The next evening at six, Alfie looked like a well-heeled commuter. He took his freshly purchased navy carry-on - full of crisp new clothes - home to his small basement room. It used to be a storage closet and barely fit his cot and chair. When he lay down, his head touched one wall and his toes the other. He stared at the wet cracks in the ceiling. The mold spread in slow inky symmetry like the web of a languorous spider. Watery drops gathered mass, congealed and dove listlessly into the bucket in the far corner. Billy's words echoed in his head. "We'll meet at my brother's - the attorney in the family - and sort out your passport. With luck, you'll be in Brooklyn by New Year's Eve." Alfie didn't believe in luck. And dreams were a luxury he had cast off along with his name. So he just listened to the rhythm of the drip, drip, drip.

Five days later, with passport and ticket in hand, plus $500 tucked in a fine-smelling leather wallet, Alfie was at Heathrow. Billy and he sat together at the departure drop-off.

"You're actually a handsome fellow, Henry Wordsworth Blaylock. Kiss your Mom for me."

He clapped him on the shoulder. "There you go now; that's a good one then. Remember, just head for first class check in. They'll take care of the rest."

Alfie stepped out of the car and headed towards the airport entrance. He turned and waved.

"How can I ever thank you? Such a thing to do."

"Good luck, Henry, just write me a note." The car sped away.

He stood in the middle of the well-ordered first class lounge. The airline personnel assigned to the area were obviously the cream of the crop. Quiet solicitation and hushed voices offered flower-infused water and full breakfast. He noted that customers were helping themselves to the coffee and water. So they must be free. But what about the food? He was hungry but didn't want to embarrass himself, so he had elderberry apple juice and vitamin water. Of course the bar was busy. Free as well? He didn't want to find out. He'd been off the sauce for almost a week now. It felt pretty good. He saw his clean-shaven reflection bouncing off a glass-covered billboard. Julie had always gone weak for the cleft in his chin. He'd forgotten about that. His large gray eyes were steady and well spaced. Being tall had advantages; it had helped him protect his corner turf. Now he commanded another kind of respect. He could see it in the women's eyes as they smiled up at him. The men took his measure, deferring to him as if he might be somebody. Who was he now? And why had he agreed to this? He found a taupe mid-century chair that faced the busy runway.

He hadn't flown in almost thirty years. He remembered the newness, coursing in hopeful swells through his six foot-four frame as he crunched into his discount seat. Now he was about to board again - but this time consumed with fear.

"Your flight is boarding, Mr. Blaylock, this way please. Gate 32."

"Good day, Sir." The captain tipped his hat as Alfie passed into seat 2A.

He was dazzled and confused by the myriad of buttons and electronics in his luxurious cubicle. But the seat was quite large and his legs stretched out as far as he wanted. He exhaled with the first sense of relief he had felt in days.

The city revealed itself suddenly, lifting like a mirage through orange-tinged clouds. The evening lights outlined a silhouette achingly familiar, interposed with strange new shapes. He took comfort from the Empire State Building, dressed in Christmas green and red. Although he knew better, he searched for the twin blocks that had been the World Trade Towers. He had never liked them architecturally but now he mourned them - lost beacons in his tenuous landscape.

He got through Customs quickly.

"Welcome home, Sir," said the agent. Alfie nodded, took his bag and headed for the exit. He flagged a cab and headed immediately to his mother's house - to his house. Better to bite the bullet right away. He clutched his wallet reassuringly; how much was a cab ride these days?

"Hendrickson and Flatlands, please."

"Street address?" asked the cabbie.

"The corner will be fine."

The trip from JFK was shorter than he'd expected. They were going against the Belt Parkway rush-hour traffic that inched like a frozen slug towards Long Island. Lucky me; poor suckers. He thought that maybe things would begin to break in his direction.

"That'll be fifteen bucks even," said the cabby as he pulled over.

Alfie handed him a twenty.

"Keep the change," he said, lifting his bag onto the curb. He glanced around as the cab pulled away. The house was a mile away. He needed the time to center himself. He saw St. Thomas Aquinas rectory and wondered if Holy Family was still around, and Father Torres - a good priest who had pulled him away from trouble when he was a kid. He walked briskly, anxious now to get home. His house, a multi-family brownstone, had seen glory days, replete with Tiffany windows and inlaid wood; and desultory times - when everything had been stripped bare.

The neighborhood had always been a kaleidoscope of shifting cultures - the new immigrants often resented and sometimes feared by the entrenched inhabitants; who, in turn, had been feared and resented themselves when they had first settled there - going all the way back to the 1600's and the Dutchman, Von Cowenhoven and the Lenape 'Indian chiefs' - from whom he had purchased most of what was now Brooklyn.

His grandfather, a dockworker of English-German stock and builder in his sparse free time, had bought the house in the Fifties and gradually made it livable - not elegant, but serviceable. When his parents inherited it in the late Sixties, they took the basement and parlor floors, and half of the second. They rented out the top two stories - sometimes a pain, but mostly, it was a reliable source of needed income for a family of five.

"Gee Mom, it's great to see you."

"Wow, Mom you look terrific. Your prodigal son is home at last."

He stood staring at his well-polished shoes - not the footwear a beggar could count on for a handout. He kept rehearsing phrases, trying to get it right. He gave up and walked the remaining twenty yards, immersed in guilt and anticipation, to the front gate. He took a deep breath and looked up.

It was gone.

The house was simply not there. No gate, no steps, no trees, nothing. I've got the wrong street. You damn fool. What a moron. His heart sloshed against his chest. Panicking, he surveyed the block. It was his street. He fell to the ground - automatically assuming his beggar's squat. The earth where his house once stood was smooth, packed down. He hadn't realized how big the lot was. An ugly gap. The block seemed to be missing its front teeth. Who demolishes a house, just like that? He sat there for a long time. His mind was numb. So were his toes. It was getting cold, very cold. He rose slowly, hesitated, then turned and ran along Flatbush Avenue towards the water, searching frantically, with his carry-on bumping behind him.

Still there. "The Neon Mermaid" glowed garishly in raunchy red, just as it always had. One of his favorite haunts, back in the day. He slowed down and caught his breath. Only half full, the after work crowd was slowly trickling in. The bar was the same - highly polished and well-worn hardwood. But the bar stools sported cherry red Naugahyde cushioned seats with silver back rests. Upgrade. Someone's doing okay. He found a spot at the end of the bar. It took a minute for his eyes to adjust to the light. Mood lighting. Hah. Fancy smancy. Summoning his courage, he sought and dreaded anyone familiar. There he is. Even from the back, Alfie recognized Tommy Allen. He had a full head of close-cropped salt and pepper hair, almost a buzz-cut. It seemed to extend to his face, the beard the same length as the hair - a monochromatic exposition of head fuzz. His powerful shoulders and ham hock neck showed no sign of age. He must spend a lot of time at the gym. Alfie waited. Tommy eventually looked his way, staring questioningly as he got closer.

"Tell me I'm not seeing a ghost. You goddamned son of a bitch. Henry? Henry Blaylock? What the fuck, Henry!"

Tommy raised his hand. Alfie didn't know whether to duck or shake. He was five inches taller than Tommy but he had never beaten him in a fight. Not that there had been many; Alfie's self-preservation saw to that. The youngest of three tough boys, the kid never backed down and never stopped punching. Even his beefy brothers gave up picking on him by the time he turned six.

Taking what he hoped was a friendly proffer, Alfie reached over the bar and grabbed Tommy's hand with the strongest grip he could muster. Tommy burst into a wide even smile.

"We didn't know whether you were alive or dead. Nobody did."

He ignored the comment.

"Time's treating you well, Tommy. The bar - is it yours now?"

"Yup, Dad's legacy. Never thought he had that much confidence in me. He was as nasty as your old man. Longshoremen - mean-fisted old bastards. We both have the scars to prove it, right Buddy?"

He wasn't smiling anymore.

Alfie was still relieved that his father was dead, some twenty years now - the last time anyone had tracked him down. His brother, Chuck, his father's favorite, was always the one to try to hold things together. "You've got to see him, Henry, he needs to talk to you. He's in bad shape. Doctors say he won't last a week. Lung cancer; those damned cigarettes. Please, come home."

"For him? Not on your life. Now maybe Mom can finally have some peace."

Chuck had hung up on him. Alfie had responded by throwing his cell phone in the rubbish. Pay as go from now on. And that had been that.

"What happened to my house, Tommy? And Mom?"

His old friend regarded him carefully.

"Chuck and Sally sold it five years ago."

"Why?"

"Because it was too much to keep up. Your Mom couldn't handle it - the tenants and all. She went to live with Chuck in Forest Hills."

"And who got all the money? Chuck, no doubt."

"Hey, man, don't drag me into your family stuff. I've got enough of my own. Don't think I didn't get this place without a load of resentment from my own brothers."

"And what about Sally?"

"Your sister and Wayne are in Philly now. Her daughter is just as pretty as she is. And your nephew, he's a handful. Teenagers! Just like someone I used to know." He winked. "We talk every now and then; still carry that torch; can't help it."

"Can you give me her number? And while you're at it, give me Chuck's too."

"Your sister never gave up on you, bro; neither did your Mom. Hey, you look thirsty. Let me get you a beer. Brooklyn is now the home of some of the best microbrews on the planet."

"What I'd like is some hot tea. Got to thaw out a bit."

Tommy looked surprised; he kept the wise-crack to himself.

"I'll be right back with their contact info - and the tea. You take milk and sugar?"

"I like my tea neat," Alfie smiled, admiring his friend's restraint.

The first call was to Chuck. He needed to see his mother. He stepped out into the small vestibule - one of those temporary affairs made of plastic and canvas that keeps the cold and snow from blowing in.

"Chuck Blaylock here."

He's answering his home phone like it's a business.

"Chuck, it's Henry."

Silence.

"I'm in town, Chuck. I want to see Mom. I'm at Tommy's bar. He told me she moved in with you and Janie."

"Now you call? Do you think time stopped just for you, you selfish prick?"

"I'm not gonna argue with you. Just put Mom on."

"Well, that'd be pretty hard to do, Henry. She died three weeks ago, you fucking asshole!" Chuck slammed the phone against the wall. Or that's how it sounded from Alfie's end. He could hear Janie ask, "Chuck, what's going on? What is it?" The phone clicked off.

"Excuse me," said a pretty young woman bundled up against the late December wind. He stepped aside to let her and her companions pass. The cold air blasted him as the canvas door admitted a steady stream of patrons. The place had filled up - the last workday before the long New Year's weekend. He turned and thought to warm himself. The tea would taste good; so would a hot toddy.

Instead, he wandered onto the avenue and headed towards Marine Park - always a refuge when he was a boy. He'd played baseball and basketball there and sometimes, a game of bocce with the old Italian guys. He'd been a good athlete.

His dad worked with his hands and disciplined with his fists. Henry was always the one who got hit. Girls were never to be struck, not that Sally ever gave her father a reason to consider it. And Chuck? He was such a suck-up, always seeking paternal attention. He could still feel the blows hammering into his stomach - he'd crumble forward as the wind got snuffed out; then the old bastard would punch his bended head. His mother would break it up. When he was fourteen, she finally realized that gentle pleading was useless against a rage-aholic. In an act of adrenalin infused strength, she took a wicker kitchen chair and smashed it to smithereens over her husband's head.

"If you ever hit him again, I will leave you. Do not test me, Martin."

Her husband had frozen in astonishment. He never touched his son again; and that included hugs. Henry had become off limits to rage and affection. That was fine with him.

He loved the biting scent of the saltwater marshes. The wind whipped through the dunes - the grasses undulating in a hoary sea breeze. An almost full moon bathed the landscape in ghostly splendor - a study in glacial white - just like his heart, stripped now of his mother's lifeblood.

He longed for spring; for the exuberant chirps of Myrtle warblers and grasshopper sparrows - the joyous cacophony that once soothed his young soul. He used to lie in the shrubs, very still. On a good day, a rabbit or a pheasant would cross his path. He thought of the horseshoe crabs; he'd discover their shells scattered among the seaweed, rocking in the tide. Through births and deaths of myriad species, continents, and new worlds - long out-lasting the dinosaurs, they still poured into this very spot, as they had for more than five millions years, seeking a mate. If he was very lucky, he'd encounter a loon (another multi-million year old survivor) bobbing offshore, as it preened from its molting and reclaimed its haunting call silenced by the winter winds.

But it was not spring. Shivering uncontrollably, he headed back to the Mermaid. Tommy was relieved when he spotted him through the festive crowd. Alfie made his way to a small opening in the now packed bar.

"About that tea," he said mustering a smile.

"Coming right up. Where'd you go? Where are you staying tonight?"

"Not sure, yet. I'll find someplace. Not to worry."

"Not tonight you won't. Everything in town is booked for New Year's. Listen, I have a friend who has a bed and breakfast just up the street. She's got a tiny room that she only rents out in a pinch. I could ask her; maybe it's available. Why don't I give her a call?"

"I'm used to tiny. Yeah, thanks, that would be good."

"And how about a sandwich to go with the tea? You look like you could stand to eat."

Alfie was hungry, and sick. He had felt it coming on since he'd been at the lawyer's office five days before; it had finally caught up with him. He wanted to call his sister, but not now. He'd wait until he got some sleep.

That night, he listened to the hot water pipes gurgle up cozily. The heat felt good. There was a decent shared bath just across the hall. He treated himself to a long, hot shower and put on his new pajamas; Billy Anderson had insisted he get flannel. They were hunter green, dotted with small beige hunting dogs shaped like English Pointers. The proprietor had given him two extra blankets - one of which was wool. He piled them on and crawled under, pulling them over his shoulders. But he couldn't get warm; a fever gripped him. It was almost midnight, five in the morning London time. The last thing he wanted to do was go out to get some aspirin.

Compared to his room in Camden, this place was a palace. There was a desk with writing paper, a comfortable chair, a small sink with hand towels stacked on a shelf, and a narrow closet. He even had a window that overlooked several back yards - three of them had Christmas trees. Their colorful lights swayed in the frozen breeze; through the darkness he could see their muted hues dancing behind the gauzy drapes. Maybe I'll stay here for a few nights, until I feel better. Drawing the covers closer, he nestled into the lavender scented pillow and fell asleep.

He was still sick when he woke up at ten the next morning. The sun was shining weakly through a tired haze. After arranging to stay the weekend, he walked to a diner on the corner and ordered eggs and hot tea. He'd picked up some aspirin and downed it with the water that, ridiculously, was served with ice. A nice American touch in the summer, but not today. He shivered and cupped his tea. He decided to order some chicken soup.

As he headed back to his room, he surveyed his old neighborhood. It had changed. What did he expect? Of course, it had. There were high-rises where there used to be wooden row houses. Tucked into the ground floors, the storefronts were either national chains or small specialty shops. Artisan this and that: coffee, tea, leather goods, handbags, spices; trendy bars. There were some remaining bodegas sprinkled here and there. And the Hispanic Center was still open for business. Gentrification was infiltrating even the more dilapidated side streets. That's probably what the neighbors grumbled about his grandfather, back in the Fifties, when he had bought the place for a song. He wondered what would be built on his property next. Not big enough for a high rise; so, probably some elaborate new brownstone. Did they have historic districts or strict building codes these days? Or was everything going to the highest bidder?

He sat on his bed and stared at Sally's number. Somehow he knew that speaking to her would make all this real. He wasn't sure he could handle it. He wrapped the blanket around himself and made the call anyway.

"Hello?"

God, it was good to hear her voice. He found it hard to speak.

"Henry, is that you? Chuck called me this morning. Henry?"

"It's me. How are you, Sally? Tommy Allen sends his love," he said teasingly.

It was a stupid thing to say; she was a married woman now, not his fifteen-year old sister. He regretted it immediately.

"Forgive me. It's just been so long. I'm a jerk. I guess that hasn't changed."

She laughed worriedly.

"How are you, Henry? Where are you?"

"Tommy got me a room at a friend's place. What happened to Mom? Was she sick? Did she suffer? I can't believe, I don't believe she's dead."

"She didn't suffer, Henry. She had a heart attack. By the time the paramedics got there, she was gone."

He could tell she was crying.

"I'm so sorry, Sally. I swear I think I knew it. A few weeks ago, out of nowhere, I got so homesick; I had to come back. But I'm too late."

He felt his eyes welling up; he stopped himself.

"You know the last thing she said to Chuck and Janie, really the only words she got out, before she died?"

He was afraid to hear.

"What?"

"She said, Tell Henry when he comes home that I love him; tell him everything will be okay. And that was it. She loved you so much, Henry. She always knew you'd come back."

He reeled back from a blow far greater than any his father had ever delivered - a merciless dagger of regret.

They were silent for a long while. He could hear her sobs; he wished he were there to hold her; to protect her as he always had. But who would he be protecting her from? He was surely a cause of her sorrow, of Chuck's rage. Coming back had been a huge mistake.

"Where is she buried?"

"She's in Greenwood, cremated, in Grandma's family plot. It was what she wanted. Oh, Henry, why not come here and stay a while?"

"First, I've got to see Mom."

"She's gone, Henry."

"Please, I need a few days. Then, we'll see. I'm so sorry."

He hung up before she could respond and sat shaking on the bed. From fever? From grief? What had he been thinking? He looked over at the desk and saw the writing paper. There was one promise he could keep. He addressed the envelope, taking the information from Billy Anderson's card.

New Year's Eve, American style

Dear Billy,

Well, you were right. Everyone here was so happy to see me. My mother is overjoyed. How can I ever repay you for the generosity you have shown me, my friend? I think I'll be staying with her for a while, until I get my feet on the ground. It feels great to be in my old room again.

They tell me the economy here has turned up; there might even be a spot for someone like me. Imagine that!

Don't be concerned if you don't hear from me for a while, I've got a lot of catching up to do.

With great affection and eternal thanks,

Alfie (aka Henry)

P.S. Happy New Year!!!!

He folded the letter, put it in the envelope and placed it carefully in his breast pocket. He considered fedexing it; but, what was the rush, he'd wait till the post office opened after the holiday.

It was bitter cold. The sun succumbed to the flurries - small white furies that swirled in the shifting wind. He walked for a while, north on Flatbush, towards Greenwood Cemetery - a revolutionary site and part of a vibrant swath of green that cut through Brooklyn, along with the Botanical Garden and Prospect Park. A visitor might find it surprising to see such gorgeous old trees- Pin Oaks, some over 100 feet tall, Birch, Elm and Ash - that had bypassed the city's wrecking ball. When he was in middle school, he had come with charcoals and a pad, hopping the graveyard fence, sometimes spending all day, sketching the native flora.

"The kid's gonna be a fairy - what with the art classes and all. What's next? Ballet? Well, he's your problem now. Remember THAT when he comes home with AIDS," his father often warned. His mom would ignore the comment and hum. You are my sunshine, my only sunshine . . ." His father would leave the room and the topic - exasperated, but checked.

By the time Alfie reached the ornate entrance, he was exhausted. The walk had warmed him; but he was clammy from the fever that had come roaring back. It was late afternoon and the cemetery was getting ready to close its enormous wrought iron gates. He hurried through as unobtrusively as possible. It took him fifteen minutes to find the plot.

He remembered coming here with his mother every Easter as she planted new tulips and tidied up the gravesite. Often, the winter would heave the earth up and partially obscure the bottom inscription on the marble stone. She would use her hand shovel to move the dirt away. Then she would get down on her knees and pray.

He couldn't bear to look, to find her name above his grandparents', but that was why he had come.

It read:

Loving mother, wife and daughter

Greta Emily Lang Blaylock

5/1/1937 - 12/5/2017

He had never held much stock in prayer, at least not since his time as an alter boy. But he had an unshakeable faith in his mother - and he never doubted the simple fervor of her prayers. And so, out of respect, he knelt on the frozen ground and blessed himself.

"Hail Mary, full of grace . . ." He tried dozens of ways to apologize to her, to explain what had happened. But he couldn't because he didn't understand himself. He assumed his beggar's pose, and for the first time since Julie left, he cried inconsolably.

It had gotten dark hours ago. He was afraid that if he left he might never come back again. His body ached, and his mind was unfocused. But something had happened. He had experienced a kind of lightness, an ephemeral glimmer of something new. He couldn't put his finger on it. But it was real.

Alfie stood with great difficulty. Everything was locked up so he climbed the fence on the high ground - the same spot he snuck over so many years before. He headed towards the church where, he had learned, Father Torres had been reassigned. Was he seeking absolution or answers? He didn't know.

It was ten o'clock, two hours before the New Year, when he finally reached the church steps. As he expected, both the rectory and the church were closed. The doors would open in an hour or so for midnight mass.

There was a cafe, adorned in holiday lights, just across the square where he could go and warm up. But he was just so tired. He couldn't walk anymore. He stretched out on the stone steps.

"Here's another one, didn't even make it to midnight," Officer Beneto said to his partner.

"He's out cold. Amateur night for the drinking crowd," Officer Mendez replied. Beneto reached over and shook him.

"This guy is more than out cold; I think he's dead. Maybe he froze to death. A well-dressed guy like this? It's not like he's a bum. You think he'd have some place to be tonight."

Mendez called for an ambulance. "Check his pulse."

"I just did. I can't find one."

The ambulance arrived five minutes later. The cops were relieved to resume their beat. It was too cold to stand around.

"He's all yours," said Mendez. "Still, it's a shame, to cash it in on the church steps, on New Year's Eve no less."

The paramedic nodded and checked for vitals. She detected a faint pulse.

"This guy is still with us. Get a move on!" she said to the driver as she put the oxygen mask over his mouth.

The flu had been especially virulent this season. In Alfie's case, it had turned into pneumonia.

Three days and no one's called or come looking, grumbled the ICU charge nurse under her breath.

John Doe was still unconscious; they were losing him.

She checked the notes to be sure - no ID on him when he came in - just a wallet with four twenty-dollar bills tucked into his back pocket. Not that it's my job but someone should give a

damn. She went down to search his clothes for herself. Nothing in the pants' pockets; nothing in the jacket; the coat pockets, no. She reached for the jacket again and checked inside; there was a breast pocket. She felt something and pulled it out - a letter addressed to some guy in England.

King's County had been a madhouse - the holidays, the drunks, the flu, the cold. And everyone was pulling double duty, understaffed and overworked. This week the docs, the social workers were the "B-team". The "A's" were enjoying their vacation.

It really isn't my job! She wasn't about to call the U. K. on her own dime, but somebody had to do something. This patient needs to hear a friendly voice if he's ever gonna make it. The fundraising office was closed until next week. But she knew they could place a call to the moon if it meant tracking down some donors.

Oh, what the hell . . . she let herself in and reached for the phone.

Billie Anderson asked the nurse to open the letter; at his request, she read it to him twice. He thanked her profusely.

"Any issues with payment, or if they try to move him out of there, please call me. And if the worse should happen, well, I'll take care of that too."

Billy's brother had come through for him again. There really was no privacy anymore. Within the space of a single afternoon, he had found out that she had divorced four years before, and recently moved to California to be near her son - an art student at USC.

She lived alone with her Maltese puppy, Franklin, who had his own Facebook page. She was free-lancing as a feature film digital artist. He had her cell number, e-mail and street address.

The situation was urgent he knew; but he felt a written text would be less startling, and maybe easier to process - and consider - than an intrusive call. These days, it was the most immediate way to communicate anyway.

"Dear Julie, . . ." he began.

About the Author:

Maureen Grace has been writing stories and poems all her life but has only recently begun to send them out for publication. She has a master's in literature and had won numerous awards for her writing in television, film and print advertising.

DEATH ENTERS THE ROOM

by Elaine Rosenberg Miller

"Did you hear that?"

"What?" he said, his voice muffled by a pillow.

The children were finally asleep. They followed a nightly ritual. She would tell them stories, sing to them. They would resist sleep. Sometimes, she would recite Shakespeare, Roman or French poets. "La chair et triste, hélas!" she would coo, "et j'ai lu tous les livres." Though they could not understand the words, she hoped that they would respond to the cadence, the rhythm, her enthusiasm. Finally, they would seem to drift off and she would begin to tiptoe out of the room.

"Maa!" she invariably heard.

It was usually the older boy, driven by some unseen anxiety.

She would return, read some more, wait and quietly slip out.

"Hear what?" her husband asked after a while.

"Television. They said something about "Acquired Immunity Deficiency Syndrome"

"What's that?'

"Listen. There is no cure."

He sat up.

"And Haitians are impacted," the commentator said.
They sat silently.

"There are a lot of Haitians in south Florida," she offered.

"Homosexuals and intravenous drug users," the voice continued.

"Lower the volume," he said, lying back down and turning over.

She continued to watch and listen.

Images of emaciated men with purple blotches on their skin flashed across the screen.

"They're dying!" she thought and shuddered with concern and fear.

The next day she drove the children to school, attended a court hearing, then walked to her law office.

"Wouldn't you like little Johnny to wait in the waiting room?" she finally said, interrupting a woman relating a story of spousal neglect and abuse as her son sat next to her, his legs swinging back and forth.

The woman looked at her.

"No," she said, slowly. "I want him to hear every word."

"I am sorry. It's my policy not to permit others to be in the room when I consult with clients. He will have to go."

Reluctantly, the woman told the boy to leave.

The day went on.

She reviewed bills, signed checks.

"Donna!" she called into the intercom. "Come here, please."

Her secretary entered.

"Yes?"

"Why does our insurance agency have a new name?"

There was a long silence.

"Didn't your husband tell you?"

"Tell me what?"

"Your agent, Anthony Russo died."

"No!"

"Yes."

"What from?"

"He had pneumonia, I heard."

"I don't understand. He was in great shape. He worked out. He went to the gym all the time."

"When was the last time you saw him?"

"I don't know. A few months ago. He has all our insurance. The house, cars, the business."

"Sorry."

When was the last time you saw him?""

Donna lowered her gaze.

"A few weeks ago."

"And?"

"He looked very thin."

"Thin? He was 32! He was a body builder! His agency was a tremendous success. He was our friend."

"Sorry."

In the weeks to come she heard little about Russo. Though he had hundreds of clients and many people liked him and recommended him to others, no one seemed to know much about him.

She realized that he had been an intensely private man.

"He was so beautiful," she told her friend. "Who dies of pneumonia at 32?"

"Well, he was gay and he died of AIDS."

"No!"

"Yes."

"I never knew. I never imagined."

"Try being gay in this small town."

Then, for the first time, she shed tears over the death of a young man who had suffered a fatal illness alone, his fate hidden from nearly all who knew him.

In the years to come, others died. They seemed to fade from view and an obituary would appear often stating that they had succumbed to a "long-standing illness"

A mysteriously transmitted disease was a now a factor in her life and community.

The news was full of theories.

One day she heard an announcement that "Haitians" had been dropped from the profiled groups.

Intravenous drug users, homosexuals and hemophiliacs were at the greatest risk, they were told.

"At least we don't have to worry about anything," she commented to her husband.

A half smiled played on his face.

"Right?" she asked.

About the Author:

Elaine Rosenberg Miller's essays, memoirs, poems and short stories have appeared in JUDISCHE RUNDSCHAU, THE BANGALORE REVIEW, THE BINNACLE, THE FORWARD, THE HUFFINGTON POST and numerous print and

A GOOD SLEEPER

by Keith Jenereaux

The condensation that crept from the bottom of the window was high enough to hide the small front yard from Holly. Any other time she would have wiped it clear with her forearm, dragging the sleeve of her shirt across the window until the glass was dry, but she wanted to stay hidden today, wanted to watch without being seen. She went up on her toes, peaking over the thin layer of water. Her vision was still distorted, blurred by tears, which she also chose not to wipe away.

She could see their breath as they walked to the cars, tufts of vapour being caught in the wind before disappearing. It gave her chills, reminded her of the cold, and she crossed her arms tight below her chest.

"He was fine," she said, turning her head toward the other room.

No one answered.

Holly looked back at the window, up on her toes again. Miss Woodrow was opening the back door of her car for the officer who didn't give his name, didn't say a single word while he was in the house. Miss Woodrow had done all the talking. Holly watched as the silent officer bent over and put her son in the car.

"He always sleeps through the night. Always. Ever since he was born." She didn't look away from the window. "When I was pregnant, people told me to get ready. 'Get your sleep now, cause your gettin none once the baby comes.' That's what Mom said. And Aunt Gert. And Mrs. Hiltz down at the pharmacy. That's what everybody said. No sleep once he's born. But they were wrong. Every single one of them. They were all wrong."

The car door slamming shut made her flinch, as though she hadn't expected the noise to accompany the action. Miss Woodrow said something, pointing at the window of her car and the officer nodded, tipping his hat before he went to the cruiser. Holly stepped away from the window when Miss Woodrow looked back at the house, scared of making eye contact with the horrible woman.

"Hateful," Holly whispered. She waited till she heard the car door close before she looked again.

"He slept like a field stone. Even when he was a newborn. Dead to the world. Sometimes he slept twenty hours a day. Not a word of a lie - twenty hours. Mom said he was part cat. Said his daddy must have mud in his blood to make a baby that slept so much."

The cruiser left first. It was on the road and pulling away before Miss Woodrow's car started to move. A fresh tear warmed Holly's cheek as she watched it back out of her driveway. She raised her hand and waved absently, then brought the hand to her mouth as the car disappeared.

"I'm sorry," she said, still looking out the window. "I know you don't like me bringing up his daddy."

From the other room came the familiar snap of the television coming to life. It was followed briefly by the upbeat music from the children's show Winston had been watching, but quickly changed to a jangle of mixed noises, too brief to be recognized. This continued until Billy settled on a show about fishing, and the quiet chatter of the men on the boat seemed to somehow suit the confusion. Holly kept watching the window.

"It's been months since he got up during the night. Not since Halloween. You remember that? The night he threw up all over the crib? That was the last time he was up before dawn. Hell, before nine. That was the only time in a full year that he got up during the night. That's it. Just once in a whole year. I never shoulda let him eat all that candy." Nostalgia forced a grin to her face. "He just loved it so much."

She heard the fridge door open, followed by the clink of a bottle being taken from the shelf. Footsteps dragging into the room made Holly turn away from the window. Billy held up a beer as he came toward her, a second one hanging by his hip in the other hand.

"Here." He lifted his chin at the bottle.

"It's only nine-thirty."

"So?"

Holly took the beer and watched Billy dropped hard into in the rocking chair by the wood stove taking. He took a long drink from the bottle before he set it between his legs. She turned back to the window. "I guess I gotta get a lawyer."

"You can't afford a lawyer."

"Don't they have free lawyers for people who don't got money?"

Billy shook his head. "That's just on television. No one does nothing for free in real life. You gotta pay if you want a lawyer. You gotta pay through the nose."

"Maybe I could sell the car?"

Billy laughed. "You'd be lucky to get a hundred bucks for that piece of crap."

He was still topless, had come out of the bedroom like that when Miss Woodrow and the officer were there. Holly wished he had put on a shirt. It might have helped if he had put on a shirt. Billy had tattoos. Several of them. The ones on his arms didn't bother her, snakes and crosses and words in complicated cursives, but centred on his chest was a picture of a naked women with exaggerated breasts reaching a hand toward each of Billy's nipples, like she

was about to pinch them with her fingertips. It embarrassed Holly when he had his top off while other people were around.

"How much does a lawyer cost?"

Billy was in the middle of a drink and he didn't lower the bottle until it was empty. "A hell of a lot more than you got," he told her. "How much more?"

A shrugged was his only answer.

Holly set her bottle on the windowsill. "I gotta call mom," she said, and started towards the phone in the kitchen.

"She ain't gonna be able to help you, Holly. She's got less money than you."

"I ain't gonna ask her for money. I'm gonna ask her what to do."

Billy followed her into the kitchen. "How the hell is she gonna know what to do? She ain't a lawyer."

"She'll know." The phone wasn't on its base. It was never on the base. In this house it was always in the couch or under the covers or on the back of the toilet. It was never on the base unless the charge was spent. "She knows stuff like this. She used to work at the Sally Anne's." It wasn't under Billy's hat off. "People were always coming in with problems like this." It wasn't on the counter or in the drawer of seldom used utensils. "She woulda heard things like this. She woulda heard how to fix it." Holly looked in the same spots again, picking up items that couldn't possibly hide a phone. "Where is the damn thing?"

"Working at a thrift store ain't going teach ya how to get a kid from social services. You're talking crazy."

"Which of these make the phone beep?" She started pushing buttons on the phone's base until a muffled chirping started in the other room. The sound led her to recliner.

"You can't call your mother now, it's the middle of the morning. Rates are through the roof."

Holly was already dialling. "But I need her help."

Billy took the phone from her. "Nothing's going to change between now and tonight. Wait till ten."

"Six. It gets cheaper at six."

"Yeah, but it's even cheaper at ten. If you can wait till six, you can wait till ten." Billy fell into the beat up recliner, tossing the phone to the couch on his way down.

There was a moment of thought, a reflection on the phone itself. Her mother had given it to her the day she left, a parting gift that served as a hint. Holly sat down beside it on the couch. "In a way, this is all her fault."

The television had absorbed Billy's attention.

"If she hadn't a moved back to the island we woulda had a sitter. She watched Winnie all the time when she lived on Aldred Drive."

"Don't call him Winnie. That's a girl's name."

"I wouldn't a left if he was awake." She looked away from the phone. "It's just he sleeps so good. He never wakes up during the night. That lady, that Miss Woodrow, she wouldn't even let me talk. Wouldn't let me explain. She didn't have to be so ..." Tears slipped down both sides of her face. "She doesn't know Winston. She doesn't know how good he sleeps. She didn't even know how old he was. Kept saying Winnie's eighteen months. He's not eighteen months, he's only sixteen. Not even. He'll be sixteen on the twenty-first. Or is it seventeen? Wait ..." Holly started counting under her breath, her fingers moving as she did. "Oh my god, Billy." She covered her mouth. "He is eighteen months. Winnie's gonna be a year and a half on the twenty-first."

"So?"

Holly took in a deep breath. "I'm a bad mom."

Billy said nothing.

She wiped her eye with the heel of her hand. "Miss Woodrow was right. I am a terrible mother."

The only sound in the room came from the anglers on the television. Holly looked straight ahead, stared at the blank wall on the other side of the room as Billy watched the fishing show.

"I wish he cried." She wiped her eyes again. "I wish he got upset when she took him." Holly swallowed hard, then took a breath. "Why didn't he holler for me, Billy? Why didn't he yell for his mom instead of just sitting there grinning, smiling at that Miss Woodrow while she took him from his home? He was happy, Billy ... Happy to get away from me." She turned her head toward the window. "But I guess that's because I'm a terrible mom."

The anglers whispered in the pause that followed.

"How do you suppose she knew?"

"Who knew what?"

"How do you suppose Miss Woodrow knew we went to the Red Line last night? How do you think she knew we left Winston here all alone?"
Billy shrugged.

Holly looked at the wall that separated their apartment from the one next to them. "Mrs. Dickson saw us leaving last night. I saw her peeking out from behind the curtain when we went past her window. She gave me a real dirty look too. One of those judging kinda looks. I bet she was the one who called Social Services. I betcha it was her."

"You're probably right. The woman's a cow."

Holly pounded the heel of her fist against the wall. "I know what you did," she hollered. "I know exactly what you did, you bitch."

Billy laughed. "Give er hell."

She watched the wall, waiting for a reaction. When nothing came she turned and hurried out of the room. Billy stared at the television as the front door opened then slammed closed. He laughed to himself at the sound of footsteps stomping across the deck they shared with the neighbours.

The wind was bitter, blowing through the thin night shirt she was wearing, but Holly didn't notice as she pounded on the door to the Dickson's apartment. "I know what you did," she screamed again.

The door opened carefully and a small woman appeared behind it. "Go away or I'll call the police," she snapped.

"I know you called social services Mrs. Dickson. I know it was you. Don't try to deny it"

"I'm not denying anything."

How casual the confession had been surprised her. She groped awkwardly for something to say.

"You left that poor child home all by itself. All by its lonesome. And it ain't the first time either, I know it ain't. You should be locked up, the two of you. You and that rotten one over there. You're monsters, that's what you are. They should lock the two of you up and throw away the key, that's what should be done."

"They took away my son, Mrs. Dickson. They took my baby."

"Good. That's the best news I ever heard. Now maybe that poor little boy will have a fighting chance, cause he sure as hell wasn't going to get one with the two of you. Now get off my deck."

The door opened further as Mr. Dickson appeared behind his wife. He was a big man - his wife only came to his chest - and Holly became frightened as he looked down at her. "You need to do as you're told little girl." He pointed toward the other apartment.

The cold was obvious now, the wind tearing at her bare legs. She felt it, felt the uncomfort, but it seemed so trivial to the situation. "He's a good sleeper," she said. "He never wakes up in the night."

"You get on home," Mr. Dickson said.

Absent thoughts of her son came to her suddenly, song enough to take her away. Holly pictured his big, dopey grin, the corners of his mouth cutting into his oversized cheeks. She loved the way he closed his eyes when he laughed, the way his whole body shook with the effort.

"What kind of people are you anyway?"

She spoke quietly at first, still caught in what she had lost.

"You think you have the right to go messing with someone's life?" She saw them now, huddled in their doorway like a fox protecting her den. "You think you're God or something? Is

that it? You think you gotta punish people who don't live just like you? You're the monsters. Both of you. You're the ones who can't just mind your own damn business and leave me the hell alone?"

Mr. Dickson pushed past his wife as he stepped onto the deck. "You little bitch."

She was not fast enough and Mr. Dickson had a hold of her arm before she could step back. He squeezed as hard as he could. "You want to know who we are? We're two people who give a damn, that's who we are. We're two people who aren't afraid to do the right thing, how about that?"

"You're hurting me."

Holly didn't know what had happened as her head snapped back. She didn't figure it out till his hand came up again.

"We're two people who spent our whole lives trying to get the very thing you treat as a burden. An inconvenience. We're two people who think a kid isn't something you gotta run away from every chance you get."

He slapped her again, the fingers catching the end of her nose. The taste of blood came to the back of her throat.

"You're garbage, that's what you are. A piece of trash." He brought the back of his hand across her face and Holly felt his knuckle rip her lower lip. "You're a whore. A worthless, two-bit whore," he screamed.

His hand was up again, ready to strike, but Holly had turned away, trying to hide from the blow. She didn't see the anger suddenly disappear from his face and she didn't hear the crack until afterward, after he folded, after his posture melted in front of her. He let go of her shoulder and his hand slid down her arm as he collapsed on the deck.

The top half of the mop handle had flung off the porch with the impact, disappearing in the loose snow that had fallen during the night. The bottom half was still in Billy's hand as he stared down at the old man. Short, thick puffs of steam came from his mouth with every quick breath, and his bare chest rose and fell in perfect rhythm.

"Morris!" Mrs. Dickson hurried to her husband.

Billy watched the woman cradle her husband's head. He noticed the broken mop in his hand, stared at it for a moment before he tossed it to the corner of the deck. "Come on." Taking Holly by the arm he pulled her into the apartment and dragged her into the kitchen. "Sit down," he said, pulling a chair up to the sink.

Holly sat down carefully as Billy disappeared into the bathroom. Her breathing was short, hurried, with terrified gasps interrupting it. She watched the front door intently until Billy stepped back into the room with an old towel. He said nothing as the water ran, kept quiet while he soaked the towel, squeezed it, then shook it open, letting the loose water drop into the sink. Holly watched as he went down on his haunches in front of her, the tap still running behind him.

"That may need a stitch or two." Billy dabbed carefully at her lip. "How's your nose?"

"It hurts," she said, and sniffed. The taste of blood came back to her.

Billy touched her nose with his finger tip and Holly moved back from his hand. "I don't think it's broken." He returned his attention to her lip, using the towel to remove blood from the edge of the cut. "We're going to get a lawyer."

Holly looked at him, but Billy didn't meet her eyes. "For Winnie?"

"That's right."

She brightened. "He's such a good boy, isn't he?"

"Yeah, he's a good kid." He stood carefully, pressing the towel against her lip. "Hold this."

The freezer was in the porch, and from the far end Billy could see the porch through the window. The wife had disappeared, but Mr Dickson hadn't moved. It would have been unsettling had Billy allowed himself to consider it. Instead he grabbed a bag of peas from the freezer and went back to the kitchen.

"Lift your head. Let me see that lip."

Holly obeyed. When she closed her eyes she felt a throbbing in her nose, but she kept them closed in spite of it. "Is he dead?" she asked.

"That old bastard?"

Holly gave a slight nod.

Billy touched her cut, watched the deep wound open as he pushed her lip to the side. "It was just a mop. You can't kill a guy with a mop. The wood's too thin."

Holly nodded again.

Billy wrapped the towel around the peas.

"Billy?"

He was quiet at first, focused on the peas, but silence forced him to answer. "Yeah?"

She licked her lip carefully, then swallowed. "I'm going to be a good mom from now on. You just wait and see. I'm going to be a real good mom."

Billy nodded. "I know," he said.

He placed the towel gently against her lip and held it there, listening for the faint sound of sirens to come.

About the Author:

Keith Jenereaux had no ambitions aimed at becoming a writer. A former child care worker, his first novel came accidentally while he was trying to record one of the stories he told the children, and since then plots and characters have pestered him constantly. He lives in Nova Scotia with his wife and daughter.

TRADIO

by Richard Luftig

I stubbed out my tenth Winston of the morning. Thank God we were nearing the end of the show.

"We're back," I said, feigning enthusiasm. "Time for two more calls. You're on Tradio. What do you have today?"

The voice sounded as parched as these Ohio fields during this two-year drought. "This is Eleanor. You did a great job helping me get rid of that lawnmower. Helped buy my meds. Today, I have two bikes, a dryer good for parts, and a rocking chair. I'll take fifteen for the bikes and dryer, twenty for the chair. Everything's negotiable except the chair. It belonged to my late husband."

 "Okay," I said, "two bikes, a dryer and a chair. Your number and best time to call?"

Eleanor gave her number. "Call anytime. It's not like I have a big social calendar."

I laughed despite my foul mood. I reached to punch in the button for the next caller and my tee shirt rode up my stomach, a not-so-subtle hint that I needed to exercise more. Okay, exercise at all. It was one of the few perks of radio▯ I could be out of shape and no one would know. Also, no dress code. Given my limited wardrobe of stuff from the used clothing stores in this depressed town, I was grateful for not to have to dress up.

"We got time for one more. This is Tradio. Tell me what you got."

"This is Robert in Wilsonville. I don't have anything to sell. I need a driver."

I was stunned.

"Hello?" the caller said.

"I'm sorry," I said. "I'm not sure I got that. You need a driver? Like a chauffeur?"

"Well, not exactly," said Robert. "See, I'm eighty years old, crippled with arthritis, and my eyes are bad. Never been far from Wilsonville. Took a trip to Chicago once and Niagara Falls on my honeymoon. But that was a long time ago."

Get to the point, I thought. We're off air in 60 seconds.

"I'm sick of summers and winters here aren't much better. So I figured I'd hire a guy to drive me to Las Vegas. Always wanted to play the slots. I'll cover expenses, but the driver has to pay his own way home."

The sound engineer was frantically waving for me to wrap up the show.

"So, you want someone to drive you to Vegas, and you'll pay the freight? Never had an offer like that before, but it sounds good. Give me your number and best time to call."

Robert left the information and hung up. "Okay," I said, "that's our show. Remember, that stuff in your garage is good for cash. This is Tradio. I'll see you tomorrow."

I gathered up my papers and left the booth. Ottero motioned me into his office. Not a good sign. The station manager never spoke to D.J.s unless they had screwed up on the air. Or about to be fired.

I tried to remember whether I had used profanity. It wouldn't have been the first time. The show was boring enough, and I didn't have patience with yokels who hadn't rehearsed their spiel. How hard could it be to remember three things you wanted to sell for fifty bucks?

Ottero was shuffling through the mess on his desk.

"What's up, boss?" I knew he liked to be called 'boss.'

He found what he was looking for. "I got this from some judge. It says I need to garnish your salary for back child support. I don't have time to be the court appointed bill collector."

I took the paper and fumbled for the generic glasses I had bought at the drug store. The station didn't offer health insurance.

I perused the paper and stuck it in my pocket. "It's nothing to worry about, Stan. I got it under control."

"How? By winning the lottery? Take care of this or find yourself a new gig. You got until your next paycheck to get this straightened out and the court off my back."

He went back to his paperwork, indicating that I was dismissed.

I was furious. Damn, leave it to Leanne to almost get me fired. Maybe I was a few weeks, all right months, late with child support for Kimberly. But it wasn't like I was rolling in dough. I was behind on everything, rent, credit cards, car. Leanne of all people knew how bad I felt about not paying support for my daughter. That ten-year-old was the one good thing that had come out of the marriage, maybe my whole rotten life.

But I just didn't have it right now. If I couldn't pay on the car, the bank would repossess it. No car, no work. Then where would they be?

And now Leanne had put my job in jeopardy. No, they would all have to get in line. Even Kimberly who deserved better.

I remembered the old guy who had called the show, the one wanting a driver to Vegas. I heard about blackjack dealers making $1,000 a night on tips. Maybe I could get a gig like that.

I saw the sound engineer in the booth. I knew that he kept a list of calls. I rapped on the window, and he came out.

"Hey, Eddie, you got the log from this morning's show?"

He handed me the clipboard. "After anything in particular?"

"No," I said, not wanting to tip my hand. "Some strange calls today. Just interested."

I scanned the sheet, found the old man's name and made a mental note of the number. I'd write it down when I got outside, away from prying eyes.

I got into my beat-up Ford Fiesta and drove as quickly as I could to Kimberly's school without getting a speeding ticket. If I made the lights, I'd be in time to pick her up for lunch.

When I reached the school office, she was waiting for me. I showed the secretary my I.D. and signed her out. "All set to go, Pumpkin?"

She seemed worried.

"I'm not sure I'm allowed to go. Mom says you owe her money."

I saw that the secretary was listening.

That's all I need, some busybody not letting me take my own daughter to lunch.

"No problem," I said loud enough so the secretary could hear. "It's just a misunderstanding. Let's talk about this outside, okay?"

Once in the car, I looked at her sitting in the passenger seat. I knew I was prejudiced, but I thought she was beautiful, with her long, brown hair and mother's eggshell-color eyes⬛ blue but often changing to green or hazel depending on what color blouse she was wearing. Given that I had what was known in the industry as a face for radio, I realized that any good looks she had she had gotten from Leanne.

"Look, Hon, it's true I owe your Mom some money but it's nothing for you to worry about."

She seemed unconvinced. "But Mom says we need it to live. Why don't you just give it to her? Then everything would be okay."

I wished I could light up a Winston, but I never smoked in front of my daughter. It was hell, but I wasn't going to kill her with second-hand smoke.

"It's not that easy. If it was, I'd give it to your mom in a heartbeat. But things are tight right now.

"Don't worry, though. I have something in the works, something that pays a lot. It's going to come any day now. And when it does, I'm going to pay everything I owe your mom and get something special for you."

"Like what?"

I spoke before thinking. "A surprise."

She became excited. "What is it?"

Nice going, dumb-ass.

I scrambled to think. "If I told you, it wouldn't be a surprise. Let's just get some lunch so you're not late and we both get in trouble."

I dropped Kimberly at school promising to pick her up for the weekend. But I feared facing Leanne. And having to come up with a surprise seemed impossible. For the first time, I dreaded my visitation rights.

I drove aimlessly. There weren't a lot of places to go in a town of three thousand people. Finally, I pulled into a space in front of Cal's Bar and went in for a whiskey. It might only be one p.m., but given the day I was having, I figured I deserved it.

I sat on a stool and ordered. When I pulled out my wallet, a slip of paper fell to the ground. It was a name and phone number. At first it didn't register, but then it hit me. Robert, the guy who wanted a driver to Las Vegas.

I nursed my drink. This could be my ticket. Out from under my crappy job. Out from Leanne threatening to garnish my salary. A fresh start.

But what about Kimberly? I pictured her face. If I was going to break her heart, let it be one final time and leave the kid alone to grow up sane⬚ maybe without a father--but sane nevertheless. I'd be doing her a favor by leaving once and for all.

I punched in the number on my cell phone. No answer. Maybe the old coot was asleep. I wondered if the offer was on the level.

The voice that picked up sounded groggy.

Maybe the guy's demented and calls radio shows for fun.

I disguised my voice. "I'm calling about the job you talked about on Tradio this morning. The one to drive you, expenses paid, to Vegas. Is the job still open?"

"Yeah," the old man said. "You interested?"

A moron. Would I call if I weren't interested?

"I might be if the terms are right."

The old man changed the subject. "Say, you sound familiar. Do I know you from someplace? What's your name?"

Maybe he wasn't as senile as he sounded.

"Probably not," I said. "Is the job still open?"

"Yeah. But first let me ask you a few questions. You got a license?"

Again with the dumb questions. Would I be calling about a driving job if I didn't have a license?

"Yeah, I got a license."

"You got a prison record?"

I was stunned. "Hell, no," I stammered.

"Great. You're hired."

"Just like that? Don't you want to interview me first?"

"Nope. I figure if you know how to drive, and you're not a hardened criminal, you're right for the job. Besides, it's not like the phone's ringing off the wall with offers."

"When you fixing to go?" I asked.

"Day after tomorrow."

"Jesus, why the rush?"

"Young man, hope you don't mind me calling you young man, but next to me everybody's young. I don't know how much time I have. I'm on oxygen and got more pills than most pharmacies. So, day after tomorrow. Take it or leave it. I'd go earlier, but I figure whoever drives me might have loose ends to tie up."

I wrote down the address and agreed to meet him in two days. Then, I stared at my cell phone.

What had I gotten myself into?

I didn't have much to pack; you can't get a lot of stuff into a one-bedroom apartment. Besides, DJs live under the radar. If your ratings were low, you could get canned that day. It had taught me to travel light.

The lease wasn't a challenge. I'd just leave and let the landlord keep whatever was left behind. Most of it was "Goodwill Modern" anyway.

I wouldn't tell Ottero. It would serve him right when no one showed up to air Tradio. What would they fill in with? I always wondered how many folks listened to the show. Would anyone notice I was missing? Or care?

But Kimberly. How was I going to break it to her? I knew I should just leave. That would be easier on both of us. It would spare me having to lie about where I was

headed. Sooner or later, Leanne would have the police looking for me. The less Kimberly knew about my whereabouts, the better.

But skipping out on my daughter would be the final betrayal. I would probably never see her again. She would hate me forever, and I couldn't blame her. I was a shit as a father.

Some things never change.

By travel day, I still hadn't done much preparation. I crammed some clothes into two large garbage bags. The rest was staying behind. I didn't know how much room the old guy had in the trunk of his car.

As for Kimberly, I knew it was best for her if I just disappeared. The less she knew, the less she could tell Leanne.

But I had to see her one last time.

I locked the apartment, stuffed the trash bags into the trunk and drove off. Kimberly was waiting at the bus stop near the house.

I took a chance that Leanne was not lurking nearby. "Hey, good looking! Want breakfast?"

"Dad! What are you doing here?"

"Do I need a reason to pick up my best girl? Hop in."

"I'll be late for class."

"I'll sign you in. What's better, homeroom or pancakes?"

She slipped into the passenger seat and glanced at me.

"Mom will have a fit if she finds out."

"Then we'll keep it between ourselves."

I drove to a diner where they served good breakfasts. We sat down in a booth in the back. I didn't need being noticed by one of Leanne's friends.

The waitress came over. "So what will you have?" she asked.

Kimberly didn't hesitate. "Strawberry pancakes and hot chocolate with whipped cream."

I ordered black coffee.

When the order came, she skimmed the whipped cream into her mouth without losing a drop. "So what's the occasion?" she asked again. "It's about the surprise, isn't it?"

I blinked in confusion.

She giggled. "Don't play dumb. The surprise you promised the other day. You're going to tell me about it, aren't you?"

I struggled to recover. "Well, it's a surprise. Just not the one you think."

"I knew it! I told Mom you were going to work things out and get her the money. I told her you were getting a new place."

She didn't even pause for breath. "That's the surprise isn't it? You're getting a new apartment. One with an extra bedroom for me. I guessed it, didn't I?"

I looked into her expectant eyes. Where did she get this from? I tried to remember if I had hinted, even slightly, that I was getting a new apartment. No, this was a just a ten-year-old's dreams running rampant.

She sat waiting, confident that she had guessed the purpose of our breakfast. I sipped my coffee stalling for time. "Yeah, something like that. But you have to keep it secret. I don't want any of this getting out until it's finalized. You have to promise, not a word to anyone, especially your mother. Okay?"

Kimberly drained the last of her hot chocolate. "Deal!" she said. "But it's going to be hard."

I felt like a heel. Breakfast had been a terrible idea.

I looked at my wristwatch. "Time to get you back."

I paid the check and drove her to school.

She reached for the door. I took her hand.

"Honey...I need to tell you that no matter what happens, well... you know I love you. There's nothing that will ever change that. I hope you'll always feel the same way about me."

Kimberly turned and gave me a hug. "I know Dad. Me too. I can't wait to see you next weekend. Maybe you can show me the new place."

She opened the door and got out. I watched her disappear into the school. Gone forever.

I had time to kill before I had to pick up Robert and drive him to Vegas. My plan was to drive across town to a supermarket near where he lived. I'd ditch the car there. It would be a couple of days before the store manager would report it to the cops. By then I'd be halfway to Nevada.

I lit a cigarette and inhaled deeply. This was it. The line I was about to cross didn't have any do-overs attached.

I sat there, thinking. When had it all gone south, my whole crappy life? Now I was about to lose my daughter. I cut the motor and sat with the windows rolled and lit up a Winston.

It was crunch time, just like in blackjack when you draw a sixteen and the dealer has a ten showing. You have to draw a card or stand pat. Either way it's a sucker's bet with the odds against you. That's why the casinos were all rich and the players poor.

Grow up asshole, I berated himself. You want to be a big shot in Vegas? How about starting now? Cut the deck. Play a hand. Make a decision and stick with it.

My mind was made up. It was time. Time to live up to a commitment for once.

I put the car in gear and drove off towards a new life.

But first I needed to make a stop. I headed toward the station. I needed to check the Tradio files. Maybe someone had a two-bedroom apartment cheap in town. Who knew, maybe that prick of a station manager might let me pull some extra hours.

And a second job. I'd need that to pay back child support.

I wondered how the old guy, expecting me to pick him up in fifteen minutes, was going to get to Vegas.

About the Author:

Richard Luftig is a Midwesterner now living California. He taught at Miami University in Ohio. He is a recipient of the Cincinnati Post-Corbett Foundation Award for Literature and a semi finalist for the Emily Dickinson Society Award for Poetry. His stories have appeared in numerous magazines. One of his published short stories was nominated for a 2012 Pushcart Prize. His book of poetry is scheduled to be released in 2019.

HOW YOU RIDE IT!
By Dave Barrett

That evening, towards eight o' clock, Swanson slipped out back and announced a change of plans.

"Haul in the gear!"

He'd startled me and I tried to cover this up by sitting down on the wood siding as a large roller tipped the cockpit. All day I'd been waiting for him to try something.

"Sure," I said, setting the brake so I could face him. "What about the cooler on deck?"

The fishing had dropped off shortly after our incident at noon. The flood of salmon we'd run into earlier might have been the tail-end of this three-day Fraser River run. But now that the tide was changing⬛ and activating a feed by stirring the ocean bottom⬛ there was a chance we could still fill the cooler with a dozen or more local Kings and Cohoes.

"Naw. . ." Swanson said, grabbing the haystack as we see-sawed over a second roller. "We'll supper tonight on a little beach I know a few miles south of here. Cook in the sand. Get out of these damn winds."

Nodding, I pushed back the hair from my eyes. A big williwaw had whipped up a few hours ago. The sun was lowering behind Swanson: putting him in a strange silhouetted light. I thought how unlike him it was to not take every fish we could get.

"What about the catch?" I asked, turning my face away for a second as a ray of red sunlight flashed in my eyes. "Aren't we supposed to deliver it at HARRY'S tonight?"

"The catch?" Swanson repeated, as though the thought had just occurred to him. "Well..."

He leaned into the hayrack as a third roller tipped the deck. "We'll put it off till the morning. That way we'll avoid the lines and get a fire going before dark."

From the wheelhouse came a loud squelch: someone trying to get through on the wire. Asking if this beach supper things was all right with me, Swanson took my noncommittal shrug of the shoulders as an O.K. Without another word⬛ without any acknowledgment of the murderous scuffle that had occurred between us at noon⬛ he returned to the wheelhouse; the hitch of his high shoulder more marked than usual because of the rolling seas.

I opted to remain out back as we approached the narrow gorge leading to the tiny bay we were to anchor in tonight. In spite of Swanson's apparent willingness to let bygones be bygones . . . I detected an underlying iciness to his manner that indicated the matter was all but forgotten. It was lurking just beneath the guise of his calm surface, waiting until just the right moment to lash out for the jugular.

Having just finished packing the last of the day's catch below deck, I sat on the cooler with my fists between my legs, shivering. I wondered why, with all these easier bays and inlets to get in and out of, Swanson had chosen this one to camp at tonight. Another reason for delaying our delivery at HARRY'S was because of our vessels size we could only get in and out of this bay during high tide. High tide having occurred at 8:14, we were cutting it close as it was.

I stood as we entered the first corridor of this serpentine gorge. The sky was already a deep turquoise. Granite cliffs rose ninety feet out of the water either side of the trawler at perfect ninety-degree angles. The waters were as narrow as fifty yards across in places. And iceberg-like rocks littered the path ahead of us: jutting thirty to forty feet out of the water as we drifted by.

When we were about a quarter mile into the gorge, Swanson poked his head out the wheelhouse door and, pointing towards the gray cliffs on our right, said:

"Petroglyphs . . ."

There were about a dozen in all: strewn across the broad-faced granite walls like inner city graffiti. They were rough hewn one dimensional figures of men and women and whales and fish and animals. I was taken by one figure hewn in stone somewhat separate from the rest about thirty yards deeper into the gorge. It was directly beneath a dwarf spruce tree growing perpendicularly out of a crevice in the cliff wall. In straight blunt lines it depicted a man with one hand over his heart and the other over his stomach. It was the simplest and least creative of the carvings: except for the strong feelings of horror and despair it evoked out of me. There was something about the man's face that made me think he was very young and very old at the same time: a sage and a fool all at once. His eyes were wide and staring and while his hand covered his heart his mouth was slightly parted and drawn down in a frown not unlike a salmon's.

Entering another corridor of this gorge . . . I began to pace deck. We were passing more of these iceberg-like rocks every two-hundred feet or so now. The limbs of the dwarf spruces growing in the crevices stretched their mangled arms out over the glossy green waters as though to reach out and touch us. Barnacles and mussels, attached to the cliffs at water level by the tens of thousands, seemed to watch us as we slid by. Forcing myself to stare directly ahead (to belay the claustrophobic feeling I had that these granite walls were actually closing in on us), I began to wonder if we'd ever make it to this fabled beach of Swanson's before wrecking the boat. I expected to feel our bulwarks come crunching in at any moment. What if Swanson had entered the wrong passage? What if this gorge suddenly came to an end? Or it became so narrow we couldn't proceed further? There was no way in hell we'd be able to turn the trawler around: we'd be like the proverbial ship stuck in a bottle! Finally, rounding one more dizzying bend of the gorge, the black green waters beneath us widened and we moved out onto the main body of this hidden bay.

After dropping anchor, I was told to bring the skiff from the roof of the wheelhouse. Untying the orange plastic skiff, I slid it down on my back and flip-flopped it right side up on the water with a loud smack. It suddenly occurred to me if Swanson wanted to kill me or something . . . this would be the perfect place to do it. There were probably hundreds, even thousands, of isolated little bays like this all up and down the Southeast Coast. Swanson had mentioned that only he and a few other fishermen even knew this spot existed. He wouldn't even need to do the killing with his own hands. He could simply abandon me here . . . leave me to the elements . . . the bears and wolves and lions that were said to inhabit all of these islands. If someone should come looking for me months later, what was the likelihood they'd even think of searching out a place like this? Staring wide-eyed at the foliage massed in green along shore, I argued that I'd become hysterical. But why else would any normal person want to supper on a goddamn beach in a hollow like this? And why had Swanson pointed out those rock carvings to me? Surely, he was trying to spook me; toying with my stupid puny little mind.

I was still musing over these matters when Swanson emerged from the wheelhouse.

"O.K.," he said a bag of groceries under an arm. "Get in the skiff."

I just stared at him.

This was too unfucking believable. Strict Hollywood script.

"Get in the skiff!" he repeated.

I got in.

Two hours later I trudged up and down the shell and gravel beach searching for more firewood. It was eleven o' clock and still we had not eaten. The moon, at last quarter, had just cleared the eastern tree line: putting the hills, mountains and trees surrounding this obscure, tear-shaped bay in a dull phosphorescent light. The air hummed with quiet: the crackle of our fire, the soft lapping of the water along shore, the crunch of my own boots the only sounds reaching my ears. Fifty yards away, following me as I moved up the beach, the Western World strayed on its anchor: its white paint-chipped exterior ghost-like in the purple gloom.

Swanson had started the fire over an hour ago, but was waiting, he said, for better embers. He sat cross-legged a yard from the flames, stirring the fire occasionally with a switch he'd broken off a nearby sapling. Although he'd shown no obvious signs that he'd taken me here to do me harm, he had appeared more interested in keeping our fire well-stoked than in engaging in any of the half-dozen conversations I'd attempted to bring about.

I stopped when I came to the beached rowboat. I'd stumbled upon it earlier while taking a leak. The rowboat was half eaten away with rot, half-hidden beneath a clump of salmonberries. Gingerly pushing aside some the shrub's thorny vines, I began to kick out pieces of wood from the skeleton of its bottom.

Along with offering a ready source of fuel, the boat had become something of a mystery to me. Its bleached weather wood had a petrified quality to it which made it hard to say just how long it had been here. It may have been only a year or two, then, just as easily, twenty or thirty years. And how had it arrived at this obscure spot? Had a fisherman seeking refuge from a downed vessel paddled here on it? The surrounding trees and mountains would have provided fortress from the rough seas and winds outside this bay. If he'd been able to forage through the summer . . . had been able to fend of the bears and wolves and lions . . . had been able to provide makeshift shelter for himself . . . would he have been able to endure the long white season (seasons?) of winter?

Searching distractedly though the dark bramble and underbrush outlining the beach . . . I imagined this Robinson Crusoe of mine had, indeed, survived and was running wild, half-mad on the island at this moment . . . that years of isolation from humankind had brought him to a Neanderthal state . . . that he'd learned to feed on the raw flesh of deer and fish and wild goat . . . and that he was, at this very moment, spying on Swanson and myself . . . sizing us up.

And it was while my head was full of such thoughts that the answer came to me. BURN THE WESTERN WORLD! BURN THE FUCKER DOWN! It wouldn't be hard to do. Our skiff was just yards away, both paddles still in it, almost inviting me to crawl in. Swanson's back was still turned towards me, and from where the trawler had strayed it would be almost out of his view. I'd start it in the engine room, of course. Swanson kept gallon cans of gas there and oily rags. Splash a little Boy Scout juice around; dump out a box of matches, light a stick. By the time I was back ashore with the skiff, the first billows of smoke would be issuing from the wheelhouse⊡

SNAP!

A knotty piece of wood popping back at the fire, followed by cursing about the hold up on the wood. Scooping up an armload of the ivory planks, I trudged back to the fire's pit.

Swanson was removing something from the grocery bag when I arrived within the perimeter of the fire's light. I stopped in my tracks. Since the moment Swanson had appeared with the grocery bag under an arm, I'd suspected him of packing a gun inside the sack. Observing that Swanson was only moving the salmon now, I moved cautiously forward.

"Mmm. . . " I said, smiling when Swanson glanced up at me. "Salmon smells good."

Swanson nodded, but said nothing.

Dropping the wood in its designated pile, I sat across the flames from Swanson; bracing me tired back against a rock. I watched Swanson reposition the salmon, wrapped in aluminum foil, between two rocks. Then he brought out a can of beans, opened its lid with a can-opener, and placed it on a flat rock beside the salmon. He peeled off some foil from the salmon and covered the lid of the can with it. Then he resumed his cross-legged position. Once again his eyes turned towards the faint display of aurora borealis shimmering pale green, pink and blue above the northern tree line.

I shifted uneasily: kicking sand and gravel into the fire's pit. There was something too damn serene and removed about Swanson tonight. And it wasn't because he was stoned: he'd gone cold turkey now for over 24 hours. There was something else going on. I was sure of it. It was almost as though he was trying to lull me off guard. I was so out of it now it wouldn't take much. Already waves of sleepiness were oozing into my head in thicker and thicker waves; getting harder and harder to fight off. If I didn't try something soon⏷ try to get to the bottom of this⏷ it might be too late.

Clearing my throat, I asked, point blank:

"What are we doing here?"

Swanson looked down from the display of lights, his chiseled features hatchet-like in the red play of the fire.

I hesitated. Maybe it wasn't smart to make my suspicions known. Still, there was this tiredness to consider: another wave of it pressing down on me now like morphine.

"I said what are we doing here?"

I leaned forward, back straight, fully alert.

Swanson grinned horribly⏷ his eyes narrowing into flint-like slits.

"What do you mean?"

I glanced knowingly at the grocery bag. The image of Swanson suddenly removing the revolver from the sack, and pointing the barrel at my forehead and firing from point-blank range flashed through my head: causing me to kick up more sand and gravel into the fire's pit.

"I mean what's inside the bag?"

I flinched at a loud hissing noise from the fire. The butter and lemon juice Swanson had earlier placed in the salmon's belly had begun to leak through the foil. Distracted, Swanson flipped the salmon over. He opened the foil pouch, and spread the steaming butter and lemon juice more evenly with a stick. Then he closed the pouch, looking across the flames as though he'd forgotten what it was we were talking about.

Again I hesitated. What if I was wrong about there being a revolver in the bag? Surely there were easier⏷ legal⏷ means Swanson could take to get his revenge of me. He could have simply called the Coast Guard and had me arrested on assault charges. Why risk going to prison? This whole scenario⏷ taking me to a deserted island to off me with a .38⏷ was no doubt a result of too many books and movies and TV. Yet . . . I couldn't help it. I had to know if there was a gun in the goddamn sack. The risk of not knowing was too great.

Suddenly, without realizing exactly what it was I was going to do, I scrambled across the sand on all fours and snatched the grocery bag right out of Swanson's hands.

"Hey!" Swanson exclaimed. "What the fuck? Give it back!"

Smiling crazily, I shuffled backwards in the heavy sand, tripping ass backwards over the pile of firewood. Scrambling to my feet, I turned the bag upside down and shook out its contents: a box of matches, some utensils and paper plated, and a can of peaches.

"Peaches!" I shouted. "Where's the gun?"

"Peaches? Gun?" Swanson said, on his feet now. "What the fuck are you talking about?"

I dropped to my knees, picking up several of the items littered at my feet. I turned the bag upside down and shook it a second time. Finally, convinced there was no gun, I let the bag fall to the sand. My face burned in humiliation. I glanced towards Swanson, wishing to explain. But it was too late. Swanson had already figured it out for himself.

"Oh, shit! Oh, jeez! Oh, Christ!" Swanson exclaimed, falling to his knees double-up in laughter. "A gun! Peaches! In a grocery bag! Bang! Bang! Oh, man! That's the funniest thing⏷ "

But was unable to continue: overcome as he was by the situation.

Realizing how utterly ridiculous I must have appeared scrambling on all fours like a crab for the bag of groceries, I began to laugh myself. First just a little snicker; then a few more; finally whooping nearly as loud as Swanson.

When we'd both calmed down enough to talk, I wiped the tears from my eyes and stammered out the only words I could think to say:

"I guess you know I'll have to quit now."

Wiping tears from his own eyes, Swanson righted himself in the sand, and answered:

"Fine. Quit. Better yet . . . you're fired!"

I gathered up the plates and utensils I'd scattered about, and after Swanson had checked the meat with a fork, we began to eat.

After a good amount of time had passed, Swanson said:

"Adam? Can I ask you a question?"

I nodded.

"All that stuff Miss Sue Ann Bonnet fed you about Mother Earth and life out of balance and thinking about future generations: You bought all that, didn't you?"

I nodded again.

There was a long pause, and then Swanson said:

"This is what I think, Adam. In the end⬜ in the grand scheme of things-- ol' Mother Earth will shake us off her like a tick off a dog's back." And, after another pause, he smiled and added:

"The trick, kid, is in how you ride the bitch."

About the Author:

Dave Barrett lives and writes out of Missoula, Montana. His fiction has appeared most recently in Potomac Review, Cowboy Jamboree and Midwestern Gothic. His story--EL PARADISIO--will appear in Issue 24 of Quarter After Eight. He teaches writing at the Missoula College and is at work on a new novel.

REVENGE

by George Carlisle

Jon Corey was my nemesis. He lay sprawled across from me with his arm around Jenny, who was his girl friend. Jon, my nemesis, was the most hateful senior at St. Bart's School. He knew I was in love with Jenny. That's why he had invited me to his party Saturday night, and that's why I accepted.

Eight of us sat together on an old rug in Jon's little hut, located in the School woods. These last days before Graduation were supposed to be special, part of the grand, final windup. Nobody knew exactly what "special" meant, but I knew it shouldn't be as painful as this; watching Jenny snuggle with Jon.

We sat there in the hut, hidden away and out of reach of the school, enjoying Jon's good pot in exchange for listening to him revisit every tiresome detail about constructing his hut — ordering lumber from town, finding roofing in the school dump, stealing the rug from the school storehouse, and hiring juniors to help put it all together. Eventually he ran out of details, and took a long drag. I hoped for some blessed silence, but this was not to be.

"Well, Albert." Jon paused for effect and continued. "Are we rich yet?" I realized that he was referring to the investment club that he and Albert had started.

"We're on track," Albert said.

Then the two of them proceeded to enlighten us about the astute purchases the club had made during the year. Apparently each member had put up two thousand, and their investment had grown to some unbelievable amount that Albert couldn't divulge.

"Oh come on, Jon. Enough already!!!" Jenny said. She and I were co-editors of "IMAGINE,"

the school's literary magazine, and I knew her gift of putting people down, but with a warble in her voice to pretend she was joking.

Only encouraged, Jon asked Albert what he thought of Starbucks. This time Jenny groaned, and I thought she closed her eyes in horror, but in the candlelight I couldn't be sure, but I hoped so.

Jon began to banter with Albert about who might run the club next year, pretending to be very important. The rest of us drifted off into dreamland without really listening. Jenny leaned her head against a big cushion. Her hand rested only a few inches away from me, and I reached over and laid my hand on top of hers. She gave me a squeeze before moving it away. My heart leapt as I worked out the possibilities of what Jenny might have been conveying.

Bored by the talk, Jenny interrupted. "Well, Jon, now that you're are all rich, let's turn to something really boring, like how many Coreys are carved on the wall.'

Instead of being annoyed, Jon seemed pleased.

"Yes," I interjected. "Tell us about Coreys you spit on as you walk past." I was trying unsuccessfully to imitate Jenny's humor. Each year the school would carve the names of the graduates on the walls of the dining hall, and students would give their family name a spit shine as they passed by. I hadn't mastered Jenny's warble, and I realized how sarcastic I sounded. Still, it didn't matter. Jon happily told us about the first Corey, who graduated in the very first class, back in 1828. And twenty years later it was his family's company, of course, that built the railroad north of Boston, right up past the school.

""Everybody buckle your seat belt. We're in for a long ride." Jenny said. There was that warble in her voice, but, I was disappointed to note, affection as well.

Then the chapel bell tolled eleven. The cool breeze carried the sound our way through the trees so that it sounded close. I took a drag and was struck by a thought I wanted to share with the others

"Strange," I said, "that only three months ago ice and snow still lay under these trees." I wanted the others to understand that the evening was surreal in some way. It was as if this place in the woods had been especially prepared just for us by arrival of spring. Yet all this would cease to exist after we graduated and went away.

Cathy, sitting next to me, said I was stoned, and the others laughed. Maybe I was, but I felt so overwhelmed that in only a week we would all be leaving forever.

"I think I'm following you," said Jenny, but before she had time to explain, Jon cleared his throat and took over.

"Now for some entertainment," he said. He rose to his knees, and everyone watched as he pulled his cell phone from his jacket and dialed a number.

"Hello, Vance Henderson here."

We all heard Mr. Henderson's voice. He was Jon's head of house. The voice jerked us into the real world of the school, even though it was only from the I phone.

A conversation continued. "It's Jon, sir. Good evening."

Hello Jon. How can I help you?" Jon had turned up the speaker so that Mr. Henderson seemed to be sitting there among us.

We sat shocked. The teacher's voice was a violation. It didn't belong here our sanctuary in the woods. We waved our arms to make Jon disconnect.

Saturday night, and I'm on duty, you know. I just wanted to affirm that all is quiet in Winthrop House. "

"Thanks, Jon. It's a comfort to know you're backing me up."

"Yes, everything is quiet."

I hated Jon, sitting there so confidently. This was Mr. Henderson's first year, and he was young and trusting, never suspecting that his house proctor was in the woods getting stoned.

"Thanks so much, Jon. I hope you're having a good evening."

"Yes, a few of us are in the woods smoking pot."

We waved our hands wildly to make Jon stop. Jenny leaned over and tried to snatch away the phone.

Mr. Henderson laughed; playing along with what he thought was a joke.

"I guess I'll say good evening, sir," Jon continued. " A very good evening to you." He turned off the I phone. "Done," he said with great satisfaction.

We sat stunned. Jenny shook her head in disbelief, moving across the carpet to get as far from him as possible.

"Now, wasn't that fun?"

No, it wasn't. Not yet satisfied that we were suitably impressed, Jon waved his I phone above his head. We might be interested, he said, to know that he saved it all. Who knew when he might need a friend in high places, a kind of insurance policy?

Nobody spoke, but just sat there staring.

Then we heard Jon's voice again as he replayed the tape. "We're all out here smoking pot," we heard again.

Jon fell backward, laughing. I wished him dead.

The next to speak was Jenny. "Really, this is nothing but shitty, and I...." She stopped, unable to find the right words. She gave up trying.

"Would someone walk me back to the dorm? I didn't bring a flashlight a flashlight."

I was the first to volunteer. I held out my hand, and she took it, and off we went, before the others.

"He was just too much," she said. "I had to get away."

These were magic words to me, but all I could manage to say was "yes."

I held the flashlight that guided us along the twists and curves through the woods, past the glows that came from several other huts along the way. The path veered around a marshy place, and the spring peepers momentarily stopped singing as we passed.

I finally thought of something to say, but I was so pathetic. "There's a log up ahead we have to step over." My voice broke.

Yes, thank you." Her voice was soft and lovely, and gathered up enough courage to put my arm around her shoulders to guide her.

The path opened up too quickly onto the school lawns, and I saw the dark shadows of the chapel and the library against the light of the moon. I just had to prolong our time together, but only managed to clear my throat. She spoke first. "I need to go back to the dorm, but thanks for being my guide."

"Any time." I said. "Any time." Oh God, I thought. Oh God, God, God. My last chance, and this was all I said? I headed back to my dorm. I was going to bed. One thought was that maybe, just maybe, she had finally seen the true Jon and decided to quit.

The next morning I stationed myself after Sunday chapel to find out. I saw Jenny and several girls walk down the steps talking together, and a moment later Jon appeared in the doorway and surveyed the crowd. He spotted Jenny and headed towards her, and I saw her smile at him. I saw that nothing had changed. The two of them walked together towards Sunday brunch. Yes, they were still a couple, and I was still the outsider.

Still I managed to console myself by looking forward to the next evening when I would have one last chance. As co-editors of IMAGINE, Jenny and would preside at the annual literary reception, just the two of us together, side by side.

We had reserved the common room of the Union and ordered for seven o'clock crackers, two kinds of cheese, and grape punch. Students would stop by after dinner, when Jenny and I would introduce our special visitor, Eric Thompson, the alumni writer. It seemed impossibly wonderful that Jenny and I together would be hosts. This would undoubtedly be the high light of my four years at school.

We left the dining hall early and walked together to the Union to tend to the final details. Mattie, the school maid, was just filling the big punch bowl from one of the big jugs that had been delivered. We said hello to her, and she arranged the crackers and cheese on the platter.

Then I set up the kindling in the fireplace. Jenny struck the match ceremoniously, and we watched the fire transform the room.

I had her all to myself, and I imagined that we were together, arranging a party in our own home. I pictured us descending the stairs from our bedroom, down to where our guests were waiting.

The dream ended when Jon entered – first -- wouldn't you know -- dressed like the lord of the manor with a bow tie and a silk handkerchief in his jacket pocket. He wore glasses with the heavy dark frames, which he thought made him look intellectual.

He strode up to us. "You've been seeing a lot of my girl working on your little magazine." He smiled condescendingly. Jenny laughed and, failing to think of a response that was damaging enough, I managed a laugh.

I watched as he fastened upon Mr. Thompson, telling him how much he enjoyed reading his work. I was sure he was lying. I was disappointed when Mr. Thompson forfeited his chance to unmask him, but instead asked if he himself wrote short stones.

Undeterred, Jon said he simply enjoyed reading, not writing. "After all," he said, "without readers, there would be no point in writing, would there? Why would you write if you had no readers?"

Finally Mr. Thompson was a bit more forceful. "Have no fears, serious writers will keep writing regardless. It's just the way we are." He looked at me for confirmation, and I looked at Jon victoriously.

Any person with an ounce of sensitivity would have retreated, but Jon continued. "An interesting way of looking at it," he said, feigning great interest. "Yes, I'll be sure to keep that in mind."

Next he joined the crowd at the refreshment table. He reached for a glass of punch, and smiled condescendingly at Mattie. "Good evening, Matilda. Your special brew I presume?"

I hated his mock formality.

Mattie laughed happily. "Get on with you," she said.

Jon made a salute with his glass and treated her to a wink. He sipped and made a clicking sound with his tongue. "Not bad, but a little weak, don't you think?" The others standing near the bowl smiled expectantly. Jon was not one to disappoint, and sure enough, after making sure Mattie wasn't looking, he removed his big silver flask from his jacket pocket.

It was full, and he poured the entire contents into the punchbowl. I was sure it was vodka, and the stream seemed to continue forever. Immediately, of course, he became the star of the moment. Never in the history of the school had anyone ever displayed such audacity.

Then he topped off his performance by asking Mattie if she wouldn't mind stirring the punch. "It seems that all that good stuff is on the top," he said.

Unaware of what had happened, she stirred and gave him a cupful to sample.

He sipped carefully and noisily and then handed back the cup for a refill. "Thank you, Mattie, much better. He lowered his voice to a whisper. "Absolutely delectable,"

"You're the best," she said.

The crowd became electrified and gathered at the punch bowl. Of course, it was Jon who now became the hit of the evening. I wanted retaliation, but he seemed impregnable. He had won. I knew it.

Jon moved up to me and said; "I thought I'd add a bit of spirit to your dull little party."

Precisely at this moment Albert suddenly pushed against me as he reached for a refill. My arm flew up, and the contents of my full cup few up and splattered on Jon's face.

I pulled back and stared. It was impossible that so much punch could have come from my cup.

Jon stood stock-still. Then exhibiting great coolness, he pulled out a handkerchief from his back pocket, took off his glasses, and slowly wiped them. Then deliberately he patted his face dry.

I couldn't believe what had happened. " It was Albert's fault," I said. "He hit my arm." I stared at him. "Look what you did," I said.

Albert simply stared at me. "You're out of your mind. You threw it. Everybody saw you." He looked around for confirmation.

"Perfect shot," someone said. A few laughed, but most everyone simply stared.

Jenny came forward with a handful of napkins and handed them to him. " My, you are a mess, aren't you?" I heard laughter in her voice.

Jon glared at both of us. "I'll leave you to your little party," he said, and marched out the door.

Standing there, I tried to relive the scene. Without a doubt If Albert hadn't hit my arm, such a thing wouldn't have happened.

I stood there repeating this in my mind as Jenny took charge and introduced Mr. Thompson, who began to read one of his stories. Only when he began answering questions did I begin to pay attention to him.

It was Jenny, not me, who finally brought the evening to a close. "We've worked Mr. Thompson too hard," she said. "Just one more question." I saw three people raise their hands. The evening was a success.

Together, Jenny and I walked with Mr. Thompson back to the school guesthouse and said goodbye to him, I suggested that we head over to the Union, but Jenny didn't hear me. She wondered about Jon and began sending him a text. He was in his dorm, she learned. Would I want to come too? At first I thought she was joking, but she wasn't. I said goodbye and headed off alone.

The last few days passed far more quickly than I wanted. My mother emailed me, reminding me to start packing. She knew my father would want us to leave soon after graduation. I deleted her message.

My room stayed unchanged, just the way it had always been and the way I wanted it to stay -- my posters of Hemingway and Paris still on the walls, the worn out Oriental carpet on the floor, the story I was writing on the computer, the books crammed on the shelves and scattered on the desk.

I realized the end was near when my Mother and Dad arrived Saturday morning, the day before Graduation. I allowed myself to be swept along with demands for small talk. Yes, I was sad to be leaving (and I was), but excited about the future (and I wasn't).

They were appalled, they said, by the state of my room, and they insisted on helping me pack. They brought in packing boxes that the school had put in the hall for seniors, and I only watched, leaning against the wall as they tore everything apart.

By five o'clock, they finished to their satisfaction and went to the hotel to change clothes for the last night party. Jon's parents and a few others had rented the local Audubon Society nearby so we could all celebrate together.

I entered the party room with my mother and father, who immediately saw old friends to hug and kiss, leaving me free to join my friends. Of course, the bar was forbidden to us because of drinking laws, so we carried our own flasks,

and the bartender secretly poured us setups that we could top off.

"I paid off the bar tender," explained Jon, who, as always, was the showman.

I pretended not to hear him. The effect of vodka began mercifully to take effect, and I walked over to some friends to talk. I began to feel better. We formed a nucleus of friends -- close, bonded, but together for the last time. Tomorrow we would be broken up, scattered across the country.

Jenny walked over to our group. Her hair was tied up in a special way that I loved. Jon followed her, of course, and gave me a superior smile as he put an arm round her waist to show me that she belonged to him.

I moved over to some others and tried to put him out of my mind, but I always seemed hear him. With his drink in his hand, he made his rounds about the room, grandstanding as usual, in a very cool way, of course,

He was too drunk to notice that he was scuffing up a wire that led across the floor to the sound system. I watched as the wire started to form a lasso around his right foot as he performed a little pirouette to illustrate something to a group of people.

" What are you staring at?" Albert asked. He tried to follow my gaze, but didn't notice what was happening.

"You lose something?"

"I thought I heard something fall," I said.

Albert shrugged his shoulders and walked away.

The noose began to tighten, as Jon appeared to be doing in some kind of dance. He shuffled from one foot to another. He thought he was being very funny, and I heard Jenny laugh with appreciation.

The wire grew taut as he tried to take a step forward. I watched Jon lurch forward and slam to the floor.

. "I'm OK! OK!" I heard him scream. All conversation stopped as everyone turned to stare.

Then, there on the floor, he did pushups, three of them. "I'm all right, just needed a little exercise!" He was trying so hard to pretend he wasn't drunk that he didn't notice he was pressing a hand down into the broken glass.

"Always do pushups this time of evening – good for the health" He tried to sound forceful, but he was out of breath, and then his voice broke as he saw all the blood. He jumped up and held the hand against his chest. Blood soaked his shirt and ran down onto his pants.

Jon's parents rushed up to him. "You're drunk, that's the problem," said his father.

"Can't you see he's hurt?" His mother tried to embrace him. and I saw blood soak the front of her dress.

"He's drunk I tell you!" his father repeated.

"No he isn't," I rushed over to him. "It was the wire. There it is. That one!" I pointed to it. "It tripped him up, and he fell."

"He's right," Jon said in a weak voice.

Mr. Tomlin, Ike's father, stepped up and guided Jon down into a chair, "We need a tourniquet," he said.

Before anyone else had the chance, I tore off my tie and handed it to the man, who doubled it up and wrapped it around Jon's arm. Someone handed him a fork, and he inserted it in the knot and twisted.

Then I grabbed a cloth from the bar and rushed forward. I pushed though the people gathering around Jon. I crouched down pressed the cloth against the blood.

" The wire. That's what did it. The wire!" There on my knees I called to the others in the room. " It wasn't his fault. I saw it happen."

"You should know," came a voice behind me. It was Albert,

"Meaning what?" I stood and forced myself to look at him.

"You were watching what happened," he said.

"Meaning what?" I asked again.

I panicked and looked around to see if Jenny was listening. I saw. She knelt in front of Jon, and cupped his chin in her hands and said something in a low voice.

She hadn't heard, but Albert would tell her everything soon enough.

"I think he needs the school infirmary," said Mr. Corey, He seemed calmer now. He stood beside John helping him to stand and supporting his arm with the tourniquet. Then both Mr. and Mrs. Corey began to steer Jon to the door. Mrs. Corey turned to the crowd and assured everyone that Jon would be all right. Everything was under control, and everybody should continue to enjoy the party. she said.

I moved towards Jenny and said. "Don't worry. It's OK," Pathetic words, I knew, but all I could manage. Jenny ignored me or at least didn't see me. "May I go to," she asked Mr. Corey

"Yes, do come, of course."

"I want to go too." said Albert. They left together with Jon in the middle. The door slammed shut behind them, and I stood alone.

If only I could relive again what had happened. Only five minutes would be enough. Then I could call out to Jon. "The wire," I would shout. Watch the wire."

Many people hurried back to the bar, but I stood there with Jon's blood on my hands and I became some kind of a hero. You're a true friend, someone said, and the others agreed. My mother whispered that I go wash, but I shook my head no. His blood needed to remain. It showed I had tried to help.

It was then I told the truth. The praise was intolerable. The enormity of the situation was too much for me. "It was my fault, I said. And then I added, "I saw him. I saw what happened. I saw the wire, and I didn't say anything. Still no one seemed to hear. or, worse, they couldn't understand.

I told the truth, but it didn't make anything any better. I tried again. I walked over to a group if parents and said, "I could have warned him." People nodded pleasantly, but didn't hear. "You're a good friend," they said.

Now they started saying goodbye to each other. The party was breaking up.

My parents walked over to me. Maybe you could wash your hands now," Mother said.

"And then we can go out to dinner," my father said.

I would go with them, of course. I had no choice. I would have preferred to go back to my room and be alone and think, but it was not my room anymore. Everything had been packed. I had nowhere else to go.

About the Author:

George Carlisle graduated from the Writers Workshop at the University of Iowa, and taught as an intern at Phillips Exeter Academy, before moving on to St. Paul's School, New Hampshire, until his retirement. His specialty was teaching creative writing and he was long-time adviser of the school literary magazine. Former students are staff writers at theNew Yorker and others have published poems and short stories in other publications. Carlisle and his wife spend time in Boothbay Harbor, Maine; Cambridge; and San Miguel de Allende, Mexico.

OUR SALLY

by Ruth Deming

Over the years, The Newman Girls followed the fortunes of their next door neighbors in Shaker Heights, the fashionable suburb of Cleveland, Ohio. It was just their good fortune to live next door to the Hunters. Each family had four daughters. Comparisons were inevitable. And inevitably unpleasant.

The Hunter's house had red shutters on the windows, the Newmans had green. The Hunters ate "shaved ham" from the deli and kept their butter in a kitchen cabinet, but not in the fridge. The Newmans were among the first Jews in the neighborhood back then. The Sherwins, on the next street, got eggs thrown at their windows.

The Hunters were debutantes, like in those Katherine Hepburn black and white films, where she'd come down the stairs with a smile and a wink. The names of the Hunter kids were as unforgettable as our backyard swing set with the blue seesaw the kids always tried to tip over.

Christina, Rosemary, Ellen, and little Sally. Four girls to The Newmans four girls. The Newmans were not allowed to have pets of any kind, while the Hunters had Pete, a black French poodle, a yapper, who followed them like a fifth child.

For the nouveau riche of Shaker there was an assortment of private schools. The Hunters attended Hathaway Brown, tucked away in the woods. A yellow mini-school bus would pick them up every morning for their special college-prep education. Pete would be outside yapping goodbye.

Trouble was unknown. When you're young, wealthy, athletic and poised trouble was one of the bad desserts that would greet you later in life.

Somehow the years swept by. Glenmore Road was no longer their home, with its "island" across the street, land that would never be built upon, perfect for baseball, building forts, and reading dirty books like Peyton Place by Grace Metalius. Sharon, Lilly, Annabell and Lynn Newman reluctantly left when Dad found new jobs in the women's apparel field in New York City and Boston.

The Hunters had indeed been "prepped" by their gentiles-only Hathaway Brown.

Christina Hunter became an expert on race relations. Wrote a couple of books on the subject. Married and divorced Kelsey, a black man. Their daughter, Judith, needed years of psychotherapy. Rosemary became a social worker who specialized in working with people with borderline personality disorder.

Annabell bought her own clothing store, "My Darling Daughter," which did quite well. Then she bought the store next door. "Hunter's Chocolateria." When her clothes bulged at the seams, she bought a yoga studio and lost weight.

Little Sally was as talented as the others. Were these in fact the modern-day Bronte sisters? Creative juices oozed from her pores like honey from Winnie the Pooh's honey pot. She was a portrait photographer, trying to get her name out to the public and much too busy to think of marriage or hooking up with a mate. Either sex would be fine.

And then came her stroke.

She lay in bed in her Manhattan flat. The morning light crept through her blinds. Today's the day, she thought, when she'd photograph the last of the twins, for a book on twins she was working on. She hoped Aperture Press, one of the best, would publish it. It was not impossible. Just improbable.

Then it happened. Slowly, like spilt milk dripping on the floor. The left side of her face, with her blue eyes, quivered and froze in place. Her entire left arm lost feeling, as did her left foot.

"A stroke?" she thought. "But I'm too young." She couldn't for now remember how old she was but she wondered how she could get help. A million thoughts came to mind. Bette Davis going blind in Dark Victory. Ray Milland attempting to kill his wife in Dial M for Murder. Of course, she couldn't remember the names of the films, but she clearly saw the famous scenes.

Her survival instinct sprang into action like a revved-up ballerina. Without a further thought, she rolled out of bed – thump! thump! – and kept rolling and crawling into the living room. Her hardwood floors scraped her elbows and knees through her pink silk pajamas. She was so dizzy the room spun about her as if she were on a Ferris wheel.

Her blond Ikea table sat waiting for her. Toast and jam is what she would have, if only she could. She stared up at it from the floor. Her land line hung on the wall, with its curlicue cord leering at her: Catch me if you can. She pulled the cord with her right arm, it flopped down onto the floor and she dialed 9-1-1.

She made a bargain with the universe. Save me and I will change my life.

It seemed to be working. Every morning Luis from the rehab knocked on her door and wheeled her down the elevator in her Hovercraft wheelchair. A water bottle sat in one of the pockets. Her sisters paid for everything and told her not to worry.

The rehab was in a former elementary school. The floor-to-ceiling windows allowed plenty of light. Cindy, her personal trainer, fixed Sally's hair. How good it felt to have her shoulder-length graying hair combed, straight down to

the scalp. Sally was one of three people who'd suffered a stroke. Others were individuals with loathesome diseases such as Parkinson's and that dreadful ALS. "Just shoot me dead," thought Sally.

She had no intention of dying.

People flocked to help her, people she hadn't seen in decades.

One of The Newmans came to visit her in her Manhattan pad. Lynn took off from her job as manager of The Merlin Theatre and stayed with Sally a few days. They'd been close as children. Lynn's birthday was July 3, while Sally's was the fourth. Since Lynn was a pack rat, she brought a huge satchel of things for her friend, including a Minolta camera someone left at the theater.

"I tell you, Sal," she said when they sat together in the kitchen. "We could open a store with the things people leave behind at the theater."

Sally visualized a darkened movie theater, with 12 different theaters. Once when she brought her nieces Juliet and Robin to see the Disney film, "Fantastic Mr. Fox," the girls did somersaults across the carpet. How they laughed and didn't mind people staring. She encouraged their playfulness and individuality.

Lynn and Sally lounged at the kitchen table. Using two hands, Sally poured Lynn a cup of cinnamon tea. Her face was immovable. She pinched it. Then gave it a playful slap.

"Will you ever be able to speak?" asked Lynn.

"Noooo," came a sort of whisper.

Lynn, who had shoulder-length black hair, pushed the Minolta in front of Sally. Sally remembered attending summer camp and all the photos she had taken of fellow campers and counselors. They were somewhere in her apartment. She smiled as she remembered the short black-haired counselor Ina. They liked one another and had written postcards for a while. Wasn't it Ina who had organized the skinny dip in the lake?

Sally had never felt so free in her life. As she lowered her skinny body into the water she felt not a whiff of self-consciousness as the cooling waters embraced her like the white gloves they wore as debutantes.

She lifted up the camera with both hands and looked tentatively at Lynn. Gingerly, she stood up. She was quite good at this now. Rehab had taught her much. Everything, however, must be done slowly. As slowly as a little mouse sneaking into her flat and helping itself to the Cheerios she'd spilt on the floor or dribbles of popcorn. Did Cinderella's mice eat everything, like hers did?

After she picked up the camera, a sound came from Sally's mouth. Laughter. Real, genuine laughter. Lynn stared at her.

"Shit," said Lynn. "You can't tell me you're never gonna recover. You know what my daddy used to say?"

Sally looked over at her, remembering Lynn's father who would occasionally change into his Marine Corps uniform, and brag to the assembled neighbors, "I'm tough as nails.

"And so are you, Sally Hunter."

Sally got up from the table and haltingly walked into her bedroom. In one of the bottom drawers was a manila envelope. Inside was a swatch of Grandma Hunter's hair. With difficulty, she sat on the floor, opened up the envelope, and spread the hair out on the floor. She could feel its softness with her right hand, and now, with part of her left hand. With the Minolta, she photographed it.

Her craving to photograph became unstoppable. If the Stones had sung "I Can't Get No Satisfaction" she made it her motto to find satisfaction by photographing everything, with the help of Luis: pies and cakes on the counter at the Broadway Deli, where breakfast went for a good fifteen dollars. Wealthy people walking their dogs. Coffee carts parked on the street with foreign-born men and women dispensing hot dogs, hot salted peanuts, and sweet-smelling French fries. And, of course, children sitting on the lions at the New York Public Library.

Sally's sister Rosemary helped her find an agent. The photographs traveled around Manhattan, appearing in top galleries. "Healing through Photography" was a sensation. How many people in Manhattan were broken down, depressed, suffering from supposedly incurable conditions. Everyone wanted a piece of Sally Hunter and her positive outlook on life.

Lynn decided to visit her friend again. She got her friend Neil, the assistant manager, to take charge of the Merlin Theater, and she took the Greyhound to Manhattan.

Sally heard her friend walk down the linoleum hallway and waited for her at the door.

"Lynn?" she asked as she unlocked the chain.

It was not Lynn. It was a man in a black ski cap, who pushed Sally aside and rushed through her apartment. He lifted up the cushions in the living room, rifled through her underwear drawer, and when he saw her camera, he put it in his pocket.

Sally went after him with a broomstick, poking him wherever she could reach. Her strength was abysmal. He had a few unkind words for her, as he kicked her and punched her in the mouth.

"Celebrated photographer killed by intruder," read the obituary notice. "Memorial service will be held at the O'Toole Art Gallery, 530 West 25 th Street. Naturally the Newman Girls made the trip. Their sister, Annabell, met them at the art gallery in her late-model Mercedes SUV.

When Lynn signed the Legacy guestbook, a cryptic message had been left. "Sorry," said anonymous. "Was desperate to buy my cocaine. Am now enrolled in a 12-Step Program."

About the Author:

Ruth Z. Deming, a psychotherapist, lives in Willow Grove, PA, a suburb of Philadelphia in the good ole USA. A mental health advocate, she writes Guest Columns for local papers to help lessen stigma for mental illness. Her poetry and prose have been published in Blood and Thunder, Pure Slush, Page and Spine, Bookends Review and other literary venues. She writes a poem a day on Facebook.

SILVER HORSES REINED IN

by Susandale

Eight p.m., or thereabouts: the usual time for the droves of kids that peeled into the diner, Four Horses, at seven, to peel out. Josh put Reggie in charge of p.m. fries and cokes before he plunked down in the back booth with a book propped up in front of him. His assignment, the bone-weary, *Heart of Darkness awaited him.

'This is the third time this week I've attempted to plod through this ball-breaking rag.'

Stubbing his cigarette, he was about to turn another page when he glanced out the window and saw Rita's jaguar racing around the corner.

'Huh, what's this? When Rita told me she couldn't make it tonight, I volunteered to short-order on my day off, so why is she coming here now?'

The perplexities falling over Josh seemed to be caught in the illumination of the sinking sun. *'No, it's not the sun; it is Rita who is sailing through sunset.'*

Narrowing his eyes, he widened his imagination to Rita's Jaguar, as a silver chariot. *'Like coming down from Mount Olympus, pulled and being reined in by a golden goddess gliding down, but down to what?'*

He widened to fully open his eyes to the stark reality of Four Horses parking lot: pot-holes, over-stuffed garbage cans, dented cars lined up and honking their horns beside rusty call boxes.

Josh dropped his book only to fall back in the booth. *'So what if she canceled our date tonight, as she does so often these days? How can I stay angry at this exquisite goddess pulling in the reins to halt her chariot? Draped in*

gossamer folds, she steps into Four Horses with silver sandals that click-click her along.'

For the first time in his confident life, Josh felt low rent: grungy apron, his nose twitched with the awfulness of it: a combination of ketchup, mustard, and pickle juice merged with the piercing odor of fryer grease that permeated his hair and body, versus Rita's goddess perfection.

Josh's was a common-enough reaction for mere humans, but until this very moment low rent was unknown to him. He looked up to see Rita poised and posed in the doorway. She seemed miles away: alabaster and shimmery one moment, and in the next, a lioness prowling the jungle for a mate. Blinded by the sun exploding over the lake in blazes of sunset, at first glance Rita wasn't able to find Josh. He saw her searching with her eyes darting through the Restaurant.

"Hey, Rita, over here," he called out in a voice he struggled to hold steady.

A nod for acknowledgment before Rita headed his way. *'As she glides through the scruffy place, the walls seem to slip back into the foundation. Her movements carefully conducted, as though she is performing: Rita, continually the presence:now, as ever.'*

When she made her way over to the back booth, she slid into the booth in the seat across from Josh.

Her perfume or was it Rita, Josh couldn't be certain___ floated over to him with its elixir of mysteries: something deep, heady, but indefinable. Her perfume, or what was it that exuded from her pores? Rita and her fragrance wrapping Josh up, while her gestures, the set of her chin, shoulders stiff, body squeamish___ were saying don't touch. But Josh wasn't seeing the forbidden signs. He was seeing Rita, as they were in the beginning of their romance when she gave him every indication of wanting them to be a couple. His hand moved over hers. Inadvertently, mistakenly, and oh so futilely, he was trying to take her back to that time.

"Don't!"

"Don't what?"

"Don't touch me like that."

Barricaded behind her words, Josh said, "Like what?"

"Like I belong to you."

'Not even the fingers his hand cover are Josh's any longer,' she thought. She belonged to someone else now, and she searched for the words, which would sever the slender thread that once connected them.

"Alright." When he held his hands up in surrender, he freed both Rita and himself from the place they found themselves to be, as of late: painted into separate corners.

He said, "I am sorry I couldn't talk to you when you called, Rita, but I was in the middle

of … "

Rita's expression stopped him cold: rebuke flashed with impatience.

"Well, you know how it gets around here."

"This isn't about you, Josh; this is about me."

"What is about you?"

"What happened."

"What happened?"

David happened before Josh; he happened after Josh, and now Rita had no place left for Josh in her life rapidly turning topsy-turvy: Josh, but a trespasser in the aftermath of secret passions that brought Rita to this place at this time. This time, this place: neither, nor was the terminus of which Rita had long dreamed: a ring slid on her finger with his declaration of

undying love, a passionate honeymoon stretching into a happily-ever-after with two children: a boy and a girl, of course. Rita's dreams she cradled in a hope chest of candlelight and whispered endearments, while inside her actual hope chest laid priceless treasures, a dowry, really. Tucked in amongst her grandma's silver and her mother's pewter, an ivory and amber bracelet from Russia, a Picasso sculpture from Antibes, and her lace baptismal gown brought from an island close to Venice. Once promised by her father, but not going to happen now___ a blow-out wedding in Grandma Porter's Cathedral in downtown Cleveland: solemn Mass, heavy with white lilies and multitudes of tapered candles. An orchestra with a trumpet would have announced her arrival down an aisle that trailed her satin train. Peals of bells greeting the guests, and from the choir loft celebratory voices would have sung out.

None of it going to occur now: Rita's lofty dreams and her father's long-held promises came to an end.

'But when? She wondered. 'On what night of soft airs and careless passions? We first met on a hot, crazy night at Catawba Beach when the three-piece-group repeatedly played "*Night Train" in diverse rhythms. A drunken sailor on leave kept hitting on me. He was icky, scary persistent until David knocked him flat. And while the dizzy sailor was groaning on the dance floor, David said, "He's not fully to blame, you know. You are unbelievably beautiful" Later, we walked along the shoreline and looked up to see a glorious array of shooting stars. We were together and then we weren't, and then we were again.'

All that dreamy history in but fleeting seconds, Rita took a deep breath to expel it. And here she was at Four Horses. 'Josh and I need only clear away the debris that we've accumulated this past year when I was, more or less, his main squeeze, even as David and I were secretly meeting. Only then can we go on. Ah, but this is going to be so very difficult.'

Laying her head on the back of the booth, Rita shut her eyes. 'Unbearable for me to look into the direct, uncomplicated blue of Josh's eyes when I reveal the deceptions, which are about to change the courses of our lives: all three of us.'

She made tight knots of her fists. "Help me out, Josh; this isn't going to be easy."

"I can see that it isn't. Quit your peek-a-booing, Rita, and play it straight with me! Tell me what it is that you have to say."

She took a deep breath and let it out slowly. "Play some music then. I don't want anyone else to hear this."

Bewildered, Josh dug inside his pocket for a couple of quarters. After sinking them into the jukebox on the wall beside them, he held his palms up in an obligatory gesture that preceded an old game on theirs. Josh dropped in the quarters: Rita selected the songs. Though she went along with their old game, this time she did so without so much as a glance at what would be playing. A short while into *Billy Holiday's, *"Autumn In New York," she sideswiped the Restaurant with her glances taking in her surroundings: rowdy teens, some dancing, some gathered in circles laughing. Flirty-busy waitresses. Car hops bustling in and out the side door holding trays, a dishwasher carting off tubs of dirty dishes.

Her heart took another tumble towards the ending of more than her and Josh. Directly in front of her but distancing themselves to further back, *'my peers, calls coming from the cars at the call boxes, the end of my carefree, privileged youth when the most pressing decision of the moment was, " leather or cashmere for Homecoming," shrimp cocktail or lobster bites when I lunch with grandma at the Yacht Club, but now ...'*

Squaring her shoulders to her new realities, Rita thought, *'I must get this over with and as quickly as possible.'*

Which was the reason she blurted- "I'm getting married in three weeks, Josh."

Josh's head fell forward. "Married?! But, but, when, what, why ... "

Rita's eyes snapped shut: unbearable for her to see the confusion flashing across Josh's face. With eyes yet shut, she arranged and rearranged the next words she planned to say

with a touch or two of tenderness to scruff off the sandpaper-edges.

She opened her eyes to, 'what is the mysterious 'happy' shining in Josh's face?'

Before she could get a grip on Josh's twinkles and glows reaction, she was hearing him say, "So, you are proposing, are you?"

Her eyes widened in disbelief. Unaware, he continued. 'So this is the reason, Rita, that you and I have hung on through all that we've been sloughing through lately. All this time you wanted commitment. Why didn't you say so before now, honey? I realize I'm a clod when it comes to guessing what you want from me, but, Rita, you gave me not even a hint."

"But, Josh ... "

"If it is commitment that you want, commitment is what I will give you and in full doses, too, beginning with an elaborate proposal and on my knee yet. The ring, well it won't be what I wanted for you, which explains why my pledge has taken so long. I didn't think; it didn't even cross my mind ..."

"But, Josh ..."

"In my wildest dreams I never let myself dare hope that you would want to be the wife of a restaurant manager. You, a surgeon's daughter, way so above me both socially and financially, why would you come down to the greasy spoon of Four Horses?"

"Josh, that's not what I'm trying to say ..."

"Three weeks though? I don't know anything about planning weddings, but three weeks; isn't that sudden for a wedding? Or are you wanting me to lean a ladder up to Doc's place, and ... "

Rita's eyes spilled over with the tears that must wash away Josh's foolish conclusions. "I am pregnant, Josh," she said flatly, but as gently as she could.

"What, what: pregnant?"

Pregnant - a foreign word too female for male understanding: a word like a treacherous curve. Presto - right out in front of Josh: too sudden for him to put the brakes on - too sharp for him to drive around.

"Pregnant, but how? We haven't ... "

Bang into a brick wall - knocked flat-out! Like a balloon with the air escaping, Josh was helplessly zigzagging through the winds of change. Soaring up when he thought Rita wanted to marry him only to spiral down with doubts and half-formed conclusions. But when the lightening truth struck him, Josh crashed with whirlwind speed into the reality of Four Horses' drudgery.

Such an immense effort it was for him to regain his balance. To steady himself, he gathered his hands within the thick mane of Rita's hair in a motion both sensual and riveting. His hands firm on Rita's scalp held the two of them in this time and in this place. Steady now. He had to wait for the room to stop spinning with pregnant, pregnant, pregnant swirling around him.

Rita shut her eyes; bar them she must from seeing the pandemonium that distorted Josh's features. With his fingers yet clutching her scalp, Josh brought her around to face him.

Feeling his fingers firm on her scalp, Rita slowly opened her eyes and looked up at him warily.

He was saying, "Let me guess the father-to-be, slash, groom."

"Josh, keep it down; there are kids all around us."

"What the hell's the difference? In three weeks, isn't that what you said, three weeks and it's a done deal."

"You needn't be so crass."

"It's about to get a whole lot crasser, Rita. Could the father of your baby-to-be maybe, just maybe, be my sister's steady: one and the same, Lea's sweetheart and your old flame still burning bright: Du'Jon?" Josh demanded in words emerging in such tight bites, they poisoned the very air they were breathing.

His hands left her head and fell to tighten on Rita's shoulders; he was yet trying to steady himself in a room dizzily swirling around him: spinning with the whirlwinds of Rita and David: David and Rita, and their deceits and lies?

"It could have been anytime, too, with me working double shifts - this fucking summer school," he spat furiously, as though it were the books, pens, and grill that impregnated Rita. "When Rita, when and where did the two of you, you and Du'Jon ...?"

"What is it that you want from me, Josh? The times and the places?"

His hands flew from her shoulders. Trying to bar her words from landing on him, he held his arms in front of his face. "My god, Rita, no! No, don't tell me!"

Rita stood. "I am leaving, Josh."

Flee she must from the pain that filled Josh's face. Nothing in Rita's privileged life had prepared her for this hell: all of it: her mother scathing her with vitriolic words, her father mute and despondent, David's silent desperation, and now Josh's agony.

Up, to be away from the booth, Rita rushed for the door; she flew out. In visibility of her car and escape when she was seeing, no, she was feeling, not Josh's, but David's eyes searing her: David's eyes piercing her through the dark. Only by the fearsome light in David's eyes was Rita able to find the father of her unborn child. Running through the parking lot, she clutched her forehead with tight fingertips; she was attempting to block out the anguished light in David's eyes.

Once, when Rita was a child, her father trapped a stray cat in the gardener's shed. She never forgot the cat's demonic desperation begging for release. David's eyes bored into Rita with that same desperation..

She had just reached her car and was opening the door when an inexplicable sickness moved from her stomach to her throat. She feared the vomit that came without warning these days. She backed up and stopped. Overcome with nausea, she bent over the open door and took deep breaths to hold back the sickness she felt burning in her throat. Thus, she didn't see Josh, suddenly beside her. But when she felt a hand over hers, stunned, she looked up and into his face gone pale.

"You canceled our date tonight, only to come here with this?"

Her mouth agape with an answer she didn't have.

"Maybe you figured that I would read your nuptials in the society page, and just like that, you and I would be finished."

"Shortly after I cancelled tonight, Josh, I had a crisis of conscience. I realized that much as I dreaded it, I had to tell you."

"Conscience!?"

"I am on a merry-go-round, Josh, going around and up and down."

A ride, however, that you've wanted to take for a long time."

"Not like this," she sobbed.

Josh's face softened with the love that he felt for Rita, *'strangely enough, as powerful now, as when I saw her in her silver chariot in the beginning of this nightmare night.'*

Rita's silver steeds versus the four old nags of Four Horses Restaurant: Josh suddenly realized that they were never going to be together again. *'Me and Rita: we were never meant to be together. I guess I knew it from the first, but I was lured by her lavish beauty and sensual ways.'*

Gathering Rita close to his chest, Josh held her torment against the tangled mess he had yet to sort through. With fury tempered with tenderness, he moved outside of himself to comfort Rita. Circling his waist, Rita sunk within the warmth of his strength.

"David is so, so ... "

"So what?"

"It's not to be explained: The light in the back of his eyes: it's fearful, explosive. He says nothing, but his eyes burn me with a terrible light."

Josh's anger mounted. He clenched his jaw so tight that it hurt. He wanted so much for Rita to share his tomorrows, and her beauty to lessen the hardness of his days___ that the very thought of David sulking around and worrying Rita, who was carrying his child, enraged him.

Of a' sudden, David's deceit to his sister hit Josh. It felt like a harsh slap across his face. *'They are, they were a couple. Everybody knew them as together. And now this: why, Du'Jon isn't as much as the dirt under Lea's feet.'*

Though he was infuriated to the brink of combustion, for Rita's sake, her pregnant, frightened sake, he tried swallowing his anger: close to impossible with the lump of rage blocked in his throat too poisonous to gulp back, and too large for words to pass around it. His words he left barred behind his grinding teeth. He was literally shaking with the enormity of his un-expelled anger. Yet and still, with clenched jaw and red-rage face, he stiffened his back to soldier on.

Holding Rita against his chest, Josh pulled himself together. He said "Maybe it'll take that bas--as⬜ e-er, take Du'Jon, take him some time to get used to the idea of being married. Some time, to, ah, prepare himself to be a fa-fa-father," he stammered with the words he surely did not want to say.

"No, no!" Rita stood back so that she might fully explain her ordeal to the right-on, steady sturdiness of Josh. Everlastingly, Josh had been Rita's on-target steady: so straightforward, and so in love with her.

"It is more complicated than that, Josh."

"Frightened, maybe, confused? Oh hell, I don't know. And what's more, I don't give a good, gawd-damn."

Slashes of rage and grief were ripping Josh apart; he felt them tearing at him. He laid his head against Rita's even as he held her so close, she could feel the sobs wrenched from his gut.

Stroking his head, Rita murmured soft caring things to Josh: tender endearments such as she wished her mother would have spoken to her when Rita told her that she was pregnant.

She felt Josh's tears bathing her shoulder. And in the grandeur of a purple twilight baptizing the horizon, Rita finally, belatedly, knew how much she would miss Josh ... his abiding strength, his decisive moves, the certainty of his love and adulation.

"Rita, I don't know where I'm going. As long as you were with me, wherever it was, it was to a future that held promises. How can I trudge on without you?"

"Oh, Josh, I don't know. I can't think beyond the baby, marriage, David's silent rage. I'm living from moment to moment. I don't know how you will carry on without me. I'm so sorry, but I can't help you. I don't know how. "

Somehow, Rita's words to Josh caused her to be antsy. She twisted away from the shelter of his embrace: not all that difficult. Exhausted with anguish, Josh's entire body had gone limp. Silent, numb, he stood alone with tears burning his cheeks as he watched Rita drive off: golden goddess with silver steeds pulling her silver chariot up, up ... and further off into the horizon of a black night, coming on hard and fast.

_____*Heart of Darkness by writer Joseph Conrad: 1857 -1924

_____*Autumn in New York by composer Vernon Duke: 1903 –1969

____ __ * Billy Holliday: Blues and Jazz singer: (1915 – 1959)

_____*Night Train: lifted from Duke Ellington's Happy Go Lucky Album and recorded by Jimmy Forest 1951

About the Author:

Susandale's poems and fiction are on West-Ward Quarterly, Mad Swirl, Penman Review,The Voices Project, and Jerry Jazz Musician. In 2007, she won the grand prize for poetry from Oneswan. The Spaces Among Spaces from languageandculture.org has been on the internet. Bending the Spaces of Time from Barometric Pressure is on the internet now.

SEA COW

by David H. Miller

Edna's knuckles cracked, a stark sound of snapping twigs that was muffled by the mud. She clenched her fists again, letting the bones grind. Open. Close. Open. Close. Hurt more each time she did it. Her calloused palm brushed against something solid. She reached down deeper and then deeper still. Her elbows disappeared below the surface, the frayed ends of her stringy, gray hair dipping into the murky water. She felt around with her fingertips, searching for the sandpaper touch of a buried clam. She had ditched her gloves early on, trickier feeling shells through rubber. She nicked herself more often since then, but she had upped her haul. Lost the top of her pinky about a year ago, though no one seemed to notice her nub digit. Dwight would have, but he hadn't been noticing anything for a while and wouldn't again. The bay water squished and slurped as she dug through the shoreline sludge. She felt her mangled pinky jam against that same solid something. Nothing but a rock.

It took Edna a few months to step onto the shoal. Verne Trotter helped her locate Dwight's trawler at the Kennersley docks, coated in seagull shit, the hull overrun with barnacles the size of silver dollars. The engine was flooded, probably from the tropical storm that hit two Septembers ago. Edna hadn't remembered the storm. Dwight was in hospice then.

She took to the job faster than most. Osmosis, she reckoned, after three decades of marriage to a bonafide merman. There were moments, echoing across her memory, her salt-haired husband bobbing just below the surface of the bay, holding his breath three, four, fives minutes. She couldn't swim nearly as good as Dwight, and she had no idea how to fix a trawler. She preferred to walk the shoals anyway,

feel the sand under her feet. Her knees appreciated the stability.

Verne said he'd never seen a waterman with tits before. Neither had Edna. Still hadn't. Because she was a water-woman.

She had made him a promise, just before they got married all those years back. The bay, that was his domain. If she wanted to jump into the ocean during a weekend in Rehoboth, by all means, but the bay was off limits. Dwight said he was protecting her. Too many local boys and girls claimed by her waters. Edna sometimes thought it felt like the bay was his mistress. Spending all that time together, away from home. Giving up her bounty day after day. Edna hated the bay most of her married life on account of that notion, but once the creditors showed up on her doorstep, she forgave Lady Chesapeake.

Now she was drowning on dry land. It started with the urgent care. Then the tests, lots of tests. Hospitals bills piled on the living room carpet, atop the couch. She had to start watching her programs in bed again, like she and Dwight had done for half their thirty years. Cost more to die than to live, thought Edna, as she dug her hands into the silt.

She hadn't found a single clam all morning. The news liked to tell her the bay was dying. Maybe so. There was a lot of that these days. She had already let go of knowing. When they told her that with the chemo Dwight had at least two to three good years left, they knew until they didn't. She had let go of Jesus too. He didn't know shit either.

She wandered down the shore, ready to call it a day. Cutters in the distance, white sails dancing across the chop. A few trawlers still trying to make their haul. And there it was.

She brushed over barnacles, looking for the edge. Her hands danced across the boss, feeling the contours, the grooves and ridges, getting more excited inch by crusty inch. A doggone bonanza. The edges of her lips turning up into what your average joe would call a grin, but anyone who knew Edna Holly would call a great big smile. She ran her hands over that clam shell nearly twenty minutes before she found the umbo.

It wasn't always clams. You spend your time digging, you find things. Beer cans. Plastic bags. Traffic pylons. Dwight found a skeleton back in '88, though it might have been '92. Someone was getting elected. Edna remembered all the signs in Gayle Dunleavy's yard. It wasn't really fair to call it a skeleton, since it was just a foot. A few toes were missing. The police wouldn't let Dwight keep it, though all he had asked for was a single bone, something to remember. Edna wished he had kept it, even if it didn't exactly belong to her late husband. It would still have been his in some way. She still had the trawler at least. Thankfully her memory hadn't gone yet. Dwight's went pretty quick.

She spent another hour digging, clearing off the mud. Then, with a heave that cracked all her joints at once, Edna's clam broke the surface, jutting out like a drowned schooner after a hurricane. Her smile went sideways. Just the hull of an old sunfish, she thought. The paint peeled off, stripped by the barnacles. Sure as hell looked that way.

But no. There was the valve, crusted shut. That there was a clam. Praised be. A big one. Enormous. She thought about calling the folks at the Guinness book. Lester Denton would want a photo for his wall; every catch of note went behind the bar at the Docksider. Jools Vanderpreiss at the paper. Lily Sweetwater and all the other ladies Edna used to see at the knitting circle. Dewey Trout. Verne Trotter. They would surely want to weigh her, feel her, slobber their tongues all over her. Soon enough the whole town, the whole county, would be wanting their piece, and all Edna would have left would be a big ol' empty shell. If she was

lucky. And Lady Luck was as a much a legend for Edna as this clam would be a few years from now, a good yarn to tell at high tide.

Of course "Luck" was a lady, thought Edna, as she wedged the knife blade into the valve and jimmied it the best she could. The only god anyone prayed to in earnest these days was the same one they cursed, the only small "g" god it was safe to call a bitch. You didn't hear the winos at the Docksider calling big "G" God a bitch. He only got their praise. He was the one who made their philly come in first. It was Lady Luck who was the whore. It was her fault when your colt came up lame. Screw them both, thought Edna.

She adjusted her grip and wrenched the knife even harder. The clam didn't give an angler's inch. So she summoned what extra strength she could and leaned all of her one-hundred and twenty-six pounds against the knife. The blade snapped off the bolster and stayed there, suspended in the thick, salt build-up.

And there was Edna's justice, landing the largest clam a woman, or man, had ever seen ⍰ bigger than anything Dwight had brought home in thirty plus years ⍰ and she couldn't even shuck the darn thing, which was a major breach of protocol given the clam was still lodged in the wet sand of the shallows. But moving it was a pipe dream if there ever was one. Heck, she had almost ripped her arms off lifting that briny bivalve out of the mud. And any clammer worth his sea salt wouldn't help her out for anything less than halves. Edna would chuck herself overboard with rocks in her boots before she let anyone else take a piece.

Rage seeped in, taking her to that same dark space she found herself when the collection agent had shown up the morning of Dwight's funeral. It made her eyes see spots and her body become like one of those marionette puppets that got its wires tangled, that is to say, she lost control of herself. She snatched up the hammer, clenching so hard her knuckles cracked again. She swung like Casey at Bat, pounding against the clamshell. Bits of boss and barnacle broke off, whole pieces of shell. Spittle whipped from her lips. A final pound, and Edna dropped the iron. Her lungs were on fire. Chalky dust hung in the air a moment before settling into the frothy surf.

"Dangitall," she yelled.

The shell creaked open.

Edna froze, waves of fear and awe hitting her like the breakers, a feeling she hadn't felt since she watched Dwight's soul slip out from between his blistered lips. She half-expected the secrets of the universe to pour out of the darkness. Her other half expected dinner at least. A choking stench of rancid grouper gills and stagnant sulfur pools wafted out instead. Edna doubled over and chundered her breakfast into the ebbing tide.

She wiped a bit of half-digested gruel from her chin and peered into the shell, making sure to shield her tortured nostrils with the folds of her shirt. A tangled cocoon of seaweed and split-ends lay at the bottom. It quavered. Shook. Writhed. Something within pressed against the bourride jumble, yearning for escape. A soggy palm shot through the morass, flexing its fingers. Human fingers, wan and waterlogged like those floaters kayakers found from time to time beneath the Bay Bridge.

The waterwoman fell back, splashing onto the shoal. The haggard hand gripped the edge of the shell, rising before Edna, a resurrected nautilus. Soggy tendrils hung like vines, masking the creature's face and body. It was impossible to tell where the hair stopped and the seaweed began. What skin peeked through the overgrowth bore a mossy hue. Folds of sallow flesh hung from all sides and angles. Edna could see the creature's nethers peeking between two pasty, brined thighs. It reminded Edna of a manatee caught in a net, an image painted for her by that nickel-and-dimer Dewey Trout, who swore he had seen it on a fishing trip down in the Conch Republic.

The creature brushed aside a slimy tress. An eye peeked through. A woman's blue iris. More mollusk than moll, her chest looked as if someone took a pin to a pair of puffer fish, resting flat against the curve of her protruding midriff, marshmallow paunch jiggling with each raspy breath. Skin pulled taut over sodden knuckles, like overstuffed sausage casings, as she attempted to unknot her tattered mane.

Lady Godiva of the Black Lagoon.

"Speak mortal," spat the woman.

The tidewater swirled around Edna, pitifully attempting to drag her out to sea. She gazed up at the sea hag. Words hovered inside her throat, jaw locked by terror and acid-reflux.

"Art thou mute? In awe? Perhaps your people possess not the words to describe my beauty?" The hag pulled back her algae-coated locks, exposing her wide sargasso see.

"So you're not a manatee," Edna surmised, earnestly baffled by the creature standing before him.

"Manatee? Do I have fins, mortal? Do I have the whiskers of a beast?" asked the woman. "Behold, Venus, The Goddess of Love!"

"If you say so," said Edna. "Still don't excuse you standing there in your birthday suit."

The hag furrowed her brow, crushing a sand crab as it skittered across her forehead. That look brought Edna back to the time her son, Gus, had taken a lighter to little Vera Daughdril's Barbie doll. Melted half its face off. The doctors had called him "emotionally disturbed" and insisted that he be placed until a professional's care, but aside from that fist fight with the Ukrainian skipper when he was fifteen, Gus had been a model citizen. Until the meth at least, but that was another thing entirely.

The woman lowered herself to the shoal, extending a mossy limb.

"Come mortal, I have taken pity upon your simpleness. Thou shalt feel the sweet embrace of the Goddess, drink of the divine nectar..." She whipped her head back, a shower of barnacles plinked into the waves. "My sacred flower shall be yours. The mighty Ulysses was not so lucky as to taste my▯ "

"There's a clinic up the road a ways," offered Edna. She dug her hands deep in the muck, searching for something solid. "They could check you out."

Edna volunteered at the Methadone clinic every Sunday. It wasn't like she was gonna be spending that time at church. At first she hoped she might see Gus there, but she gave up on that dream pretty quick. Lately, the clinic felt less crazy than the rest of the world. At least the people at the clinic got better sometimes.

"Hear me, simpleton. This is a godly gift I have offered to bestow upon thee. My sex⬚ "

"Hear ME, bitch," interrupted Edna, her mind retreating once again to the comfort of that dark, angry space. "I ain't got no problem with lesbians, but that sure as shit ain't no invitation for you to get groovy. Now I think it best we get you some sorta health inspection before your tits fall off."

"Mortal. You freed me from my prison. Let me reward you," she begged. "I have spent millennia trapped in that accursed crustacean. I yearn to quench my thirst. To do that which I was created for..." The hag's words trickled out until no sound came from her lips.

Edna cleared her throat. She thought of Dwight. The cooper had messed up the gravestone. "Living husband," it said. Edna had to land a larger haul than a waterwoman or man would find in a lifetime to pay them to change that "i" to an "o." But they'd already laid it in the ground, years back. Edna didn't want to disturb Dwight again. That's why she hadn't considered selling the clam before she opened it. She hadn't forgotten her husband.

She pushed herself to her feet. She was a head taller than the sea hag. Algae dripped from the woman's once-golden tresses. Salt-cracked lips framed a dying reef, her teeth pocked and rotted from centuries of binging on the bones of bottom-feeders. She was a drowned goddess, her beauty soured in a clamshell sous vide. And in that moment, like the mirrored surface of the bay on a windless winter morning, Edna saw herself. She hadn't yet built up the courage to fish for suitors at the Docksider, but she probably didn't look too much different to those land sharks. Dewey Trout had called her a sea cow last week. He and the other crabbers had mooed under their breaths as she refueled the trawler.

"You want something to cover yourself?" Edna wiped her sandy hands on her shirt. "Got a jacket in my truck."

An ocean poured from the eyes of Venus, the Goddess of Love, all the salt water soaked into her innards, now oozing out. Her bloated body quivering. She looked up at Edna with her pale blue eyes. "I have temples in my name..." She reached out to steady herself against the clamshell.

"Good for you," said Edna.

"The bravest men fight wars at my word. Kings lay their swords at my feet. None can resist me..." Her words trailed off, lost in the sloshing tide. She stared off, out past the waves, to the artificial calm of the horizon, her divine motivations incomprehensible to a mere mortal like Edna.

"Maybe we can wash you up first. I'm sure you'd like that seaweed outta your hair," offered the waterwoman.

The sea hag's shoulders slumped. She gripped the shell's edge, straining to pull herself back into the safety of her clamshell prison. Her hands slipped. She tumbled onto the shoal. Seaweed, sand, sagging flesh, splashing about, a tantrum unfit for a goddess. Her fists pounded the sea, sending small tsunamis harmlessly lapping against Edna's boots. Her feet kicked up sludge, unearthing buried fish bones and sloughed crab skins. Edna thought she looked even more like a manatee caught in a net, trapped, drowning in the ocean it calls home. It reminded her of something Dwight had said, back when they had first heard Dewey Trout tell his tale. *They're like them water buffalos, the ones out in 'Nam. But someone forgot to give 'em feet. Not fit for the land and not fit for the ocean. Ain't got a place in the world, manatees.*

"Brought low by a fishmonger," Venus tore at a tuft of seagrass. "Hippolyta led armies!"

Edna cracked her knuckles, unsure what else to do with them. "I got a fireplace at my house. It ain't much, but it's warm and pretty dry."

The goddess's eyes seemed an even lighter hue now, having liquidated their excess stock. "This happens not to Mars. War, death, murder fail to change. But beauty, love has not the stasis that evil, that cruelty, possesses." The sodden goddess rose to her feet, wiping the tears from her face. "Hast thou heard my tale, mortal? The story of my birth?"

Edna felt the acrid temper of her words. She shook her head.

"I have heard it. I have heard it for millennia, from the gilded halls of Olympus to the bilge of a Cretian trireme," the goddess closed her eyes, summoning her story. "The dismembered phallis of fallen Uranus was flung into the sea and out of it, I emerged. Beauty born from the discarded genitals of a deposed divinity."

The sea hag dislodged a coil of kelp from her mane and held it to the sky. She breathed on the swollen pods and, from within, small flowers broke through the carapace, reaching for the warm rays of the sun. They fluttered in the cool ocean breeze, verdant and alive, but in an instant, they were dead. Shriveled. Rotten. She dropped the refuse into the waves. "We are at their mercy, as we have always been."

Edna twisted up her fingers. She felt the joints grind. She didn't know what she wanted, this Venus of the Dunes. It was hard enough looking at her, the grotesque way her body hung, out there for all the world to see, not a lick of clothes on. She hoped Dwight didn't look like that, down in that casket. Most she could hope for, that he was just bones at this point, like that skeleton foot.

The sea hag bent her head, performing a corpulent genuflection. An invocation, a plea. Her lower half disappeared into the murky sea swirls, watery blue eyes begging Edna, for what, she couldn't suss.

"Tide's running high," the waterwoman said, "I think I'm gonna head on home. You're welcome to come with. Haven't had a friend over in a long while."

Thunder clapped in the distance, a storm on its way inland.

The goddess waded out into the chop, her hair buoyed by knotted kelp strands, spreading out like sinuous digits. A snapper splashed about, caught in the hirsute web. Venus kept her course, stepping deeper and deeper into the unwelcome sea.

Edna heard a slurp behind her. The clamshell twisted back and forth, an unseen hand jimmying it from its marshy entanglement. Squish. Squish. Splosh. Edna quickly stepped aside as the shuck burst from its confinement, looking like a mastless schooner as it sailed out to the fleeing goddess. Snatching her up in its craw, the sea hag uttered not a word of protest. And with a faint pop, the shell sealed itself once again, and dove below an approaching wave.

Edna stared at the spot where the goddess, Venus, had stood only moments before, and saw her reflection in the mirrored surface of the bay.

She kept her eyes on the road ahead. Too much to think about. Edna just wanted to lay down and forget about the creature, forget about everything. Even Dwight. Especially Dwight. It was too hard, all the digging, and the living. She had already decided she wasn't going to tell anybody about it. Not like there was anybody for her to tell. Anyway, it could've just been something she ate. And she hadn't really been sleeping much lately, at least since Dwight passed.

Lightning flashed on the horizon. The storm had landed. Rain pelted the windshield. Edna's wipers creaked. Right, left. Right, left. Leaving translucent streaks across her field of vision.

Ka-Boom! A tree beside the road exploded. Flakes of wood and tinder peppered Edna's cab. She swerved to the shoulder, dodging a free-falling limb. Her tires squealed as the car fishtailed across both lanes and finally stopped next to the shattered elm.

Edna took a big breath. She'd have cursed if she could have thought of the right god to curse. It had been a confusing day, and the bolt had left her rattled.

Wisps of smoke rose from the ashen heap, the tree split straight down the center. Edna rolled her window down to get a better look. She heard the soft hiss of rain drops on the glowing embers. From between the cleaved tree stepped a hulking man. Cartoonish muscles bulged every which way, his genitals flopping in the wind. He waved his hand and the storm calmed. A matted, white beard framed his gnarled face. Glowing white eyes scanned the dented pickup. "I am Jupiter. King of Olympus. Father of the Gods…"

Edna stomped on the gas pedal and slammed her chassis into the naked deity. His body bent limply over the hood before it disappeared beneath the undercarriage.

She was halfway home before she looked back. The sun dipped below the horizon, dyeing the sky a bubblegum pink. Dinner sounded good right about now. She had some leftover oyster stew from the day before last. Hopefully it had kept. Edna never took away Dwight's place setting, even after they'd put him in the ground. She knew he wasn't coming back, but it had made her feel just a bit brighter, eating by herself. But she didn't need it tonight. She wasn't alone anymore.

A GUEST AT THE CLUB

by Henry Simpson

"That was a delightful performance, counselor," said a man with a voice that easily pierced the sound and fury of the courthouse hallway.

I opened my eyes. Standing before me was a tall, imposing man about sixty in a perfectly tailored suit. He had the look of Ivy League and aplomb of a Rockefeller.

"Do I know you?" I said.

"Doug Evans," he said.

"What do you want?"

He smiled, cool and unoffended by my rudeness. "We have mutual friends, Mr. Costa. I wonder if you'd mind talking with me. Won't take long."

"Mutual friends?"

"The Gentry family. It's about that suicide over at Macarthur. The police have arrested my son and Steve Gentry. The arraignment hearing is at two o'clock today. I am their defense lawyer. I would like to know everything possible about the evidence before I go to court."

"You'll find out soon enough. I can't help you much. I'm not involved in that case at all. I don't know anything."

He smiled. "Ah, those familiar words. Do you mind if I call you Joe? I believe you are being disingenuous, Joe. My sources tell me you are directly involved. You know Dougie and Steve. Do you seriously think they would murder one of their best friends?"

I got to my feet. "I witnessed your son kill my dog and skewer her with a bayonet. He also threatened me with an air rifle. Does that answer your question?"

"An air rifle?" He chuckled. "Listen, Joe . . ."

I put my hand on his chest. "You don't know me. Don't call me Joe. Please get the hell out of my face."

He backed away, straightening his Yale necktie and smoothing back his thinning dyed black hair. "Douglas is a blockhead, not a murderer. The only things he has ever shown any talents for are football and close order drill. I am sorry about your dog, but my son has feared all dogs since he was bitten as a small child. He is cynophobic. He was protecting himself against attack when he killed your dog. It is unfortunate, but I am sure a court would interpret his actions as justified. As for the air rifle incident, it is hard to take seriously. Now, if he had pointed a loaded firearm at you, it would be entirely different."

I walked away from him to the exit. Moments later, I was on State, thinking about lunch. "My club's in the next block," Evans said from behind. Catching up, he was soon beside me. "Come on, shipmate. Be my guest at the University Club."

"I'm not a member."

"I will vouch for you, Mr. Costa. Does my calling you that help? Loosen up a scoche." He surged ahead, then turned to face me, standing opposite the elegant tile and wrought iron doorway of his club, pointing at it like a shill.

I had never entered it before, never been invited. It was for millionaires, bluebloods, Ivy Leaguers, and their ilk, not commoners. The doorman greeted Evans with a broad smile and ushered us inside, where he handed us off like a relay runner to a maitre d' who led us to a reserved table in the middle of a compact dining room. The floors were covered with thick mauve carpet and the walls with dark wood panels and gilt-framed oil portraits of prosperous white men. I scanned the room. I counted two judges and three attorneys who looked familiar and at ease among all the other nice suits, high cheekbones, confident expressions, and easy laughter. They owned this exclusive little oasis and much outside it as well. Before I knew it, a bowtied waiter set Cobb salads and tall glasses of ice water with lemon on the table. "Gentlemen, enjoy yourselves," he said in parting.

"This is my usual lunch fare," Evans said. "Quick and healthy. Hope it suits you."

I lifted a salad fork and tasted. "Very good."

We ate without talking. Evans finished before I was halfway. He signaled a waiter. The waiter quickly delivered a crystal Old Fashioned glass half filled with amber liquid.

"Care for a cocktail?" he said.

"Nothing, thanks."

The waiter left.

"Do you have a son?" Evans said.

"A daughter. She's fourteen."

"Good. You will understand. We are protective, fathers. We want the best for our offspring. It is fundamental to our being. When they are young, we try to aim them in the right direction, and hope they will do well in the world. When they err, we help them recover. Sometimes we make excuses for them."

"Is there a limit?" I said.

"Of course. There must be. People in our profession are especially aware of limits." He drank and, for a moment, seemed to admire the splendid crystal. He set down the glass and looked me in the eyes. "Your father is an impressive man, a leader and a hero, a genuine asset to Macarthur."

"How do you know my father?"

"I chair the oversight committee at Macarthur. We pass on all professional hires. I reviewed his resume and interviewed him. With his background, he is highly qualified for a post at

Macarthur. The committee so recommended. It would probably be best if you did not mention to your father that I told you about my role in his hiring. I just thought you should know."

"I won't say a word."

"Now, about my son, and Steven . . ."

I said, "I don't have anything to tell you, Mr. Evans. My only connection with your two young clients is that Steven is . . ."

"Max Gentry's brother. I know. He was your close friend. Steven explained all that to me."

"What else did he say?"

"That he likes you. He said you have been like a mentor to him, and have given him good advice. What's your opinion of him?"

"Nice young man, polite, good family and prospects, undoubtedly a catch for some debutante."

"Not exactly how I'd put it. Let us stop this chess game. I am due in court in fifty minutes. What I need before I face the lions in that arena is some inside information. Help me. You have been where I am. What say?"

"The bluesuits want to put away some murderers and close some cases."

"What's the evidence?"

"A bruised and broken neck."

"What else?"

"That's all I know."

"Is political pressure involved?"

"The mayor has taken an interest. I believe she's made it clear to Homicide."

"You mean Pete Romero?"

"He's the ambitious one over there. Do you know him?"

"Of course. Do you have any advice?"

"Why ask me?"

He smiled. "Professional courtesy. Surely you've played devil's advocate before."

"Well, if the prosecution focuses on your son in particular, consider an insanity defense."

"He's not crazy."

"Who cares? Let a psychiatrist muddy the waters."

"Ridiculous."

"You could try shifting blame to Steven."

"Some friend and mentor you are."

"No, devil's advocate."

He raised his glass and finished it. As soon as he tabled it, the waiter whisked it away and left a fresh one.

"What happened two years ago?" I said.

"I have no idea what you mean."

"You were involved. I'd bet my life on it."

"Don't ever bet your life, son." He raised his glass. "Quite a puzzle, isn't it?"

"Two years ago, a burning death, this year Max's murder, and now Bobby Hughes. They're connected."

"Prove it," Evans said sarcastically.

I slammed my hand on the table with a bang and clatter of silver and glass. All eyes faced us. "You son of a bitch. You played me. You're like every other rich asshole in this cave. You get away with murder without a murmur of conscience."

"You really should have a drink, Mr. Costa. Believe me, we seldom get away with murder, and most of us carry heavy burdens of guilt as we live our lives. It comes with the responsibities we bear and the difficult decisions we must make to hold together the thin fabric of society. Your father would know what I mean. I am surprised you do not. Just to show you how fair and broad-minded I can be, I will let you look at a confidential case file that will interest you. It deals with the pranks and mischief that got three juveniles into trouble. Alas, I do not have much time, and would violate the law if I let you borrow it, so I will give you exactly two minutes to examine it." He reached into an inside pocket of his jacket, pulled out some folded pages, and laid them before me. He checked his wristwatch. "Starting now."

I leaned over and went into speed-reading mode. The papers comprised a two-year old juvenile case file involving Douglas Evans, Jr., Steven Gentry, and Robert Hughes. The three were charged with assault on several homeless men, resulting in one charge of involuntary manslaughter of a man who died of burns. D.C. Evans defended, presenting as character witnesses family friends, two high school coaches, and a teacher. The prosecution had no witnesses and slim circumstantial evidence. In a plea bargain, the defendants admitted guilt to one charge of battery and malicious mischief. They were sentenced to 180 days in juvenile detention and two years probation. At defense counsel's request, the judge agreed to allow the defendants to attend Macarthur Preparatory Academy under close supervision for two years in lieu of juvenile detention. Before I could finish reading, Evans pulled away the papers and pocketed them.

"Why did you show me that?" I said.

He looked at his watch and stood. "I must leave now. Let us part as friends." He extended his hand, I accepted it, and soon heard polite applause from several nearby tables; again, all eyes were on us from these fine, well-bred people.

"I'll expect an invitation to join," I said.

"Don't get your hopes up. A parting thought. Your father has a bright future at Macarthur. He has many good years ahead of him. He could aspire to any job he wants there. It is always helpful to have a friend in the front office. Marines cherish loyalty. It is one of their prime virtues, a wonderful thing. It's reciprocal."

It surprised me how quickly he left.

About the Author:

Henry Simpson is the author of several novels, two short story collections, many book reviews, and occasional pieces in literary journals. His most recent novel is Golden Girl (Newgame, 2017).

WHEN LOVE WAS A STORY WORTH TELLING
by Mathieu Cailler

Maybe it's because I'm a writer, maybe it's because I'm a romantic, maybe it's simply that I'm a sucker for a good story, but I'm envious of older folks' "how we met" tales. My generation does many things well, but romance isn't one of them. We don't possess these epic love stories, nor do we date or, god forbid, court. Rather, we "hang out," which is exactly what it feels like⬜ clinging to something that's difficult to grasp. And if we continue down the "right swipe" and "you up?" path, I'm afraid our love stories may soon be slotted on the endangered-species list, sandwiched right between the Amur leopard and the black rhinoceros.

My parents have one of these perfect yarns⬜ one that Pablo Neruda himself might deem muse worthy, one that makes me feel as daunted to take on love as Michael Jordan's son might be to try his hand at basketball. It's a story that always regales and lives up to the hype.

In college, my dear friend, Sam, met my folks⬜ my French father, my Midwestern mother⬜ and later, in the car ride home, he asked me how they'd met. I'd heard my mom and dad tell the story at dinner parties my whole life, but I'd never told it, and I was curious to see how it would hold up under my delivery.

I didn't make a long story short. I indulged in details and filled him in on backstory: it was June of 1976, and both my mother and father were in their early thirties. My mother and her friend and my father and his brother all boarded a cruise ship in Finland and headed for Russia during the height of the Cold War. Like most "meeting stories," this one began with someone catching someone else's eye. My curly-haired, Gitane-smoking father spotted my mother in the dining area on the very first night. She didn't notice, but he says he tried to find her whenever he could. My mother spoke no French, my father no English, but that didn't stop him. He waited and bided his time, and when the ship finally docked in Leningrad, my father joined her on a tour bus designed for English speakers. He snagged a seat next to her, and when the tour guide pointed out different historical monuments, my father followed the passengers' stares. When they craned their necks to the right, he followed suit. When they rotated left, he did the same. He and my mother didn't communicate with anything other than smiles and giggles⬜ the Esperanto of emotion. She said she thought he was kind and handsome, and silly, too, for stepping aboard the wrong bus. For three days, he boarded the wrong bus, remembering some English words he'd learned here and there. "Nice, no?" my father would say. "Yes, very nice," he would say. And my mother would grin and laugh and agree that things were nice. Very nice.

When the cruise ended, they exchanged more than just soft gazes, swapping addresses and phone numbers, with my father saying that he would write immediately and would learn English in a year's time, too. Then, each returned to their continent and home, surrounded by different time zones, rivers, and ranges.

Oh, and I forgot to mention, they also returned to their significant others to which they were both engaged for some time.

Each of them immersed themselves into their old worlds and obviously struggling relationships. My dad dove deep into his work as a lawyer (he'd told my mother on the ship that he was an avocat, the French word for lawyer, but she had understood that he was an avocado farmer). My mom did the same, putting in longer hours in her special-education classroom in Boston. But even with all the work and distance, they stayed rooted in each other's minds, and if thoughts had been phone calls, both of them would have needed to take out small-business loans.

My father did as promised: he wrote her. It took him time to craft a worthy letter, and he asked friends who spoke English for advice and enrolled in a class at a nearby school. My mother waited patiently for his words to arrive, checking her mailbox every day, but nothing. Weeks passed, and she began to think their romance was of the perfume variety: sweet, yet ephemeral.

Some eight weeks later, however, the letter arrived. My father's dad⬚ a postman, no less⬚ had accidentally sent the letter via boat instead of by plane. The spot-on English was scrawled in loopy, purple ink, and it was imbued with my father's charm. He drew margin doodles recalling their Russia trip, and he often joked that he was "trying to be like Keats."

My mother, too, had been honing her language skills, practicing her French with a neighbor who had lived most of her life in Belgium. If my father was Keats, then my mother was attempting to be Baudelaire, and she wrote and wrote whenever she could, and my father did the same.

One night, both my mother and father still engaged, my father called my mother. The English class and his constant listening to Elvis had paid off, as had my mother's lessons with her neighbor, and two of them communicated with ease. The feelings were as palpable as ever, even through all the miles of wire, and hours later, when they ended the call, my father broke up with his fiancée. My mother did the same after two more phone exchanges.

They spoke via phone weekly, and the relationship strengthened with each question and sweet nothing. About ten months after they'd initially met, my father invited himself out to Boston. "Patricia"⬚ though my father pronounced it Pa-tree-zee-ah⬚ "when can I see you again? I am coming out to Boston. I was thinking I could take all my money out of my savings and stay with you until I run out."

My mother agreed. And the plan proceeded.

My father arrived at Logan, speaking English, exactly as he'd promised. He wore a Cuba t-shirt and tight pants, and my normally cautious mother found that their relationship picked up right where they'd left it. Every time a "what am I doing?" thought popped up, it was assuaged by their love.

They indulged in a lavish time in Boston, my father spending money like a man who only had a few weeks to live. They shucked briny oysters on the Cape, toured the creaky floorboards of the Old North Church, and took in a thrilling Red Sox game at Fenway. When my father's money ran out weeks later, my mother said it was her turn now to spend the same amount, and thus the American travels continued with my father driving my mother's green Pontiac Le Mans all over New England, New York, and even down to New Orleans.

The last night, before my father had to return home, he asked my mother if she would like to come stay in France, and also if she would like to get married. After my mother made sure my father understood exactly what he'd asked, she happily agreed, but only if she could bring her Irish Setter.

After quitting her job and saying hard goodbyes to students, family, friends, she arrived in Le Mont-Dore with her dog and stuffed suitcase. She clucked at markets to ensure she was buying chicken, ate her weight in Camembert, and rode shotgun in my father's Citroën DS.

They were married in Paris. My mother in a red dress, my father in a white suit. It was July 1st, 1977, fifty-three weeks after they'd first met in search of nothing more than a cheap cruise and the midnight sun.

Just as I finished telling this story to Sam, we exited the freeway and pulled up to our college. He didn't get out of the car, though. Instead, he peppered me with questions⬚ wanting more.

For the next few years at undergrad, Sam often asked me to tell the story to friends and fellow students, some who I barely knew, but the story always seem to deliver. Maybe it's just pleasant for people to sit at the hearth of one of these tales and feel the flickers of its flames, if for nothing else than to see that love isn't totally on life-support.

As for me, I try to tell myself that there's no better time to be alive than in this current present. That it's just a story, and that it doesn't matter. If my father were dating today and met my mom online, the results would be the same. Love. Marriage. 42 years. That the real story is what happens next, when love has found its targets and had time to settle into each person. That's what I tell myself: it's the second act that's important, and that while I would love an epic story like my parents' yarn, I'll probably have to make do with it just being a part of my DNA.

About the Author:

Mathieu Cailler's poetry and prose have been widely featured in numerous national and international publications, including the Los Angeles Times and The Saturday Evening Post. A graduate of the Vermont College of Fine Arts, he is the recipient of a Short Story AmericaPrize for Short Fiction and a Shakespeare Award for Poetry. He is the author of Clotheslines (Red Bird Press), Shhh(ELJ Publications), and Loss Angeles (Short Story America Press), which has been honored by the Hollywood, New York, London, Paris, Best Book, and International Book Awards. His newest book, May I Have This Dance? (About Editions), was recently named poetry winner of the 2017 New England Book Festival.

THE EXPERT

by Virginia Hoeck

My dad was a reluctant expert in death.

Though he was a psychologist by training, it was the losses of two children that qualified him to help others cope with grief. Ten years into my parents' 53 year marriage, my older sister – 9-year-old Elizabeth – was killed in a boating accident. A decade later, my 17-year-old brother Pat, died in a car crash.

People from all over would seek out for his unconventional brand of counsel that stemmed from his education, personal experiences and an unshakeable faith in God. I couldn't go anywhere - grocery stores, business meetings, Little League games – without bumping into someone who would share with me the story of how my father helped them heal from a tragedy. Isn't it so hard, I asked him, always talking about such devastating losses? He shrugged. "It can be so, so sad," he said. "But it's what I can do."

When at the age of 85 his generous heart began to weaken, my dad had no trouble talking about his own demise. He spoke about it somewhat frequently, and was completely at ease with the idea of his death. "I'll get to see Elizabeth and Patrick again, and my parents," he once said. Another time, "I hate the idea of your mother being alone. She'll miss me I know but she'll be fine." Her children, grandchildren and friends would stave off loneliness. He was light-hearted when he said, "I'm ready to go when God wants me. But I don't think he's ready for me. Not just yet." he said smiling, as if he were playing a game of Duck, Duck, Goose, and was wondering when it'd be his turn to be tapped on the head.

His good humor was tested on the morning of my mother's 82nd birthday. For the third time in just a couple months he was rushed to the hospital, this time in an ambulance. Breathing had become impossible; he couldn't get out of bed. At the ER, he was agitated. I asked him what was wrong. Was he afraid? "No, it's not that," he said. "I didn't want this to happen today. Not on her birthday."

After a while the tube pumping oxygen into his nose and the one draining liquid from his lungs began to help. He could breathe a little easier and speak a little more clearly and yet he kept his eyes closed, though he didn't seem to be sleeping. I wondered, despite what he had said, if he had been thinking that even if today wasn't the day, it might be coming soon. But when my mom stepped out of the room, he spoke up.

"Get a pen and paper," he told me. "I need to write a letter."

Of course: A birthday note. There was never a holiday that my mother didn't wake up to find a note from my dad, propped against a vase of flowers, on the dining room table. Though his love letters were publicly presented, they were never shared.

"To my darling wife….." he began. It made me feel both sad and privileged to witness this intimacy.

"I'm so happy that in spite of the difficulties of these last few days that we have been able to spend so many wonderful hours together…." He paused for a moment, caught his breath, then continued. "I am so happy that we are on

one page and that we both have total confidence that whatever is to come is ok."

His voice was soft, barely a whisper, but his message was clear and strong. He spoke of falling in love with my mom in an instant; of her beauty, still after all these years; and how proud he was that they had made such a good team, in spite of tremendous heartache. His words were more eloquent than that, but, won't be repeated here.

When he was done dictating, he squeaked out instructions to get money out of his sock drawer to buy flowers and go out to do it now, please, so they'd be there when she got home that night.

When it appeared that my dad was, in fact, likely to make it through my mother's birthday, I ran to the florists and he was moved up to the cardiac ICU. Over the next few days, he was mostly his old self: Caring, compassionate, curious. Sometimes my siblings and I were stuck out in the waiting room because his visit with a nurse or doctor or orderly had turned social. My dad always wanted to hear their stories; for some reason, they were always willing to oblige. But he was often tired and uncomfortable, if not in pain. The medley of medications being used to control his blood pressure, heart rate and diabetes were in conflict. Blood draws from his parched veins were tortuous. And some inexplicable pain in his back could not be managed.

A memory from a few years ago flashed before me during those early days in the hospital. I had been out to dinner with my parents. We were following the hostess to our table but moving slowly because an elderly woman, confused and barely mobile, was ahead of us, nearly being dragged forward by her son.

"If you ever have to lead me around like that lead me right to a cliff and give me a little push," Dad had said. "Don't ever let me be like that!" I shook my head and chuckled; the idea of my father as a frail, old man was unimaginable.

One afternoon my dad's close priest friend came by for a visit. The two men were personal confidants who had deep respect for each other, even if they didn't always agree. There is

no doubt that this kind and wise man loved my father and wanted only the best for him and our family. On his way out of the hospital, he stopped by the waiting room to offer his love and support to my mom, my sister and me. He also had some advice. "He's ready, you know. Don't get in God's way."

The bluntness of his statement shocked us. But it corresponded with what I, and I think some of my siblings, had already been thinking: Enough was enough. My dad could no longer do many of the things he loved to do: Drive, go to Mass, visit his grandchildren or friends, eat a good meal. Plus, this back and forth to the hospital was exhausting and distressing to both my parents. Given my dad's attitude about life, and death, I wondered whether he thought it was all worth it.

He didn't. Within a day or so, he and my mom talked and decided together (they always decide everything together, he reminded us), that he was going to stop treatment and let nature take its course.

Dad's cardiologist didn't take the news well. Tears streamed down her face as she tried to convince him that if he only let him she was sure he could get more time. My dad smiled as he told her: "It's not up to you, it's up to God."

They unhooked my dad from his various machines and moved him into a comfortable room, a room more suitable for receiving visitors. Family and friends, former patients, even some of the hospital staff came to say their goodbyes. Off medications and mechanical contraptions, he was able to sit up and talk with the people who'd adored him over the years.

For a couple days, it seemed that maybe the doctors had been wrong. Maybe he could go on for a long time like this. But then he started sleeping more, his breathing got slightly more labored.

We played music for him and talked about every important thing we could talk about. He continued to dispatch pieces of advice to all of us and offer observations about dying. He encouraged me to write about his death. "Are you getting this down?" he sometimes asked.

"People need to know," he once said, "there is nothing to be afraid of. It is as beautiful as birth." Seven days since leaving the ICU, he'd been wondering why it was taking so long for him to die. "I thought I'd be annoyed with God, but I'm not. This is just fine. It's very peaceful."

Nine days into it, with mom sitting by his side and my siblings standing nearby, he opened his eyes and began talking to us about choosing love, a topic he'd shared with each one of us children before we married.

He motioned to my mother. "We chose to love each other," he said. Then looking at us, he said, "I chose to love her," and then he looked at my mom and said, "I chose to love you. And you know what? It was easy." He looked around at us again and continued. "Choose to love and embrace that decision. There will be hardships and ups and downs but when you choose to love, it's easy. Choose to love."

And the next day, with my mom holding his hand, he looked up at her one last time, then, with the peace and resolve of the greatest of experts, he closed his eyes and was gone.

About the Author:

Virginia Ryan holds a degree in journalism from George Washington University and an MFA from Lesley University. She served with the Peace Corps in Thailand and worked first as a journalist and then as a nonprofit marketing director before settling down to a life of writing from her home by the sea in Massachusetts. She is currently working on a novel.

DANCING WITH MY MOTHER

by Nancy Nau Sullivan

My mother left me for three months with my Aunt Margaret when I was a newborn. She went to San Francisco to meet my father who had survived World War II and the torpedoes shooting at him throughout the Pacific. They had never had a real honeymoon, given that my father called my mother one day in 1943 and said, I'm coming home to Indiana and let's get married. Which they did.

I don't regret that unremembered time with Aunt Margaret. She was an ample, lovely woman with a gap between her teeth, already in her 30's and unmarried. I never think of her that I don't see her laughing. I miss her to this day...

But I do carry a certain amount of disappointment that I never really had time with my mother. Just the two of us. That old bonding thing.

When she picked me up after that rather long honeymoon, she was pregnant again.

And by the time I was six, she was expecting her fourth.

She left me again, this time with my grandmother in Florida for six months, and I really can't say I blame her. In fact, I thank her every day. First off, she was overwhelmed with all those babies. And second of all--but first in my book--was that I adored my grandmother, and those days still remain the best I've ever had. Endless, unconditional love and pampering with no dripping, crying babies around. I still flee to Florida every chance I get. I'm there now, listening to the birds, squinting in the sun, looking forward to a swim and a walk on the beach.

My mother always said, I left you down there too long.

I went home when I was seven, and the babies kept coming. Seven in number, finally. My siblings and I were always happy with the announcement of another, but my mother not so much. She was pregnant nine times, and once when she knew she was miscarrying with number eight, or maybe nine, a friend told her to run up and down the stairs. It wouldn't have mattered. Seven it was, nine not meant to be.

One time, my sister and I found a strange calendar in our mother's bottom drawer. It was tucked under the Playboy magazines and Tampax, which we figured had something to do with sex. Did she put these little white tubes in her bosom--a word we looked up in the dictionary and snickered over. Boobs were the only evidence of anything having to do with sex that we could think of. The Tampax must go there....We put the cardboard tubes with their cotton innards, which we pulled out, back in the drawer, with the frayed pink elastic belt and cotton pads. And we studied that calendar. The X's on the dates had nothing to do with holidays or birthdays, or any other special event we could figure. Except for another blessed event.

My mother always said, Rhythm doesn't work.

She just wasn't meant to have so many children. The youngest of four, she'd never been around babies. She was shy, and beautiful, and although strong and disciplined about meals and the endless, tiring regimen of practices, lessons, Girl Scout cookie sales -- even doughnut sales (What were they thinking?) -- she wasn't cut out for it. She ended up drinking: vodka (vanilla) in the afternoon and Canadian Club (chocolate) in the evening.

Growing up, I grudgingly helped out. Diapers, dishes, dusting. I babysat when I was nine for 25 cents an hour, and I had to clean and vacuum three times a week, which I saw no point in doing since my family continually scummed up the thread-bare carpet and sticky coffee table.

When my brother developed juvenile diabetes at four, I was finally able to do something worthwhile. I gave him his insulin shots that I learned to do by practicing on an orange. When my mother found out about Felix, it was the only time I saw her cry. The doctor told her he wouldn't live to 30. An accomplished swimmer through grade school into high school, mostly due to my mother's tireless efforts to weigh what he ate and drive him to practice, he is now collecting social security.

She expected a lot out of me. But we just sort of danced around each other, my father in the middle. My mother and I were never close. Until she died.

But that was years later. 55 to be exact. In the meantime, we had our moments, and it's the weird shit I remember.

She said I looked like a monkey because my hairline was low. One day, she was eating an apple from my grandmother's orchard. She gave me one bite, and one bite only, and grabbed it back. I wanted more. She told me my ass was too big. Well, I wish she could see me now. What a walking fashion statement I turned out to be.

And that may have been part of the problem. I looked like her, and my father adored me. We danced around him like he was a hot rack of clothing at a department store sale. He gave me authority, she declined. He preferred my bridge playing and praised my drive and school grades. He wasn't so happy with some of the parties I threw while my parents were at football games or the country club. My hooligan friends tore the place up, drank the booze, broke the dining room cabinet, stole his Knights of Columbus sword. I wonder where that sword is today. Probably defending the northern edges of Hammond, Indiana.

When I graduated from college, I was offered a fellowship at Northwestern, which would have put me close to home, back in the Midwest. It was either that or the Peace Corps, but I really wanted that fellowship at Medill. She steered me away. Get into the market place, she said. So I did. I went to New York. Only later did I earn that graduate degree--20 years later--and join the Peace Corps--nearly 50 years later. Many a commencement speaker has cautioned, Don't listen to your parents. They only want what's best for you. If Steve Jobs had stayed in college and listened to 'the noise of others' instead of his 'inner voice' (Stanford, 2005), would I be writing this on a legal pad? Probably not. But I did listen to my parents, and it cost me.

Shortly before my mother died, the two of us were sitting in the sun room of her condo. She was curled up on a love seat, a satin pillow behind her neck, a mohair throw over her knees. She was wearing a blue gingham bed jacket. I hated that bed jacket. I'd given her one years before, and she had lent it to a friend with cancer. 'I never got it back,' she told me, and I went out and bought her another. I'm sorry I did. It was just another reminder.

We were alone that night. Shocker. With six siblings and spouses, twenty grandchildren, and one needy father in the vicinity, this was a rare moment. The oxygen machine clap-clapped behind her. It was the only thing that relieved the cancer that was eating her up, that and the valium. She was past the vodka stage.

She napped, and I sat glumly, staring at her, and then suddenly she jerked awake. Our conversation went something like this:

'I haven't done anything with my life,' she said.

I was stunned. 'What? Why do you say that?' My responses to her were usually clipped. I was always trying to temper my conversation with humor, or philosophy. One time she told me I was full of shit. Point. Score. Always be honest.

'Why would you ever say such a thing? You and Dad put all seven of us through college. You rented a castle in Ireland. You've traveled from China to London, and some other places. And you make the best chicken tetrazzini in the world.'

She laughed, nearly expelling the plastic tubing from her nose. Something cold whirled around me. But I laughed, too, remembering a night in Germany in 1972, when my parents came to visit us during our stint in the Army, and she raged and sang, up and down a dark street: 'I am woman.' As I recall, there was Steinhager involved. Dad called her the female bull. Something came over her with the women's lib movement. She never wanted to be Donna Reed, or that Cleaver woman.

My mother struggled to sit up. 'Well, I missed the boat. But you haven't.' Her eyes were startling blue. 'I'm not afraid anymore, and don't you ever be. You're right .I've had so much.'

She rarely said I was right about anything. I took it.

Her voice was strong. I thought of a candle, pooling and burning out in a final luminescent white glow. My mother waved me over, and I sat next to her. Even when she was sick and kind of helpless, there was very little talk along the way, no light bantering down the stairs to hell. Suddenly here we were. In hell.

She said: 'How can I ever thank you? I want to tell you something. I know being the eldest makes you feel responsibility very seriously. You're different because you're you, and you're the first born. You know how I go on... There are so many good things about that; you're strong, independent, smart and a great achiever. That's a lot of good stuff. Besides, God made you beautiful. Isn't that nice? And you're blessed with good health....'

I didn't move. She said: 'Seems like you're going through a giant rough spot now.'

Right again. Find husband with another woman. Get divorce. Be pissed off at the world.

'Please,' she said. 'Try not to look back. And try to forgive. I know that's hard but it's the only way you'll have peace. Peace is what we need. You don't have to say or act out forgiveness. Just know that you do...'

I leaned closer. We stayed like that, together, the cold rain dinging the patio stones. I went over her words that filled the room to bursting. I locked them in. I held her hand.

I think about the last time I danced with my mother, and my mother danced with me.

About the Author:

Nancy Nau Sullivan is a writer, teacher, and former newspaper journalist. Her memoir, The Last Cadillac, was published in 2016 and won an Eric Hoffer Award in memoir. Her writing has appeared in magazines and collections, including Gargoyle, The Atherton Review, The Blotter, Akashic Books, skirt!magazine, Red Rock Review⏾ and, most recently, in Literally Stories online. In 2014, she taught English in the Peace Corps in Mexico--and, prior to service, at the City Colleges of Chicago, in Argentina and at a boys' prison in Florida. She has a master's degree in journalism from Marquette University and worked as a reporter and editor at newspapers throughout the Midwest. She lives in Northwest Indiana near the lake⏾ and on Anna Maria Island as often as possible.

IN LOVE AND WAR
by Dufflyn Lammers

I couldn't bear watching him walk through the rain with his head wet, so I bought two umbrellas, one for myself and one for my boyfriend, the first Spring I was in Paris.

He lost the polka dot umbrella from Monoprix after I'd left to go back to Los Angeles, which I still officially called home, and where I had no need for an umbrella.

When I returned to Paris in October he was starting a new job so he carried the Samsonite with him. I like this umbrella. It's automatic, and black, and light as a feather⏁ perfect to carry in your purse for, literally, a rainy day.

This left me umbrellaless.

On my way back to his apartment one day that Fall it started to pour. I stepped into a baggage shop on Avenue de Clichy and bought yet another umbrella.

Somehow two weeks later all things umbrella had ended up at my boyfriend's office. Friday night I texted him at work to please bring my the new one home. I was a little ticked off. How many umbrellas did I have to buy?

That was Friday November thirteenth, 2016. The day of the Bataclan terrorist attacks in Paris.

We sat in his apartment all night listening to sirens cross and re-cross the city. There was nothing else to do.

I forgot all about the umbrella.

The next morning the real estate broker he works for decided to close for a few days. Nobody wanted to shop for apartments in Paris that weekend.

A friend called and asked if I would join her; there was a group of (mostly women) meeting at St. Elisabeth's Church. This church is near the Place de la Republique, just blocks from where the attacks took place. I was afraid to go. How could we know it was over?

But I wanted to connect.

At the meeting, one woman told me how she had run when the shooting started and a stranger had pulled her into an apartment. She hadn't wanted to go inside, the whole thing seemed surreal, like it wasn't really happening, but the stranger insisted. Later, she realized this woman may have saved her life.

As I listened I wanted to go back home and tell my boyfriend that I love him.

We had been together for a year at this point. Neither one of us had said those words. Not even last winter after "Charlie," although I wanted to say it then too. I was waiting for him to say it first.

I believe the things we want most are also the things we fear most.

That Summer he had come to stay with me in California and we ate Dim Sum with my father. Then we went back to France and took the train up to meet his family in the North. But I didn'tknow what the future would hold.

If we said we loved each other, what did that mean? I was afraid of how those words could change us. That he would feel some sort of pressure. That he wouldn't say it back. That I would lose my power in the relationship and become a groveling mess.

This is the first relationship I have been in since my last one ended, quite badly, thirteen years ago. I'm forty-five now. I don't know how many more chances at love I will get.

When we met in Paris I was on a three-month visit from Los Angeles, taking some time to work on a book. It was only my second trip to Paris and I didn't know the city then. I stopped to ask a handsome Frenchman for directions one day and then ran into him again two weeks later in the same spot. He invited me to lunch at a cafe. After that we saw each other more and more.

He made me laugh. He was persistent and reliable. He held my face when he kissed me. I was ready, I thought, to try again.

Toward the end of that stay I had planned a ten-day trip to Italy. I didn't want to leave Paris and the man whom I was by that time calling my boyfriend, but I had already bought my plane ticket.

I went to see the Sistine Chapel in Rome, the ruins in Pompeii, and the birthplace of pizza in Napoli. It was the low season so there were no boats running from where I was staying in Laverno to Positano. I took a train, then a subway, then another train, and yet another train, then a bus, until at last I arrived in the seaside town dizzy with motion sickness.

I stopped at an empty boutique that I was sure in summer would have been swamped. One frilly blouse was all I could afford. As I waved goodbye to the shopkeeper and stepped back into the alley, a fierce rain came slobbering down. I pulled back and gasped.

"What's the matter you don't have an umbrella?" The shopkeeper said.

"I don't..."

He held up his palm in a gesture universally accepted to mean stop, wait, pause and disappeared behind his counter.

I watched the rain slap the cobblestones outside. It was getting dark.

The shopkeeper reappeared and handed me a red umbrella.

"But I'm leaving today. I... I can't bring it back to you."

"That's okay."

I opened the umbrella and pushed up the hill to the bus stop.

I made it back to Laverno, then to Paris and my boyfriend in time for Thanksgiving. I carried that red umbrella with me every day until my 90 day tourist Visa was up and I had to go back to Los Angeles.

When I told my boyfriend the story of how the red umbrella came to be in my posession, he said that in parts of Italy there was a wartime law which remains on the books◻ it says that if a fugitive, or someone in need, comes to your door you must help him.

Odd the unexpected inheritance of war.

A year later, after the Bataclan attack the president of France declared a state of emergency. The markets closed, the theaters too. We were advised not to go where there would be crowds.

The tension in the city moved like a fog. Nothing looked the same. We squinted at each other in the streets.

Then one morning I went to the Muslim bakery in our neighborhood for my croissant. There was a young Gypsy girl, maybe fifteen years old, who for weeks would sit outside the doors. She wore the same beige hooded jacket every day. She had a cup on the sidewalk where people gave her money. Usually, when I passed she would say hello to me. I would smile and say hello back. But I never gave her money. I didn't want to be taken for a fool.

Who could say if she was just lazy and didn't want to work. But then again, what if she was an orphan, or a refugee, or if the horrible rumor was true that the Romany husbands beat their women if they don't bring enough home at the end of the day?

I was thinking all of this as I walked toward the bakery. I took a deep breath and turned to her. "I'm getting a croissant, do you want one?"

She shrugged.

I went inside and bought two croissants and I handed her one as I came out.

It seemed to have taken more courage than it ought to.

I remember thinking: maybe I should buy the gypsy girl an umbrella. Maybe the next time it rains I will get a whole box of umbrellas and stand on the corner handing them out.

The weeks passed faster than I would have liked. When it was time for me to go back to LA, my boyfriend left for work in the morning like he always did. But on that day he knew I wouldn't be there when he came home.

He kissed me at the door and he said, "I love you boo."

"I love you too," I said, and I watched him all the way down the stairs until the top of his bare head disappeared. What if it rained? Or worse? Who would have the courage to give him shelter?

It's hard enough to love anyone in this world, but doing it from eight thousand miles away was stressful. And expensive. So I have decided to move to Paris.

In the meantime there have been more attacks: Nice, Normandy, Champs Elysee. My family is worried.

I tell them it's not different from living in the states: Orlando, San Bernadino, Las Vegas. I worry about them too.

But I am in love. And with a little luck, and patience for the French bureacracy, we will sign our civil partnership papers next month.

What if it doesn't work out I am left stranded in a Foreign country? What if these attacks lead to a full-fledged war? What if our cultural differences prove to be too much?

I'm seven years older than him, what if he wakes up one day and I'm old? What if he falls in love with someone else? What if I fall in love with someone else?

I remind myself what the Dalai Lama says: "Take into account that great love and great achievements involve great risk."

Yes. I am completely terrified. And I am going to do it anyway.

About the Author:

Dufflyn Lammers is veteran a writer and performer. She is a regular contributor at thefix.com the world's leading resource for addiction and recovery. Her essay "Tinder in Paris" won a Silver Medal in the Love Story category for the Twelfth Annual Solas Awards, 2018. Her one woman show DISCOVERED was a 2017 Duende Distinction Award nominee in its debut at the Hollywood Fringe Festival. She has been published poetry in Iowa Woman, the Museletter of the National Association For Poetry Therapy, and in Poetry Slam: The Competitive Art of Performance Poetry edited by Gary Glazner. She has appeared on RUSSELL SIMMONS DEF POETRY JAM (HBO), CRIMINAL MINDS (CBS), ENTOURAGE (HBO), and in countless independent films and commercials. Lammers co-edited the spoken word anthology Chorus with Saul Williams, 2014 (Simon & Schuster). In 2011 Lammers wrote, produced, and starred in the short film "Raven," winning Best Experimental Short at the LA International Underground Film Festival. Lammers was Slammaster of the Los Feliz Slam team 1999-2002, leading her team to three nationals. She was 1993 National Silver Medalist in Poetry Interpretation for Phi Rho Pi. She graduated from Sara Lawrence College in 1995 with a BA in Creative Writing. She lives in Paris France and is also now an International Recovery Coach.

OF KIEV, COWS, AND COUNTRY FOLKS
by John Walters

In 2011 I received a modest windfall, which any sensible person nearing retirement would have added to his modest nest egg. But this money was unlike any money that had ever entered my bank account. It had no interest in compounding; it begged to be spent, not in part but in whole, perhaps because it knew I hadn't earned it, or perhaps because I feared that the benefactor, even in death, would change her mind and gift someone or something worthier than I⬚ and I couldn't imagine anyone or anything that wasn't. This money arrived on fire and had to be disposed of quickly.

It so happened that I was in a squandering mood, kindled in online conversation with an engaging Russian woman, a medical doctor working for an international health organization based in Kiev, Ukraine. What more promising scenario to separate a fool from his money? Anna grew up in a village on the Volga River, coming of age in the 1970s, as did I. We were children of the Cold War.

I loved the pre-Soviet literature of her country, which as an undergraduate I had studied extensively, even if without much understanding. My reverence for Dostoevsky undermined my ability to summon Cold War hostility toward any tribe from which sprang a genius such as he.

My initial indifference toward the demise of the Soviet Union gave way to unbridled giddiness as I discovered that the departure of Russian Troops from Eastern Europe allowed for the arrival of the Russian Five, who were not, as the name suggests, a Vladivostok based-band covering the hits of Michael Jackson. This was a quintet of supremely gifted athletes who fashioned Russia's Red Army hockey team into an Olympic juggernaut. For a princely sum these lads brought their breathtaking brilliance to Detroit, giving life to my beloved Red Wings, known formerly, and deservedly, as the Detroit Dead Things.

I set out to impress Anna with my knowledge of her country's sports icons and literary legends, hoping to demonstrate straightaway that I was not just another ugly American unappreciative of the achievements of other cultures. But were my heroes her heroes? There were reasons to think not. I supposed that a proper Soviet education, which Anna had received, dismissed Dostoevsky as a reactionary and enemy of the people. But would not intelligent Soviet citizens, such as aspiring physicians, see through the ideological claptrap? By 2011, I imagined Dostoevsky having fully ascended in stature, his countrymen, in overwhelming numbers, acknowledging and revering him as a national treasure, along with the resurging Russian Orthodox Church.

In our first Skyped conversation, I launched into effusive praise of The Brothers Karamazov, certain that Anna would receive my commentary as both erudite and winsome. In her quite perfect English, she responded plaintively, "Please tell me you're not Christian."

Having stumbled badly on what I presumed to be the terra firma of Dostoevsky, I less confidently broached the subject of the Russian Five, fearing that all Russians, even those of tepid national feeling, would sooner forgive the toppling of an empire than the poaching of ice hockey superstars. But my allusions to the Russian Five elicited shrugs of indifference, even the kind of eye roll for which my daughter was famous. How the names Slava Fetisov and Igor

Larionov fail to animate a Russian national is beyond my comprehension. Only Sergei Federov drew a response from Anna, who commented not on his skating prowess but on his highly publicized dalliance with Anna Kournikova.

My heroes clearly were not Anna's. In things that truly mattered (classic literature and ice hockey), I was more Russian than she. As it turned out, Anna, perhaps like millions of post-Soviet Russian girls (even accomplished middle-aged women) just wanted to have fun.

In the time it took Boris Yeltsin to polish off a keg of Nevskoe Imperial, Anna took an exhilarating flight to an unknown future in Kiev, a rising commercial star streaking on a trajectory toward political independence, despite persistent efforts of corrupt public officials to knock it off course. Cosmopolitan Kiev offered much that hitherto had been inaccessible to Anna, including a world without boundaries, where the fluent speaker of four languages found ample opportunity to exercise her linguistic talents as did her professional responsibilities, which included recommending treatment regimens in underdeveloped regions. Anna quite justifiably considered herself a Citizen of The World (COW) who wanted to have fun.

This particular COW found fun and purpose in Latin dance, transmitted, perhaps, in the Soviet kinship with Cuba. Kiev provided numerous venues to indulge one's passion for latin dance, Club Salsa beihg Anna's favorite.

I did not share Anna's enthusiasm for Latin dance, or for dance of any origin or description. In my early teens, a traumatic event rendered me dance phobic. Ever since, I have rebuffed every attempt to draw me into the simplest of musically inspired movements, even those consummated at a snail's pace and calling for no greater dexterity than that of a thumb wrestler.

I arrived at this unhappy state in my 14th year, up to which time, however incomprehensible as it now seems, girls considered me inordinately cool. Indeed, it was not unusual for older girls to favor my affections, even over boys a few years their senior, thereby establishing as indisputable my bona fides of inordinate coolness. I was in a really good place.

My perceived coolness, I am convinced, derived from my older sister who enjoyed a fully established reputation for inordinate coolness. I'm not sure why we kids of the 1960s embraced the theory of family branding (if the eldest sibling possessed inordinate coolness, so, too, would the brothers and sisters who followed), especially when evidence abounded of the randomly spawned dork, muddying the gene pool.

In 1966, a new lounge for young teens opened its doors, which demanded my attendance. My mates and I welcomed an indoor gathering place for cute girls, never imagining that a dance floor imposed a protocol for picking up said girls quite unlike the skating pond, where girls, as eagerly as boys, pursued a straight and unmediated path toward a warm embrace. It got cold; we got close.

In the lounge, the girls demanded dancing. They wanted to dance The Jerk, specifically, but needed an exemplar of inordinate coolness to demonstrate. I felt the weight of a collective female gaze.

I really thought I could pull this off, even as beads of sweat formed on my forehead. I was gracefully athletic, an essential and widely acknowledged component of inordinate coolness. I saw my sister dance many times at home, and I watched with pity as the dorks danced on American Bandstand. Then as now, I believed that cool guys did not dance, that dancing originated with dorks to give dorks a chance to gain proximity to girls, that inordinately cool guys sustained their inordinate coolness by refraining from activities fraught with dorkiness, like dancing and studying. But I could not imagine a cool guy shirking when pressed into a vital public service.

As the Kinks belted out You Really Got Me, I, of James Dean caliber coolness, began a roughly three minute journey (a precipitous descent from the happy heights) by the end of which I had so thoroughly diminished in stature as to join ranks with the Leonard Skolnick's of the teen world. My adoring admirers, who only minutes earlier gazed upon me longingly, recoiled in incredulity as the image of each spasmodic movement imprinted upon their formative brains.

Dance had routed me, exposed me as an imposter, and hurled me upon the ash heap of fallen teen idols, where I commiserated with Troy Donahue and Frankie Avalon, where we prepared a place for the toddlers destined to replace us, like David Cassidy and Leif Garrett. I had become so despondent that I even considered studying.

As Anna and I proceeded in our rolling disclosure of significant deal breakers--my inability/ unwillingness to dance; her inability/unwillingness to discern the greatness of Dostoevsky; my Judeo Christian proclivities; her unwillingness to acknowledge ice hockey as the apogee of sport, if not the whole of human activity-- it became clear that Anna and I were not a couple destined for a lasting relationship.

Except for an aversion to marriage, Anna and I had little in common, to be sure. Despite our differences, I had never known a COW and longed to meet one; as for Anna, she got to collect another American man, even if this one she fully intended to discard. I also felt a nudge from my maternal ancestors, who came from the Ukraine. What better way to honor the Motherland than to stimulate her economy.

Anna agreed to serve as tour guide and advisor on all matters regarding East Europe.

This was my first trip abroad. I recall sharing in the rollicking good times of U.S. domestic air travel in the 70s and 80s, decades before domestic airlines institutionalized the perverse practices that have kept otherwise adventuresome feet grounded. I assumed that the practice of subjecting passengers to the most abject of conditions had extended to foreign carriers.

Upon boarding a Lufthansa airbus bound for Munich◻ the first leg of my journey to Kiev--I discovered to my astonishment that one doesn't have to fly like a refugee. To board a Lufthansa airbus is to enter a land of enchantment, or so it seems to anyone conditioned to the horrors of U.S. domestic carriers.

Everything about the airbus emitted an air of unreality: the seating was comfortable and spacious, even in coach; the food was abundant and delicious and served continuously throughout the long flight. If this weren't

enough to dumbfound the provincial U.S. passenger, the stewardesses were of such extraordinary quality and substance that I thought of them not as stewards but as highly skilled professionals in the German Foreign Service, whose purpose was to treat you as an esteemed guest in the Democratic Republic of Lufthansa, not in a servile or unctuous way but in a way that acknowledged and honored your humanity, that evinced no desire to be your jailor, that responded to inquiries graciously in the passenger's native tongue, without a hint of contempt.

These are remarkable young women of uncommon intelligence whose lovely faces are devoid of vapidity, who move effortlessly from one language to another. Their elocution in English, which is impeccable, wholly belies their Teutonic origin. I imagine the Lufthansa stewardess as masterful and at ease in translating an emergency session of the United Nations as in auctioneering at the Nebraska State Fair.

It occurred to me, minutes after boarding a German airliner in Chicago, that I satisfied the requirements of my European trip. I sought a COW and found myself amongst a coterie of such, in what felt like a leisurely glide down a placid river, scarcely aware that I was aloft, barreling toward a distant continent. In bringing to bear civility, high culture, and uncommon aeronautical expertise, Lufthansa was reversing the course of passenger airline history◻ which I found joyously disorienting.

These were ten hours of undiminished contentment. Upon landing in Munich I had no desire to deplane, even as the opportunity to smoke presented itself. Who was this person inhabiting my nicotine deprived body?

I arrived in Kiev later that afternoon, eager, finally, to succumb to the demands of Lord Nicotine. In baggage claim, I eyed the door opening to the out-of-doors with great anticipation. As I stood outside inhaling deeply, enjoying the bright October Kievan sky, an officious looking man approached. Making no pretense to excuse my ignorance, this formidable looking functionary, speaking a language I did not comprehend yet fully understood, directed me forthwith to Customs, where I was roughed up mentally--and just enough physically--to make me feel as if I were home, in a U.S. airport.

It took at least 90 minutes to travel the 15 miles separating the hotel from the airport. My driver, a gregarious young man commandeering a Hugo, did his best to advance us beyond each imposing obstacle, construction being the chief impediment. Clearly, Kiev was rising.

The trip to the hotel was a jarring experience. We careened headlong into the wild west of Kievan vehicular traffic, streaking by one unobserved traffic light after another. I was grateful for each construction zone that brought us to a screeching halt, giving my internal organs a chance to sort themselves into their proper anatomical position.

Kiev is a city of great beauty adorned by towering chestnut trees that drop their nuggets on unsuspecting visitors, who wish they had packed a hard hat. These trees grace boulevards of such magnificent width as to accommodate at least 20 persons walking arm in arm.

The streets were remarkably free of litter. Walking several blocks through population dense sections of downtown Kiev, I noted an additional departure from the American landscape: I saw no army of destitute and homeless persons. It didn't seem possible for a city transitioning to a market economy not to generate as many losers as winners--even if only temporarily--and that the number of displaced and dispossessed would be considerable. (Anna assured me that the homeless of Kiev are legion, but painstakingly kept out of view, relegated to areas where visitors are not likely to find them).

The leather jacket--invariably black--is the indispensable item of clothing for Kievans, regardless of age, body shape, or climatic conditions. I can report that not all leather is created equal. In east Europe, I expected the swarthy of appearance to predominate, or at least to constitute a sizeable demographic. Kiev is not the place to find them. There I saw mostly pale, fair skin, lots of elevated cheekbones, and heads crowned with blondish hair.

To their credit, the Soviets preserved many of Kiev's historic buildings, the most impressive of which are the Orthodox Churches, which draw throngs of pilgrims, particularly to St. Vladimir's Cathedral. To my surprise, the religious impulse is strong and widely exercised, despite the seven-decade long atheist hiatus⬚ or perhaps because of it.

Americans are accustomed to walking life's tight rope without a net, mindful that the descent into poverty is as swift and certain as one catastrophic illness. Prior to independence, Kievans walked confidently, without fear of stumbling, knowing that a generously cast safety net undergirded their steps⬚ even while taking each step under the watchful eye of an unyielding bureaucracy that, for many, sucked the joy out of living.

Membership in the Soviet empire had its privileges, which it considered rights: pensions for the aged, education for the young, subsidized housing, universal health care⬚ all of which faded away in the post-Soviet period⬚ and which, by 2011, had become a source of growing nostalgia, as Kievans struggled to find balance on a decidedly American tightrope.

For many inhabitants of the former Soviet Union, including Anna's elderly mother, Erika, dependence had become the ironic consequence of independence. No longer able to live independently in Moscow, Erika had recently moved into Anna's flat, where along with room and board, she received free doctoring from her daughter, an arrangement that often impinged on the free wheeling movements of our Dancing Queen. As the infrastructure of their social welfare system collapsed, many Kievans found freedom and independence priced beyond their reach.

Financial uncertainty in no way diminished the ferocity with which Kievans exercised the freedoms of speech and assembly. I arrived in Kiev shortly after President Yankovich (he of suspected ties to the Kremlin and for whom the eminently indictable Paul Manafort served as impresario) arrested Prime Minister Yulia Tymoshenko (she of perceived westward leanings). Her arrest elicited massive crowds of sympathetic protestors gathered in Independence Square.

A large contingent of heavily armed military police separated the protestors from a much smaller gathering of counter-protestors who supported Ukraine's Putin-backed President. A medium sized high school gymnasium could easily have housed the counter protestors, whose lack of enthusiasm amused me. Anna recognized several dignitaries of the East Orthodox Church from among the stiffs lined up on the side of the President. They gave the appearance of wanting to be elsewhere. (Whom did Anna favor: the Prime Minister or the President? "Neither of them is an angel").

The military police▫ all gym enthusiasts by appearance--made no attempt to feign impartiality. They exercised their muscle (I thought excessively) for no purpose other than to subdue the prime minister's supporters.

Anna and I kept a safe distance, observing events from the perimeter of the larger crowd. I, a foreigner who stupidly left his passport at the hotel, was particularly vulnerable to arrest, or so Anna thought. Further, my voice, according to Anna, drew unwanted attention, even in the din of this raucous political demonstration. She accused me of speaking like a "country person;" a euphemism for ear-splitting uneducated lout. "Please try to speak like a city person," she pleaded, in hushed urban appropriate tones. She warned me also of my impending death, diagnosing my hands as too chronically cold to sustain life.

I assumed that the hostility expressed toward the Putin friendly President was as much directed, if not more so, toward Russia, a traditional villain that I doubted Kievans had even begun to absolve from historic injustices, let alone transgressions of recent vintage. But I was quite wrong.

Centuries of intermarriage have saturated this relationship in a deep well of ambivalence. I encountered no Kievan without at least one familial tie to Russia. In shops, restaurants, hotels▫ wherever Anna engaged Kievans in conversation and revealed her Russian heritage▫ the locals received her enthusiastically, telling of Aunts, Uncles, Grandparents, who settled in or near Anna's hometown of Saratov. From these encounters, I witnessed a rich

reserve of affection for Russia, even as Kievans prized their independence.

Poor Anna, I thought, as my forefinger extricated a chunk of rhubarb from an incisor. The embodiment of sophistication and urbanity wasted an entire day tutoring a village idiot in the art of city dwelling, answering his incessant questions, delivered invariably in the pitch of a carnival barker. She must surely have been eager to abandon this dance deficient bumpkin in favor of busting a groove at Club Salsa, if for no other reason than to shake off the day's embarrassments. She would have been wholly justified in doing so.

Even though she could have been less imperious in regulating the volume of my speech, Anna otherwise had been a good sport, responding thoughtfully to my inquiries, as I dragged her to places of little appeal to her but of great interest to me. She had earned her deliverance. As I was about to hail a cab and release her into the night, an exasperated Anna asked, "If you don't like to dance, what do you like to do?" "I like to drink," said I. "Thank God," said Anna reverentially, which had the effect of extending our association for several additional hours.

PS. Anna and I spent an evening of prodigious drinking, which▫ as it so often does in even the most urbane of city folk--revealed in Anna the existence of a country person, a slightly debauched Tammy Wynette, I thought.

About the Author:

John Spencer Walters lives in the Rocky Mountains. His non-academic work has appeared in such publications as Defenestration and Foliate Oak Literary Magazine.

THROUGH THE FOG OF TIME

by Jeffrey James Higgins

All your dreams are on their way

See how they shine

Oh, if you need a friend

I'm sailing right behind

Like a bridge over troubled water

I will ease your mind

Simon and Garfunkel, "Bridge over Troubled Water" (1969)

I drove along the George Washington Memorial Parkway under a slate gray, northern Virginia sky, with thick fog hanging over the Potomac River beside me, vapor tendrils twisting and curling off the black water. Beyond the river, the Washington Monument peeked through the turbid stew. I'd lived in Washington, DC for over a decade, fighting terrorism as a special agent, and often passed that monument on my way to war in a distant land. Now, I drove by that landscape of my adult life in search of my past.

Fifty years ago, my parents, James and Nadya, moved the three of us to Vestal, a quiet town on the outskirts of Binghamton, New York. I lived there from the ages of two to ten and despite going to high school and college in Massachusetts, I always considered Vestal my childhood home. My earliest memories were there, surrounded by loving grandparents, aunts, uncles, and cousins, exploring the world as a young boy, my dog by my side.

The idea of visiting Vestal had percolated for some time, but as I lay on my couch reading a book, Jim Croce's 1972 hit, Time in a Bottle, came on the radio and evoked a flood of memories, the way only music can do. The impulse to revisit Vestal was overwhelming, so the next morning I packed a bag, kissed my wife, Cynthia, goodbye and left to find my childhood. Cynthia was supportive, but I saw the questioning look in her eyes. I had the same question.

Why was I taking this trip?

Many people revisit their childhood homes to confront demons in an attempt to heal old wounds and find peace. Many memoirs become literary roadmaps to childhood trauma, but my experience was quite the opposite. I had parents who loved me, food on the table, a safe home, a wonderful dog, and family and friends nearby. I idealized my life in Vestal, romanticized it, cherished it. Thoughts of home conjured deep feelings of love, safety, and happiness, but were my memories selective? Were they fanciful reconstructions of reality or were they genuine?

Merriam-Webster defines nostalgia as "the state of being homesick" and "a wistful or excessively sentimental yearning for return to or of some past period or irrecoverable condition." I was certainly experiencing that, but why? Was I thinking about the 1960s and 1970s because I was having a midlife crisis at age 52? Was I contemplating my finite existence and hoping to view the beginning of my life through wiser eyes? I had recently retired as a supervisory special agent and had returned to my childhood ambition of becoming a writer, so was that career change the reason for this field trip to 1967?

The fog worsened as I followed the river, passing the cold, stone arches of the Key Bridge and the woods of Arlington County. A blanket of rust-colored leaves lay on the thawing ground, moist and decomposing, below thin branches on barren elms waving in the wind and the limbs of sturdy oaks twisting upwards like ballerinas' arms. I drove north on the interstate highway into Maryland, the silver sheen of rain turned the black pavement into a sugar-covered gumdrop, below clouds, hanging like apostrophes, barely moving as they unleashed a heavenly mist. The brume thickened, creating a hazy canopy over the highway, enveloping everything beyond the road before me. It obscured the earth and reality, allowing my mind to drift back through the fog of time.

In Pennsylvania, the sky was as gray and bleak as it was on this day in 1975, the year my family left Vestal, over my futile protests and broken heart. I could see nothing but the road in front of me, my car a time machine transporting me through the misty vortex to 50-years in the past, where my memories were as murky as the fog. Einstein said, "…Physicists believe the separation between past, present, and future is only an illusion, although a convincing one."

Memories

The innocence of my childhood comes back through fleeting images and a contented feeling, like being wrapped in a warm blanket. It was a time surrounded by loving family, a time before I knew of the cold ugliness lurking inside people. Today's youth, with their bicycle helmets, computer games, and peanut allergies wouldn't recognize 1967. It was an era of personal freedom, especially for a young boy.

I remember climbing trees, riding my bike, and walking with my best friend, Treasure, a golden retriever with a golden heart. I can smell the earthy woods and feel the cool, sweet air of the Bunn Hill Creek behind our house as I jumped from stone to stone hunting for crawfish and salamanders, my explorations as much in my imagination as in reality. I remember the smell of fresh oil on my baseball mitt, getting sap on my hands as I climbed the pine tree behind our house, the bristly hair of my GI Joe, and my bike with the blue banana seat, chopper handlebars, and baseball cards affixed to the spokes.

Holidays were magical, visceral, exciting, and full of bright colors, flavors, and rituals. I recall trick-or-treating in vampire fangs and a black cape, a plastic jack-o-lantern filled with candy corn and chocolate, ghosts fashioned from white sheets, and monsters and goblins trolling through the neighborhood. Christmas was red and blue lights, hanging ornaments, the smell of the evergreen, and presents stacked high under the tree.

I remember watching the Watergate hearings and Vietnam War on television, playing with Treasure on the floor, and reading, always reading. I was transported by Charlotte's Web, Lassie Come Home, The Hardy Boys series, and my favorite, Treasure Island. I remember playing with my cap gun and wearing cowboy boots, chaps, a white cowboy hat, and a mustard yellow shirt with shiny buttons.

Vestal

The fog lifted as I descended out of the hills, crossed the New York State line, and entered Binghamton, a city only three-hours from Manhattan, but a world apart. Binghamton had been a thriving industrial city for more than a century, but businesses fled, leaving a fossil of past affluence, a place where hope turned to despair. I drove over the Susquehanna River into Vestal, the hills around me familiar beacons of home. Businesses and people may have come and gone over the past 50-years, but those were the same hills and trees I stared at as a child daydreaming of adventure. I thought of all of my extended family members, who had lived here, and smiled out of happiness and out of longing.

Simon and Garfunkel played on the radio and I felt as if my time machine had returned to 1967, my past now before me in living color.

I drove into my old neighborhood and turned right down my street, Lauderdale Drive, passing the same evergreen trees I'd ridden my bicycle by as a child, the scene of my youth. Along the lush and winding street, beyond yards covered with fluffy white snow, yellow lights glowed warm behind living room windows. The ranch style homes, built with red-brick and white trim, were well maintained and it still looked like a place where I could ride my bike, take after-dinner walks with my parents, and explore the creek with Treasure by my side.

To my right were Martha Road and the house where Mandy lived, the thin brunette with the fair complexion and red lips, the object of my innocent affections, the girl who made my chest flutter. I remembered racing my bike down the block and doing wheelies in front of her house, a ten-year-old boy's mating ritual for a girl who probably never knew I was there. It was an urge I was too young to understand.

I passed Avondale Court and remembered riding my bicycle down the street with my friend, Josh, and hiking through the woods to a candy story where we bought Big Buddies, Sweet Tarts, candy cigarettes, Bazooka Bubble Gum, and Archie comic books. To my left was the oak tree where I played tag with all the neighborhood children as the night grew dark and my mother rang a brass bell signaling me to come home. I could see the crew cuts of the Polanski brothers who bullied all of the neighborhood children and the day when I finally had enough and dove into the older brother's legs, knocking him to the ground and the air from his lungs, then walking home a victor, my enemy vanquished.

The road curved to the left up a hill where my father taught me to ride my bike, holding the banana seat and running along beside me as I talked and talked until I realized he had stopped holding the bike and was standing near the bottom of the hill. A wave of insecurity had passed through me and into the bike, which began to wobble and I crashed, leaving me simultaneously angry and proud.

At the base of the hill was my childhood home.

Home

My house was a small ranch-style home with three bedrooms, one bath, and an attached garage. To the left of the front door were large living room windows and to the right, the bedrooms lay behind a red-brick wall with small windows. A light glowed from inside and my first thought was that someone was in the bedroom, my bedroom. The gray-shingled roof was covered with a white blanket of snow. The house looked almost exactly the same.

I walked up to the house and climbed the stoop, where I'd played with Treasure when we brought her home from the kennel. She was a puppy, I was five-years-old, and we were best friends. I pulled back the screen door of the house and realized it was the same screen we had in 1967, the moment catching me off-guard.

With a lump in my throat I knocked on the door.

I introduced myself to the owner, Frank, telling him I'd grown up here, and he kindly invited me inside. Frank bought the house from my parents in 1975, when he was a young man with a baby, and now he was retired with grown children. To my surprise and delight, the interior was relatively unchanged since the day we left. The bookshelves were shorter than I'd remembered when I would climb up them in my footed pajamas, hang a bright orange Hot Wheels track off the top shelf, and launch toy cars across the room. My muddled memories were suddenly alive in front of me.

I looked out the large living room windows at the snow and thought of winters as a child, when my mother stuffed me into a blue, hooded snowsuit with racing stripes and tucked my feet into rubber boots. I'd make snow angels, roll snowmen, and dig forts, the snow falling over the top of my boots melting under my feet.

I stepped into the kitchen and froze. The cabinets and counters were the same I had used when I was two-years old. I was in one of my dreams, but wide-awake, seeing the dark grain of the wood, the design of the bronze cabinet handles, all of the detail that had faded in my mind. This was where my mother froze homemade popsicles from grape Kool-Aid and orange juice and I blew birthday candles out on my cake.

I felt like a giant inside a child's memory.

Out back, the patio was white and barren. Cardinals and blue jays had once nested in trees along the creek, but Frank had cut the trees down. I remembered trying to identify the birds darting passed our windows, watching them disappear in flashes of red, brown, and blue. In the summer, I'd play in a sandbox with a hot metal bottom or lay on my back in a shallow, inflatable pool. I remember running through the green grass chasing Monarch butterflies and catching lightning bugs in a Maxwell House coffee can with holes punched in the top.

Of course not all of my memories were good, like the time my parents invited a couple from the neighborhood over for drinks and the husband arrived drunk and chased me through the house. Terrified, I ran out front door into the yard and when I looked back and he was right behind me. I ran to the big pine tree behind our house, swung myself up the first branch, and climbed out of his reach just as he lunged for my foot. I was panting from fear and exertion and when I looked down, to my horror, he was climbing after me. I clambered up the thinning branches as quickly as I could, my heart beating out of my chest, going higher than I'd ever gone before, not knowing if the branches could hold my weight. The tree began to sway.

The man slipped in his loafers and his wife yelled for him to come down, so he stopped and lowered himself to the ground. He had been intoxicated and was probably just showing off, but I didn't like the cold, black look in his eyes or his darkening expression as I evaded him. I sat in the tree for a long time, watching the man talk with my parents and caught him glance back at the tree with dead eyes. He was waiting for me to come down. I felt angry and betrayed because my parents hadn't stopped him, but I was proud I'd saved myself and I knew I was safe if I stayed in the tree. I was always safe in my tree.

Frank and I looked out the rear windows of the house at that pine tree. It had grown much taller, as had I. The trunk was impossibly thick and a wave of disappointment washed over me when I saw the lower branches had been cut off, making it impossible to climb. That tree had saved my life.

When I lived here we watched three VHF and two UHF channels on a small black and white television, with a rabbit-ear antenna, and all programming ended sometime after midnight leaving only static. I was captivated by old movies of swashbuckling pirates and daring pilots

flying into war, stories that probably instilled a sense of adventure and propelled me to war as an adult. On Friday nights we would watch the Brady Bunch followed by the Partridge Family and if I was really lucky, I could stay up and watch Love American Style. I remember my parents waking me up to watch the moon landing in 1969. I was an only child until I was seven, so that television played an outsized role in my life and when we bought our first color television in 1975, I felt like I was losing an old friend.

I remember slipping out of my bedroom and crawling under my mother's desk as she sat there typing, listening to the clack of the metal type bars striking the paper and the ding of the bell when she hit return. I felt safe. When I was a little older, I would sneak out of bed to write stories, the words coming faster than I could scribble them down. I knew then that I would become a writer.

Frank walked me out to the front yard and I could see Treasure running after a ball, her tail wagging and joy on her face. I can still feel her soft hair, the pads on her feet, her cool nose. There is no stronger bond than between a boy and a dog and though it has been 37-years since she passed away, I still think of her every day. I remember running through the yard with her and diving into a pile of red and yellow leaves, the smell strong and earthy, the leaves dry and papery, laughing as my father raked the pile over me.

I told Frank he lived in a perfect place and he smiled widely, seemingly pleased that someone else recognized what he had here.

School

Images from kindergarten flickered in my memory, my Woody Woodpecker lunch pail with the smell of baloney and cheese, a ring ding wrapped in foil, and a thermos that smelled like sour milk. I remember sitting in the grass in a large circle of classmates playing duck, duck, goose and not wanting it to end, taking naps on matts, and the day my classmate Francis wouldn't come down from the monkey bars.

I attended Willow Point Elementary School through the fourth-grade. When I was in the first-grade, I missed my bus and my mother told me she didn't have time to drive me to school. She didn't mean it, but I walked out of our house, driven by stubbornness and a sense of adventure. I remember looking over my shoulder as I turned the corner at the end of our street and realized she wasn't coming out to stop me. I made the 1.3-mile walk, across the Vestal Parkway and up a long hill, excited at my independence. To this day, my mother feels awful about my walking alone; showing what a good mother she was then and still is today.

I drove up the hill where I thought the school was, but found a building with a "WSKG Radio Station" sign and satellite dishes looming behind it. I pulled into the parking lot triggering a vivid memory of yellow school buses parked in a line, the air heavy with the sweet smell of diesel fuel, and searching for the number of the bus that would take me home. I remembered the ripped green vinyl seats with exposed metal bars and yellow foam sticking out, and the older girl, with long brown hair and a fluffy sweater, the one who always smelled like perfume.

This was my old school.

I walked behind the building and saw the short hill I would run or roll down every day with dozens of children, fleeing the confines of the classroom for recess. In the distance, three rusting baseball backstops stood like ruins from my past. This was no longer a school, but there were dozens of little footprints in the snow, like the ghostly tracks of children who once played here, frozen echoes of the past. In the wood line I saw three jungle gyms with flaking red and yellow paint, the same equipment I'd climbed on in elementary school and forgotten about until that moment. Suddenly I was back in first-grade, hanging from the monkey bars, pulling myself hand over hand up the hot metal hot pipes. I looked back at the school expecting to hear the teacher blow the whistle for us to return to class.

Nana and Baba

My mother's parents, Nejm and Najla Aswad, were first-generation Lebanese immigrants who arrived at Ellis Island as children, met years later in Niagara Falls, then settled in Binghamton and had three sons and a daughter. My ten cousins and I all affectionately referred to them as Baba and Nana and they were the epicenter of the Aswad family.

On Sundays my parents would take me across the bridge over the Susquehanna River into Binghamton for dinner at Baba and Nana's house. For the Lebanese, family and food are the center of life and Sundays at Baba and Nana's meant eating grape leaves, stuffed squash, fresh Syrian bread, and salads with dandelions and tomatoes from Baba's garden. I would start to salivate on the way there.

Sometimes we stayed overnight and my cousins and I would scamper up the steep stairs to the third-floor bedroom, the sound of the wood creaking under our weight. We would push the beds together then jump onto the old mattresses, as loose as waterbeds, bouncing around and giggling. The beds would slowly slide apart and whoever was in the middle would slip between the mattresses, pulling the sheets and covers with them onto the floor, eliciting uncontrollable laughter from all of us. I remember Nana yelling for us to quiet down from her bedroom across the hall, a room filled with odors from creams and perfumes, but I would laugh until my abominable muscles ached.

Baba passed away in 1987 and Nana in 2000. The last time I saw Nana she was laying in a bed in her living room. She told me she was dying and I wanted to say everything would be okay, but I couldn't lie to her so I just said I was sorry. She looked at me with love, communicating without speaking.

I drove up Front Street and the excitement I'd felt as a child returned and I could almost smell grape leaves cooking in tomato sauce. I turned onto Cypress Street, and there was Baba and Nana's house, a three story, 1,305-square foot house was built in 1890 and except for new siding, it looked the same as it did 50-years ago. I had the momentary urge to go inside to see Baba and Nana, and then remembered they were gone.

Between the house and the detached garage I looked into the backyard at Baba's garden and I saw the grape arbor my parents had built for him was still there, the wood dark and aging. I couldn't believe it still stood, 43-years later. My memories had faded with time and I had assumed everything I remembered had faded or gone as well. My childhood was gone, my grandparents had passed away, and I thought this place only existed in my memory, yet the homes were still there, the terrain was still the same; the artifacts of my life still existed. While the memory of childhood had slowly dissipated, the structure of my previous life remained in the physical world.

I had left, but the grape arbor stood, waiting for my return.

I knocked on the door, half expecting it to open and to see Baba sitting in his favorite chair wearing a grey fedora and a cardigan sweater, with newspapers stuffed inside to keep him warm. It's strange that the house is here but they are not. Baba and Nana were buried in the cemetery at the end of the street, but I don't associate them with their graves. I feel them here, with me.

An elderly woman with short white hair and a dirty tee shirt opened the door. She wore a grimace, set into deep wrinkles likely formed by years of scowling. I told her my mother had grown up in the house and I had spent a lot of my childhood here. I asked if I could walk into the backyard to take a couple of pictures of the garden my grandfather had planted. She asked why I was bothering her then told me to come back later when her daughter was home.

My grandparents were the warm and caring people who exemplified the Lebanese tradition of welcoming guests and now a bitter, old woman stood as the gatekeeper to their home. I told the woman I would come back in the afternoon, knowing I wouldn't return. It was the same house, but not the same place I had loved, because homes reflected the people who inhabited them and Baba and Nana no longer lived there. Some things do change.

Grandma

I drove to Cleveland Avenue, where my father was raised with his parents, James and Madeline, and his four siblings. I recognized the house immediately, though I hadn't seen it in decades. It was three stories, with concrete stairs and a rusted pipe handrail leading up a short, steep hill to the front porch. My grandfather passed away before I was born, but I knew Madeline, though only as "Grandma." She was Irish and German, with fair skin so thin I could see blue veins beneath and so slender and frail and I could feel her bones when I hugged her. She wore horn-rimmed glasses with a chain dangling around her neck and support stockings that slid down her ankles into worn slippers.

Grandma kept a clean, and orderly house and I remember the cuckoo clock ticking in the hallway, the smell of the old wood steps leading to the second floor, the same stairs my father climbed up and down as a child. From her kitchen with old appliances and a linoleum floor, she would serve us potato pancakes, roasts, boiled potatoes, with gravy on everything. This wasn't the comfort food of the Lebanese and where Baba and Nana were effusive with their expressions of love, Grandma was more reserved, probably a result of her difficult life and the remnants of Irish and German culture.

I remember the heavy, black telephone on the hallway table and waiting for the neighbor to get off the party line before straining my finger to dial a number. Most of all, I remember Grandma humming and sitting in her green chair with the extendable foot rest, a stack of National Geographic magazines in a basket beside her and Reader's Digests piled high on the coffee table. I can see her knitting a blanket with long sharp needles, her arthritic fingers and deformed joints rapidly moving as the needle tips clicked over and over.

Every year Grandma renewed my subscription to National Geographic magazine and I covered my walls with the maps inside, which probably inspired me visit more than 50 countries since then. Grandma passed away in 1991, but if I close my eyes, I can still see her humming, rocking, and knitting, with a twinkle in her blue eyes.

Reflections

I felt deep loss when we moved from Vestal, but the values I learned there followed me throughout my life and Cynthia, the prize I'd earned by searching for those virtues, was now waiting for me at home. Moving from Vestal had taught me to accept new challenges, which I did when I moved to Florida to become a police officer and to New York City to become a federal agent, and later to Afghanistan and Washington, DC. Maybe leaving Vestal was what gave me the courage to test myself against the world.

I grew up knowing I would be a writer, but when I was between jobs as a newspaper reporter, I took a position working for a private investigator, thinking the experience would help with a novel and soon became enamored with law enforcement. Now, after an exciting career chasing the world's most dangerous criminals, I was ready to write again. I felt guilt at not following my calling sooner, but I was proud of the work I had done and I didn't regret my career choice, because it was the adventure I had fantasized about as a child. I wondered what that little boy would think about the path I had chosen. Would he feel betrayed or happy? I know he would be glad I

was writing now. Maybe this trip was a way for me to reconnect with my young self, to validate a 25-year divergence. Maybe I wanted that five-year old me to know that I was back on course, that I hadn't forgotten.

When I was a child I did things because I enjoyed them, not because I was supposed to do them. Maybe who I was as a child was my real self, the true evolutionary pneuma, before society and experience influenced my genetic predispositions. Maybe I wasn't just grasping at fading memories. Maybe I was grasping for the real me.

I drove south on Interstate 81 towards Virginia and I felt more complete, more peaceful than when I arrived. It was so comforting to learn those wonderful places from my childhood still existed and knowing my past was still there somehow made going forward easier. I came looking for my childhood and found it to be everything I remembered. Those memories and feelings had carried me through the hardest times of my life, like a bridge over troubled water. All the way home, the skies were clear of fog, as clear as my memory had become.

Cynthia met me at the door, her eyes wide and teary from longing. She kissed me and pulled me into a warm hug, pressing her soft cheek against mine, her embrace filling me with unconditional love. We were talking about having a baby and I knew we could share this love with a child and give it the childhood I had been fortunate to have. Everything I'd learned in Vestal about family and love, I'd sought and found as an adult.

I sat in my home office and began to write. Listening to my recorded notes, I realized my Vestal accent had returned after being dormant for almost half a century. The toy police badge I'd worn when I was five years old sat on the bookshelf behind me, not far from my gold retirement badge. My toy swords were replaced by antique Afghan sabers, souvenirs from a war zone. Gone was the cap pistol of my youth, in its place a Glock handgun.

In front of me was the writing I'd promised to do.

I left on my trip assuming everything had changed, hoping to find shadows of my former life, but instead, I discovered the setting of my childhood largely preserved. I had grown and my family had moved or passed away, but my old house and Vestal were the same. There is fragility in humanity, but the physical world can endure. I'd lived in so many places, done so many things, and grown so much, yet home was the same.

In many ways, I was too.

About the Author:

Jeffrey James Higgins is a former reporter and supervisory special agent. He recently completed a nonfiction book about the first narco-terrorism arrest and conviction. Jeffrey is represented by Inkwell Management and is now writing his first thriller. Jeffrey has appeared on CNN Newsroom, Discovery ID, CNN Declassified, and numerous other television programs, radio shows, and podcasts. His recent articles and media appearances can be found at JeffreyJamesHiggins.com.

DOES BURKE MATTER

by Judson Blake

When I was small, in what seems like pre-history now, I had passionate arguments with college students about the National Debt, which I believed was a problem that would grow out of control. I was vehement and convinced. I was told that my views were "conservative" and I pretended to know what that meant. One student suggested that I read the work of Edmund Burke who had laid out the conservative mode of thinking two centuries earlier and so was way ahead of me.

Well, Burke's prose was beyond me (I was ten), but I could see the gist in his respect for tradition and natural human instincts. His famous work "Reflections on the Revolution in France" won my attention years later. There I learned some history, how Burke's analysis prompted opposing thinkers, notably Thomas Paine, and how Paine replied with a powerful rebuttal in "The Rights of Man". With such salvos between these two great minds, an historical crystallization came about; the difference between Left and Right became more defined, at least in England. What had before been isolated disputes now became colored and enriched by this clash of powerful ideas. Are these ideas relevant today?

 Today America has shifted strongly and haltingly toward the right, and one naturally wonders what "conservative" means for us. Going over Burke's resounding prose, I wonder today if any of it matters in America's version of conservatism. Would Burke have recognized what we have today under this name? Would debates of the kind he engaged in the Eighteenth century even be possible today? Would anyone listen? Burke's persuasive arguments were opposed by articulate thinkers

who disagreed entirely, but nonetheless listened and took seriously what he said. Could such discussion hold an audience in America today? Obviously not. No one would attend. Clear distinctions such as separated Burke and Paine have effervesced for us; they no longer can contain our passions, our dilemmas or the complexity of our experience. These men offered context in the Eighteenth Century, but their ideas seem to have been overborne, exploded by passions, ignorance and weaponry more extreme than any in their time. So I am driven to ask: what trace of Burke might still persist in America's version of conservatism? This is important because in times of radical change like ours, understanding antecedents can give balance and perspective we need.

 It seems obvious that our national dialogue lacks concepts, since the opponents, Left and Right, have grown up spontaneously, as if in total ignorance of what went on in England at a time when America was just forming as a nation. One can sketch some of Burke's thinking and those of his opponents in a rather simple phrase: the conservative is reluctant to jar what has worked before, especially if the jarring is proposed by novel ideas; the liberal is suspect of the rigors imposed by the past and so is more welcoming of ideas that spring from new conditions. Placed in this context, one might expect some sympathy from each side, not an impassable chasm of scorn. Such concepts, were they seen as a context for discussion, would help us understand the transitions we are going through and which are forced upon us. Is there even a shadow of these ideas in our modern ad hominem cannonades (mutated into tweets)? Do political figures we see today, without the patience to read either Burke or Paine, reflect any ideas at all?

I believe they do. I suspect American vehemence and American impatience with rational argument flow from deeply felt human character and human differences that we do not yet understand. Vehemence, bigotry and ad hominem attack look at first like only grandstanding and bombast, but there may be natural forces that this bombast obscures. We are in danger of dismissing as stupid what is only inarticulate outrage exploding on the right. Yet very often we see that the outrage comes from a place that even the speaker does not understand. So how are the rest of us to see through the bombast to some meaning? I suggest that there is a way to understand these things in a setting very different from the context of Burke, but one of historical force that parallels his.

Let us take for instance a remark made by a conservative politician not so long ago. Rick Perry, then governor of Texas, opined that he had a solution to the complex problems of the Middle-East: "Bomb them into the stone age." Since many people have said this or something similar, Rick Perry is not alone. If the literal intent of what he said seems questionable, then the outrage and violence of such a statement are likely to be dismissed or taken for granted rather than looked at carefully. So much violence is repellent to thoughtful people and leads them to simply turn away. If I go into any bar or public place I'll find people who second Perry's view. They even applaud Perry for being so direct, for saying plainly what they think but have no podium like his.

What does such an expression mean? Is there anything in Perry's remark besides simplistic thinking and faith in brutal means? His remark radiates from visceral impulse unmodulated by learning, compassion or reflection. As such we are faced with the raw reactions of a primitive but emotionally honest mind. This is unusual and quite forceful. Emotional honesty, with no regard for honesty of any other kind, has force because it is unusual in American politics but it speaks to feelings untampered by thought. This emotional honesty is a great strength of American conservativism today. It does not even need the cunning of lies. Political speeches filled with vague generalities meant to offend no one have worn so thin that a speaker who dispenses with such niceties is fresh air. And emotional honesty has the advantage that the speaker and the hearers need not be troubled by honesty about fact. The successful modern politician need not extend himself to careful articulation of ideas; such would only bore his listeners. But if he can speak from his gut they will listen. If he has clarity of his visceral feeling that will hold them. His emotional honesty brings raw expression to instincts that have been repudiated and disrespected in our enlightened liberalism. And there is where the shadows of Burke and Paine might be extended to inform the apparent irrelevance and chaos of American dialogue.

Burke praised human instinct as a surer guide to the future than theoretical speculation. Conservatism today trusts primitive instinct more than mental exertion and it wishes passionately to dispense with complexity and the need for intellect. Thus one sees in modern American dialogue an unformulated new dichotomy: that between instinct and culture. Trust in "the old ways" has become freedom from strictures of science, diplomacy and careful thought. Today's conservatives are reacting to liberalism they feel is forced upon them and has gone too far. We see in conservative initiatives not just hatred of ideas over experience, but even a hatred of practical science and human compassion. If scientific ideas are unwelcome, then blank denial can be imposed by simple repression, a kind of bureaucratic dropping of Perry's bombs. My quotation from Perry expresses gut impatience with careful negotiation and the arduous task of understanding the minds of other people.

We can find other threads from Perry's violent but simple remark. One thing is its imperious machismo. I call this monotonic machismo because it blankly insists on not listening to anything that would alter its willfulness. The macho dismisses subtle questions and leaves it to someone else to pick up the pieces. The ideal is that there will be no pieces. Then the macho will leave a clean slate and the future will be a beautiful fresh start, with no connection to the complexity before us now.

In with this machismo we also see that it is in love with its own maleness. It refuses to be compromised by what could be feminine tact or circumspection. So it is no accident that we see on the right today so much disrespect of the female. The monotonic macho will ride roughshod over any delicate niceties, especially those of women. This would have been too primitive for Burke.

Since his day the intervening centuries have brought a deep shift we don't understand. Between instinct and culture, or instinct and intellect, there has arisen a dark divide. Burke leaned toward the valuing of instinct, but to him that implied stability, the tried and true, not the acting out of violent emotion or the denial of culture. In America today, this natural dichotomy, between primitive instinct and the culture that would civilize it, has become a stark divide that has calcified because we don't understand it. In much of human history this duality has played out as opposites circling each other. Now American experience has thrown these distinctions into a drastic light and added deadly force to what was before a logical leaning or preference. Primitive instinct armed with modern weapons threatens chaos and massive destruction of life, but our lack of understanding of these instincts has forced them to explode with no need for logic or science. Modern American machismo has gut insistence that has surprised those who side with culture over primitive instinct (the liberals) – and this surprise springs from too much trust that science and intellect could decide all problems. The liberal believes that people will behave rationally if given a chance; the conservative sees, as Burke clearly saw, the naiveté of such a presumption.

Burke saw the naturalness of ordinary life as a better guide than intellect and he felt that culture, far from opposing instinct, informed and enriched it. Tradition was the main avenue of this enrichment and should be trusted first whenever possible. For him breaking with tradition would require strong justification but he did not rule that out. For instance, Burke argued heavily in favor of giving the American colonists the independence they desired. The new nation was started out on a strange logical theory, a serious and practical application of new ideas. So we see in this the traces of culture (meaning logic, ideas and science) overcoming instinct (meaning adherence to historical experience and its ancient mores). It is my belief that this dichotomy--between instinct and culture--is the American evolvement (or blurring) of the dichotomy between Burke and Paine. Perry's instinctual dismissal of intellect, honest in his gut, is opposed by thoughtful people who doubt that complex problems can be solved by gut instinct alone. Yet today, instinct, like a beast that has been trodden over by the mass of inevitable scientific research, resurges and demands its time, even dominance, in a world it believes it knows well enough without science, diplomacy or careful reflection. What we see today is resurgence of primitive trust in instinct.

Our modern dialogue has descended into name-calling. But the outrage expressed that way should press us to understand it. We would be greatly helped if each side, left and right, could see these concerns as having a human basis, a basis on the one hand in instinct and macho privilege. On the other hand in the importance of science, compassion and careful study due the complexity of our modern world.

The primacy of gut instinct has meant a remarkable hostility to science. We see that the evidence for global warming is attacked by vested interests in fossil fuels. But the vehemence and connivance of these attacks suggests natural expedience ("Just burn what you like.") is feeling defensive in the face of new technology and knowledge. Hostility to research in space is reflected in resistance to funding the International Space Station. The conservative feels threatened when natural assumptions of the past are called into question by the mass of statistical research. The gut instinct of men like Perry is to summarily dispense with all this. Repress it if possible, if not, just ignore it.

Another conservative aspect that is greatly under threat is ancient instinctual tribalism. Conservatives today are regularly accused of racism. By assuming that legislation could make people live together with indifference to tribal distinctions, our culture set the frame for instinctual backlash we see today. This has meant the ascendency of instinct that disregards all compromises that stand in its way. Culture, represented by liberal thinking, is swept away by the force of gut passion.   A leader who speaks with gut honesty (and no honesty of any other kind) finds a following among tribalists. Now, it is natural that they would feel threatened, for today, due to modern technology, every nation on Earth shares a boundary with every other. Contrast this with the world of Burke. In an Eighteenth Century town such as he grew up in, practically every person a child saw looked like himself.   Everyone spoke in the same language. The mindset of that day remains as our heritage, and is affronted now when hearing foreign speech is a regular occurrence for Americans.   We are a nation of immigrants and it is possible we will one day become a modest cross-section of the whole world. Where will tribal feelings go then?

This is a deep problem, yet today the premise of American democracy is struggling toward a solution. It will come about from understanding and compassion to bridge these radically opposing views. What this is coming to, and what will help America move into the future, is awareness of the root feelings that separate these two sides. For only if there is understanding of why these differences arise, can some viable firm direction be worked out. The naturalness, regard for instinct and tradition that guided Burke should inform our modern discussion.

Author about himself:

A little about myself: BA, Literature, UC Berkeley; MS, Mathematics, UNM. For many years I worked in Wall Street (didn't save a dime) and the scientific community, doing technical writing and programming. For several years I directed and acted on stage in New York. These days I tutor math and go to various cafés to sketch people, usually without their knowledge. For a long time, my writing was hardly coherent but recently it has grown so I'm proud enough to show it to you.

LIFE JACKET

by Leslie Tucker

The veins in the man's thick forearms are distended and his biceps bulge. He squats with thighs stretched wide, corrugated soles of his boots balanced on the pile of rubble. He grimaces and groans, straining to lift a hunk of roof. I squint at the big screen Mitsubishi from my leather chair but cannot read the yellow lettering on his sleeve. A German Shepherd, snout to the ground, is whining and pawing at the heap of shingles and sheetrock. I am riveted by the virtue of this first responder's heroism; how he and his sniffer dog manipulate chaos with vigorous clarity.

The camera pans to a lanky reporter in red Gortex, his baritone booming into a sponge-topped microphone. We viewers learn his name, that he's first on the scene for his media outlet on this May day in 2013. He points at the man and dog, tilts his square jaw and drops his lower lip exposing blinding white teeth. "The situation here in Moore, Oklahoma is becoming more desperate by the minute," he says.

Later the same evening, the identical film footage runs and a news commentator mentions that televangelist Pat Robertson has offered his perspective on the tornado disaster. I leave the room, return, have missed Robertson's sound bite and open my iPad to find his self-staged 700 Club interview. The spindly female interviewer asks Robertson why an all-seeing, all knowing God wouldn't have intervened in the Oklahoma catastrophe, perhaps even prevented it. Robertson faces the camera, tilts his not-so-square jaw and speaks. "If there were enough people praying, He would have."

Still later the same evening I lie in bed as four decades of personal encounters with evangelicals thrash around in my brain. Like snakes in a bag.

"You're busted."

My body shifted involuntarily and urine splashed over the seat, trickled down the outside of the bowl. I'd thought I was alone in the public bathroom but the voice got louder.

"You're evil."

In 1988, I was a Piano Performance and Pedagogy Major at Oakland University in Rochester, Michigan and had just completed the final exam for Advanced Music Analysis. Our professor, who'd felt nauseated, asked me to deliver the exams to his office while he went straight home to bed. On the way, I'd rushed into the bathroom.

I heard heavy breathing, yanked my jeans up and scanned the beige metal panels of the confined space. A long, damp nose protruded into the stall with me — between the wall and the spacer panel. I recognized the snarling voice.

"I knew you were up to no good..."

"I had to pee."

"You looked at the exams. You're evil."

Sharon was a Music Education Major who relished sacred organ music. I'd once walked into the university auditorium at a predetermined time, to practice on the concert grand for an upcoming performance. She sat at the organ, swaying, slopping through Bach's E minor Toccata, a marked deviation from her diet of Palestrina and Cavallo. Later, in music theory class, she'd astonished us by declaring that repertoire building and concern over grades was foolish. The fundamentals of life were clear, she said. God had a plan, would take her into His hands after graduation and place her in a small church as Music Director.

In the public bathroom, her voice trembled and the pitch fell several intervals.

"I call you out in the name of the Lord. You. Are. Evil."

Was I? I'd dropped the stack of exams on the floor inside the stall, noticed that the class genius' was on top and skimmed the first page. Seeing that my solution for the second problem was different, I'd rifled through the pile, found my exam and compared the two, relieved that either answer was plausible.

My skin prickled. I'd done something wrong, but how wrong? Sure, I'd looked at finished products but only after the exam was over. Sharon was jeering and exhaling into the stall, her nose bent slightly toward me.

"How many answers did you change?"

"None. I was curious, but..."

"Get out here." The nose disappeared.

I zipped my jeans, lifted my tweed overcoat from the door hook and slipped it on, feeling for a glove in each pocket. Cracking the door a few inches, I spotted Sharon kneeling on the muddy tile floor, tears flooding her face.

"Get on your knees. Pray with me."

I did not get on my knees. She frightened me. I assumed she'd tell her story to an authority figure and who knew what her version would be? I sped home, called our professor and explained how I'd compared the exams, how detective Sharon had tailed me into the bathroom.

He already knew. Sharon had badgered his assistant for the address, driven to his home, pounded on the door and barged into the vestibule. Dropping to her knees, she'd implored him to pray for me too.

It should have been easy to dismiss this bizarre confrontation, but the subject of evil had been raised with me before. I'd been surprised by another fundamentalist the previous spring.

***

Strings of red chile pepper lights drooped between fat nails in the knotty pine paneling and icy air blasted from a ceiling vent above our table. My friend, Susan, blew her nose into a sodden napkin and I shivered in my damp Speedo and hiking shorts. Our lanky blond waiter, Hawk, who looked about my daughter's age, sauntered over, grinned a mellow Taos grin and flipped his ponytail over one shoulder.

"Hit ya again with the Margaritas, Ladies?" I'd guzzled my first one, was invigorated after a rip-roaring day on the river.

"Sure, and we need menus."

I reached across the table, felt Susan's quivering wrist. "Relax. You've got a crazy story to tell your grandchildren someday."

"You flew out of a raft!"

"And Cisco pulled me in."

I was preoccupied, watching Hawk's suntanned calves ripple. He nodded at the bartender and I noticed that even his toes, one with a silver ring, were perfectly formed. I'd often theorized that beautiful people were drawn to beautiful places, and Hawk, in Taos, proved the point.

Susan gripped my wrist like a vise. "You're alive because Jesus saved the whole raft because I can't swim."

"You were wearing a life jacket and no one can swim in Class IV rapids. You just float, feet first, till the water eddies."

"You don't get it. You're with Jesus or you're with the Devil."

Nearly thirty years later, I wince at my lack of sympathy for Susan, but must admit to remaining unmoved by religious declarations that seem irrational to me.

Susan and I had met in September 1987, a year before our trip to Taos. Seventy-seven year old Ronald Reagan, who boasted of daily praying and napping in the Oval Office, was the most popular U.S. President since Franklin Roosevelt, but not with me. I was incensed over the Ollie North-Iran Contra scandal and horrified that the leader of the free world had told the Washington Press Corp that he consulted his wife's astrologer before scheduling world travel.

Susan and I were mature women in our thirties, returning to school for advanced degrees in music. We skipped out for a lunchtime falafel one day and I wisecracked that our President was a puppet, that Ed Meese was running the country. I believed Music and Art schools were liberal environments and it never occurred to me that I was offending Susan until she fired back. "He's a Christian. I'm a Christian too." I was dumbstruck as she continued. "When I married Rob, he'd been born again and I needed a faith I could live with, with him."

I'd hit a tender spot with Susan, hadn't guessed her beliefs because she didn't fit the profile of fundamentalists in our community. She was a hip dresser, a talented classical pianist, played jazz and directed musical productions too. Both times I'd met her husband, Rob, a brilliant sax player, he'd been stoned and needed a shower. Neither of them resembled the evangelicals I'd seen on TV, or the squeaky clean zealots who carried grisly posters and picketed abortion clinics on Southfield Road.

***

I was baptized and confirmed in the Methodist Church. Dad told me that faith had kept him steadfast through his family's economic collapse and the loss of their home during the Great Depression. He said that faith kept him alive through a perilous landing at Normandy and gruesome front line combat afterward. Jesus fortified Dad's soul as he led the battalion that liberated Dachau, examined evidence of Nazi atrocities and prosecuted war criminals at Nuremburg.

Dad told me once, when I pressed him, that he came home from the War a strong and able man because his Savior had walked beside him. Yet he never proselytized, said that what people believed was their own private business.

When my eleventh grade Honors Lit class read Being and Nothingness, I got cocky and told Dad that Sartre made more sense than the white-bearded-sky-god-virgin-birth-myth I'd learned in Sunday school. Dad was calm, said he understood the allure of radical thinkers for bright young minds and urged me to consider carefully. I did, and at seventeen, made the lonely decision to stop attending church with my family. I turned my back on religion over five decades ago, but it keeps springing up, squeaking and wobbling like a rusty jack-in-the-box.

The confrontations go back further than the bathroom stall and the Mexican food joint in Taos.

***

Oak leaves rustled like newspaper on a blistering July afternoon in 1976 and my two-year-old, Becky, hopped on the balls of her feet as I opened my friend's back gate. Cara's blond Afro popped up behind a row of organically grown tomato plants, "Iced tea?" She pointed at the child-sized picnic table and we squeezed into the benches, legs crumpling up to our chests.

Cara and I had met in 1972, as volunteers for the McGovern Campaign. We fed our families from The Diet for a Small Planet, were advocates of Roman beans and rice, and leafy Chinese tofu, food most people didn't recognize. We reviled plastic bags and paper napkins, carpooled to the health food store for millet and the alfalfa seeds we sprouted in gauze-covered-jars. We wore natural fibers, lived on tight budgets and sent money to Green Peace anyway.

Cara grabbed my hands and pinned them down on the tiny table. "I have to tell you something."

Oh shit, I thought. She's moving or getting a divorce. I'd never trusted her husband, who ridiculed the Rolling Stones, wore polyester and ate MacDonald's food. I'd ignored neighborhood rumors that he brought his secretary home for hours whenever Cara and the kids left town to visit her family. Cara tugged on my hands.

"I'm saved."

"From what?"

"Eternal damnation. I've accepted Jesus Christ as my personal savior and been born again."

Sure, most people in our city of 32,000 went to church, but they were Methodists, Presbyterians, Episcopalians and Catholics, people who kept their beliefs to themselves. Cara squeezed my knuckles, "Pray with me. Our Father..."

"Stop it. You know I quit church in eleventh grade."

"That's why..." Her eyes reddened, spilled onto the little wooden table. "You're damned..."

"I'm not damned. How did you come up with this?"

"I collapsed on the couch, kids were napping and the 700 Club came on. Pat Robertson was preaching and I started listening, really listening."

"To Pat Robertson? Does Tony know?"

"That's the miracle." Cara choked back a sob, said they'd watched The 700 Club together, that Tony had made a prayer vow contribution by phone, that someone had saved him right that moment. The same day, a prayer counselor from the show called back and recommended a nearby church. They'd been attending for three months.

"They saved Tony on the phone?"

"Don't make faces. Yes. He gave himself to Jesus on the phone. Our marriage is brand new."

Four months later I learned that Tony had received a political appointment in the Reagan administration and that he and Cara had moved to Washington, DC. Her jubilant letter to a mutual friend described how they were home at last, in their community of Fundamentalist Christians. And by the way, President Reagan was one of them, and in the District they preferred to be called evangelicals. Cara's faith was resolute, her hopes for her husband's career, boundless.

What exactly is this fundamentalism? This stringent belief system that bathroom-stall-Sharon entrusted with her post-graduate employment? This robust faith that Cara credited with saving her marriage and advancing her husband's career, the same one that allowed Susan to dismiss the life-saving skills of a white-water river guide.

Karen Armstrong, former nun and renowned religious scholar, addresses the issues of world-wide fundamentalism in her book, The Battle for God. "Fundamentalism is one of the most startling developments of the late twentieth century...a militant piety that has emerged within every major religious tradition with sometimes shocking manifestations." Christian fundamentalists identify themselves as wanting to go back to the fundamentals of the faith, which they identify as a literal interpretation of Scripture.

Armstrong's research demonstrates that in the middle of the twentieth century, it was generally taken for granted that secularism was an irreversible trend and that faith would no longer play a major part in world events. It was assumed that as human beings became more rational, they would either have no further need for religion or would be content to confine it to the personal and private areas of

their life. In the 1970s, however, fundamentalists began to rebel against secularist beliefs and wrested religion out of its marginal position and back to center stage.

In 1978, two years after Cara and Tony moved to Washington, D.C., a heavy woman in a farm-animal-print dress introduced herself after an evening PTA Meeting. "Leslie, I'm Annette Redman. I doubt you remember, but we met at a pre-birth orientation at Beaumont Hospital. Our daughters are in the same nursery school now."

We'd never spoken in the four years since the orientation but I recalled our walk to the hospital parking lot. She'd examined the facilities to satisfy her curiosity, but would never give birth there because she delivered her children at home, with only her husband and God present. She'd experienced three glorious births in the bed where she'd conceived, just as God intended. I thought to myself that if I'd given birth to my daughters where I'd conceived them, one would have been born in the back seat of a Mustang convertible and the other on a blanket in the grass in our backyard. I was tongue-tied but Annette wasn't.

"Bring Becky over Saturday morning, our new swing set has a tall slide..."

Annette opened the door with one hand and grasped my wrist with the other. "C'mon in, want a Pop Tart?" Her cuticles were raw, nails chewed down to the quick.

Six small children huddled around an oblong Formica table in the cramped breakfast nook and Fruit Loops and a pitcher of neon red liquid stood precariously near the table's edge. Several children had Pop Tarts squashed on their napkins and Annette handed Becky a lump of blue goop.

"We'll sit on the porch, they'll be fine. We've had a misunderstanding."

"What?" I was bewildered, had met this woman twice for several minutes.

"How are you feeling after your surgery? You almost died this summer, people at the swim club were shocked...you looked so healthy."

"Yeah, well, I had surgery, but..."

"What caused your attack?"

"Cecal vulvulus, twisted colon. Sometimes it's genetic. I went to Emergency with abdominal pain, ended up in surgery." Annette shook her head.

"It was a sign. He struck you down. Do you know why you survived?"

Her face was fierce as she leaned toward me, breasts heaving, and for a moment I thought it was a practical joke – something my wise-ass friends who knew the 'Cara and Tony Saved on the Phone Story' had cooked up. But her eyes were gleaming – this was no joke. Annette repeated, "I said, do you know why you survived?"

"World class hospital, excellent surgeons?"

"No. You survived God's wrath because I organized a prayer vigil for you in the locker room. I gathered women from my prayer group and

we bent our knees for your good health. You've never thanked me."

"What?"

"You didn't know? Well...now I can forgive you."

As decades pass, I wonder what it was about me that attracted such aggressive proselytizers. Did I provoke these encounters? Did my immediate dismissal of their evangelism exacerbate their fervor? Did my insistence that I could live a virtuous life without Him infuriate Them?

Recently, while rereading sections of The God Delusion, by Richard Dawkins, preeminent scientist and outspoken atheist, I was reminded of a scientific initiative funded by the Templeton Foundation in 2006. It tested the proposition that praying for sick patients, specifically those who had had coronary bypass surgery, improved their health. The experiments were done double blind and patients were assigned strictly at random, to an experimental group (received prayers,) or a control group (received no prayers). Those doing the experimental praying were told only the first name and initial letter of the surname. Scientists ridiculed the study, even though belief that "evidence for the efficacy of intercessory prayer in medicinal settings" was mounting at the time. The results, reported in the American Heart Journal of April 2006, however, were clear-cut. There was no difference between those patients who were prayed for and those who were not. Whew.

Sometimes, praying for each other, or for afflicted strangers, is enough for those who pray. Certainly those who pray establish a fellowship - I know that the ladies who knelt in the musty locker room stopped at the Whistle Stop Cafe for pie and coffee afterward. They must have believed they were helping me, when in fact, I would have preferred a tuna sandwich delivered to my home when I was recovering from surgery. None of them called, inquired what I might need, or visited. Yet praying for a stranger was important to them.

I believe that specific circumstances ignited the zeal of the missionaries I've encountered, and that there have been people in every age who have fought the modernity of their day, and that they have indeed, been motivated by the common fears, anxieties and desires that respond to the peculiar difficulties of life in the modern secular world. And I'm thinking praying feels good too. Studies demonstrate that religion fires the same neurotransmitters and spurs the same chemical reactions in the human brain that romantic-sexual love does.

My secular spine tingled when I attended Christmas Eve service with Dad the year before he died. Trumpets heralded the processional march, double stops resonated on the Aeolian Skinner and sapphire satin robes glistened in the candlelight as the choir entered. Dad held the hymnal for both of us, just as he'd done when I was a child, and his eighty year old face was radiant as he sang, "O Come all ye faithful." The oaken sanctuary I'd deserted as a teenager morphed into a gothic fortress of optimism and love.

I longed to believe that story in that place.

What I do believe is what I learned from Sartre at seventeen: that in order to be free myself, I must desire the freedom of other people. To treat another person as an object for my use is to make an object of myself. To be free, I must respect the freedom of others. As disturbing as it is for me to listen to second-century-like-talk of deities, I never attempt to dissuade anyone from their religious beliefs. I aim toward a life of doing no harm and wonder why that isn't enough for the pious people I've encountered.

Western monotheistic traditions hold that human beings are made in the likeness and image of God and are thus equal in the sight of the Lord. Yes, equal. If Christian fundamentalists believe this, it should be easy to recognize that with or without TV evangelists, telephone prayer vows, locker room vigils and bathroom stall raids, there is indeed, more than one way to build a virtuous life.

I still think about the four women who confronted me. Susan, tossed like salad in an army surplus raft, saw me flip into the roiling waters of the Rio Grande. Cara sobbed with a mouth full of peanut butter on a summer day, and angry Annette pronounced my damnation from a rusty porch chair. Sharon, the most vehement, accosted me in a public bathroom stall.

It seems that embracing rigid fundamentals, specifically, the literal interpretation of Scripture, made life's dilemmas less complex for these women during the cultural earthquake of the 1970s. They welcomed Jesus into their hearts, attended church where Christian behavior was strictly defined, and formed supportive bonds with like-minded fundamentalists, lauding the handholding sisterhood of their prayer groups. No stressing over the efficacy of Phyllis Schlafly's philosophy versus Gloria Steinem's. If abortion is a sin, women's rights are irrelevant.

All four women said they were certain that God, their Father in heaven, stood sentinel over their minds and bodies. He had drawn the blueprints for their lives and they needed only to listen for His voice and follow. And that, I believe, was the conflict that flummoxed we educated young women of the 70's. I'd watched my father take care of my mother, had seen how flawlessly their system of well-defined roles worked. Yet I wanted to be in charge of my own life, and knew it, even as a young teenager.

Frankly, I could have used an omnipotent guiding voice, some help riding the tidal wave of rebellion that swamped traditional American values during my teenage years. I took inordinate risks during the 1960s when authority was challenged and anything anyone believed was up for grabs. When youthful energy and experimentalism dictated, "If it feels good, do it," I did, and lived with the consequences. Yet for better or worse, I have never considered returning to the comfort and confines of the Methodist Church.

Marilynne Robinson, American novelist and essayist, describes herself as an intellectual Christian and says in Absence of Mind, "It is the quality of the science and the religion that determines the nature of the conversation." During her 2010 interview on the Jon Stewart Show, she identified herself as a Christian who believes in the science of evolution, said she knew many others like herself, and that they were not to be confused with zealots on either end of the scientific or religious spectrums. I acknowledge that the religious statements I've confronted, and the lack of any rational conversation with those who have advanced them has influenced my ever-skeptical view of organized religion. And, living where I do now strengthens that skepticism.

Thirteen years ago, after a lifetime in the Detroit area, my husband and I retired to the mountains of South Carolina, the buckle of the Bible belt, as locals call it. A majority of people we meet here believes President Barack Obama is not an American citizen and that the Earth is not old, that climate change is a fabrication of the liberal media. Many are Creationists and are also certain that our African-Muslim President will order the confiscation of their guns. Offices of doctors, dentists, and veterinarians are plastered with religious messages such as, "We Care, God Cures."

One Sunday morning while hiking with my dogs at Jones Gap State Park, a pink-faced Park Ranger tapped the flat brim of his hat and warned, "Be careful, Ma'am, all the good people are in church." It sounded ridiculous at the time and I chuckled, assuming he was joking. Years later, however, with a clearer understanding of what locals believe, I can imagine the judgment he passed on a lone woman, trekking by a boulder-strewn river instead of attending indoor worship.

What I have concluded is that all of this ruminating boils down to virtue, which requires a life of action, of choosing one's own behavior as if choosing it for all humanity. And I can define virtue because I've seen a man who saved people. A man who believed in justice and charity, a man who knew that faith coerced is no faith at all. The man who let me quit church.

In 1984, Dad was newly retired from his law practice and I accompanied him on a volunteer Visitation Monitoring session for Oakland County Probate Court. Parents who had lost custody of their young children were allowed short visits with them in public places, in the presence of a court appointed monitor. Dad wanted me to see his volunteer work firsthand, and we planned to meet in a Big Boy Restaurant in Pontiac, Michigan. When I arrived, the

social worker had already delivered the tow-headed boy to Dad's table.

The scrawny teenaged mother arrived fifteen minutes late, ashen as dirty snow, collarbone protruding through a stained tee shirt. She shivered, sitting on trembling hands, and asked if either of us had a smoke. Gazing at her son, who seemed not to know her, she was unable to communicate with him. Dad excused himself and returned quickly with two cigarettes he'd bummed and a Big Boy matchbook. Tears brimmed in the girl's eyes as she inhaled. Dad joked with her son, insisted they order food and picked up the tab.

As the girl stood up to leave, Dad asked if she was getting better. She scowled, said she was in a shit load of trouble, might have to go back to jail. He pulled a card from his wallet and pressed it into her hand.

"Call me. Maybe I can help."

It wasn't dramatic enough to lead the six o'clock news like a burly young man at building collapse rescue, but in its own way, Dad's gesture was just as important. One human with resources trying to ease another's suffering, because it makes sense, and makes life more profound for all of us.

***

Back in my leather chair that May evening day in 2013, I blink as Minnesota Congresswoman Michelle Bachman shakes her finger at the camera. "The IRS will soon be in charge of a huge national database on health care," she says. My mind clicks back to speeches from her last campaign, shrill warnings that we are at the end of days, that as true Americans we must accept Jesus as our savior, as she did at sixteen, or suffer eternal hellfire. I shut my eyes to shut her out, but can't. I do the math and deduce that thirty-eight years after televangelist Pat Robertson saved my friend's husband by phone, Robertson is still on the air -- blaming tornadoes on those who do not pray.

Armstrong's research (which preceded publication of "The Battle for God" in 2000,) supporting the concept that secularism was an irreversible trend in America, has not yet stood the test of time. Instead, fundamentalists of all brands have gained worldwide momentum, fueled by an increasing digital audience of zealous believers in our wired up world.

I can't get Bathroom-Stall-Sharon out of my head today and recall her confidence in God's plan for her, how convinced she was of my damnation. Although I wonder if she is still as certain of the manifestations of good and evil, I like to believe that it all worked out for her. That perhaps she's mastered the tricky fingering on that Bach Toccata and is playing it in a small church where her God has placed her, waiting for the devout to arrive.

Meanwhile, I'm still floating free, feet first, until the water eddies.

About the Author:

Leslie Tucker, a former Detroiter, lives on a Carolina mountainside and refuses to divulge its exact location. She is an avid hiker and zipliner, a dedicated yogi, an ACBL Life Master in Sanctioned Bridge, and enjoys anything that requires a helmet. She holds degrees in business and music. Her work has appeared in The Baltimore Review, So to Speak: A Feminist Journal of Language and Art, Shenandoah Magazine, The Press 53 Awards Anthologies, where her essay "Lies That Behind" won First Prize for Creative Nonfiction, and Fiction Fix, where her essay "Reckless Abandon" was shortlisted for Best of the Net Awards.

MOTHERS

by Beth Mead

My grandmother lived in bed. Her ankles were swollen, hard to walk on, but she wasn't ill. Not really, not physically. Depression was shameful then. My grandmother's bed was in the living room of her small home, the kitchen to her left, the closet with her portable toilet to the right. Her husband died of cancer. Her youngest son shot himself in a field. She died in front of a television. As children, we climbed up next to her and listened to her stories about the teddy bears who lived in the woods in the painting above her bed. She would draw me paper dolls to cut out and dress, girls with wide eyes and curled bangs and beauty marks on their cheeks. My grandmother was an artist.

My mother sometimes worked three jobs, three shifts, to pay the bills that my father would not pay after he left, to raise the children he no longer saw. She married another man to help pay the bills, told me later how she knew on her wedding day, standing in our backyard in her powder blue dress from a red tag sale, that she was making a terrible mistake. That man drank every day. He was accused of things that my mother prayed were not true. My mother's youngest daughter punched her in the stomach in an emergency room, stole from her, asked her how much money she'd leave behind when she dies. With husband number three, my mother got a new home away from the past, and road trip vacations, and finally retirement. She talks me off ledges and takes me to lunch, to musicals, to movies. My mother is a survivor.

I am a terrible mother. I somehow missed that my youngest son has been depressed and suicidal since he was eleven. I somehow missed that he has been drinking and doing drugs for years. Until a policeman knocked on my door at 3am, I somehow missed that my son was sneaking out of our house, meeting up with people in the neighborhood park where I took him as a child, where I pushed him on swings and wished he'd get tired enough to nap. I took my son to counselors and doctors and clinics. I gained a hundred pounds. My husband lost three jobs. Every morning I dread getting out of bed. But some days, there is art. Some days, we survive. Some days, I hold my son close and remember how to be a mother.

About the Author:

Beth Mead is a Professor of Writing and Director of the MFA in Writing Program at Lindenwood University, and she is the editor of The Lindenwood Review. Beth received her MFA in Creative Writing from the University of Missouri-St. Louis. She has won the Jim Haba Poetry Award and was an Honorable Mention in the River Styx MicroFiction Contest.

FRIDA KAHLO, BARBIE OR BARBADA

by Emily Peña Murphey

Well, I guess I saw this coming when a few months back I chanced on an ad for a children's picture book about Frida Kahlo, featuring a very cutesy, Disney-fied image of her on the cover. If there's one popular figure I thought our culture could never succeed in sanitizing, it would be la Frida! But come to find out that it's actually happened now in an even worse way: that she's been incarnated as a Barbie doll! ¡Increíble! Apparently this has been made possible by the rights to her image have been sold by a member of her family.

There's been a lot of complaint about this in the media, I'm glad to say, but of course most of it has focused on the doll's appearance, which strongly resembles that of Salma Hayek, the Mexican-born Spanish-Lebanese actress who portrayed Frida on film. It was actually a decent movie, I thought, though it seems to have produced most or all of the images of the artist that most Norteamericanos have encountered. For example, few or none who have spoken out about the appearance of the doll seem aware that Frida Kahlo had not only the infamous unplucked "unibrow" (a dumb expression!) omitted in the Barbie version, but also a very visible black mustache, of which the openly androgynous Frida was very proud. The doll's standard Barbie skin tone and inauthentic "Mexican" clothing are hardly worthy of mention.

Would it have been asking too much of these designers to have looked at a few of Frida's numerous close-up photographs or her many self-portraits; or to have read, say, the Wikipedia article about her life? Perhaps to have done so would have given the project too much

depth and authenticity for the American consumer. It might also have forced the manufacturers to confront some aspects of their subject which might prove too controversial or unsettling for even many 'feminist" potential purchasers of sexualized plastic figurines. But then, Americans would always prefer to be passive recipients of superficial bits of reality doled out to them by mass media than to actively engage in research that might lead to some deeper truth!

So (though none of these points are at all objectionable to this blogger) here for readers are few seemingly lesser-known fun facts about Frida for those who want to use her as raw material for a prettified and wholesome Latina "icon:"

She is generally believed to have been bisexual, though her primary love was her philandering husband, the muralist Diego Rivera

Her pelvis and reproductive organs were horribly mutilated in a traumatizing accident she experienced as a teenager, as the result of which...

She endured disability and chronic pain for most of her adult life, resulting in her eventually losing one of her legs to amputation

She was a Communist who reportedly went so far as to have a love affair with Leon Trotsky

In later life, she was arguably an alcoholic and/or prescription drug addict

She was fond of profanity and off-color humor--and eccentric or outrageous behavior in general.

As an expression of her suffering, imagery of blood, woundedness, maiming, and death were frequent themes of her art work.

A pretty picture for your little girls? (Lots of "teachable moments" there!)

Most scholars of Kahlo's life and art agree that what is most significant about her legacy is not her facial hair or her exotic clothing and hair-style, but her ability to transcend her difficult existence and transform it into a life filled with creativity and meaning. But this reality can't be conveyed by means of something as concrete and superficial as a stylized mannequin.

So in closing, I might suggest that the manufac-tures of Frida Barbie develop a few accesso-ries to go with the doll and lend her a bit more verisimilitude, as follow.

Crutches, a wheelchair and an old-fashioned, wooden prosthetic leg.

A phial of sugar-pill faux opiate medications, with instructions for use printed in Spanish.

A "baby" doll in the form of a miscarried fetus.

A back brace and plaster-cast corset

A man's suit for purposes of occasional cross-dressing

A sugar Muertos skull bearing the name "Diego" on its forehead

And--most importantly--an artist's canvas, pal-ette, brushes, and paints.

Empowered, ¡Sí! Pretty and conventional, ¡No!

About the Author:

Emily Peña Murphey is a retired psychothera-pist with training in psychology, social work, and Jungian psychoanalysis. She has family roots in the Río Grande valley and the Smoky Mountains of North Carolina, and sings and plays the traditional music of both regions. She uses writing to explore her identity as a mixed Latin/Anglo-American, and has published short fiction in several online journals. Her current projects include a collection of short stories and a trilogy of trans-border novels. She lives in Philadelphia.

A LOST VIOLIN, A LAST LETTER HOME

by Mike Dillon

The spoil of war is our knowledge of the world. Wislaw Szymborska

In 2013, a few months before her death by cancer, my 87-year-old mother, a beautiful, stoic woman who loved to swim the cold waters of Puget Sound, held back tears as she handed me a browned, brittle piece of paper. I had seen the paper once before, shortly after my grandfather died.

With a strange, out-of-body feeling of fulfilling a part in a story written a long time ago, I accepted the last letter home from my grandfather's brother Melvin, the uncle my mother never knew. Dated June 26, 1918, it was posted from Le Cendre, France.

Melvin's epistle was one of hundreds of thousands posted by American boys from the Great War. The day after Congress declared war on Germany, my great uncle and his little brother, my grandfather, joined up in their hometown of Coeur d'Alene, Idaho, to keep the world safe for democracy. They were 18 and 17, respectively. My grandfather fudged his age, an easy thing to pull off in those feverishly patriotic days.

He returned home alone.

"The war is beginning to look pretty good now & I suppose we will be up on the front one of these days to help with the finishing touches, at least we hope so," Melvin wrote with his fountain pen in a tidy, backward-leaning script.

In September 1918, before moving up the line for the Meuse-Argonne offensive, Melvin left the violin he brought from home with a pretty,

dark-haired young woman in a village in eastern France. In October, as their unit crossed a field toward the German positions, a shell fragment killed my great uncle as my grandfather jogged beside him.

The violin remained remains unclaimed.

November 11, 2018 marks the centenary of the final hour of the final day of the final month of World War I, a catastrophe that took perhaps 18 million military and civilian lives 110,000 of them American over "some damn foolish thing in the Balkans," as Otto von Bismarck had prophesied. The politicians will have their day on the podiums, their rhetoric drifting over the killing fields and military cemeteries of France as they remember "The War to End All Wars" which laid the seedbed for an even greater inferno.

My mother said my grandfather, a man averse to self-disclosure, spoke just once about how his big brother died and the story of his violin. It came out of the blue one day as he drove her home from high school. He chose his words carefully, she said, like an assayer weighing nuggets of gold. This would have been in the early 1940s, in the middle of World War II.

My grandfather, tall as Lincoln, gaunt as a blackthorn cane, lived until 79 and is buried in Seattle beside his second wife. Once, at a family gathering in the 1950s, I shyly watched from the margins as his eyes drifted from the conversation to stare off into the ether. The conversation continued without him, accompanied by the ice tinkling in a half-dozen highballs. Watching him maybe I was 8 I felt like one of God's spies. Over the years, I spotted those psychic excursions a few more times. That was a normal part of the household scene, my mother confided after he was dead: He'd disappear into himself and return, slowly, as the world continued around him.

I first read Ernest Hemingway's "Big Two-Hearted River" in a schoolbook anthology when I was 10 or 11. As Nick Adams's fished and camped in Upper Michigan, I was right there looking over his shoulder. "Big Two-Hearted River" is the last story in Hemingway's first full-scale book, "In Our Time," published in 1925. The story mentioned neither war nor trauma; those who had read the preceding stories from that collection knew Nick had suffered both. I had no way of knowing that, yet I sensed something was off with him, especially when Nick came to the swamp he refused to enter ⏸ "in the half light, the fishing would be tragic." Whether baiting a hook, pitching his tent or cooking flapjacks, Nick did everything just so. So intentionally right, in fact, that his skilled acts became a kind of ritual to keep some mysterious, inner tide of fear at bay ⏸ Huck Finn back from a world war.

My grandfather was a reader. I don't know if he read Hemingway but he would have understood Nick Adams. His brother Melvin never made it far enough to look back in anger or anguish.

Melvin, like many of his doomed comrades, lived his last months in a patriotic, pre-battle glow, like the soldiery of Europe in August 1914, marching off into the maw of mechanized warfare accompanied by the resounding cheers the Western Front would render brutally ironic.

"I had a wonderful trip last evening to the top of the Plateau de Gergovie," Melvin's letter continues. "When we got to the top we could see for many miles ⏸ ranges of mountains and the many wonderful picturesque villages." The area, and views, near Le Cendre in the Massif Central is now a big selling point for the local tourist board.

After noting he had enclosed some "characteristic French embroidery," Melvin writes: "We have been having some wonderful moonlight nights lately and they sure make me homesick." The wonders of the Internet confirm the moon was full on June 24, two days earlier.

"We could even see uncultivated lands & forests which is a rarity in this country, as all of the lands are cultivated and all yielding some of the richest crops I have ever seen."

The voice of agrarian, American innocence pushes on: "It is too bad tho the way the old people have to work to get their crops in. The American soldiers help them some and they appreciated it very much but never-the-less they have almost more than they can take care of. If the crops in the states are anything like those over here the war is practically ended for they say wheat will win the war."

Melvin closes: "Write to us soon."

"They say wheat will win the war" ⏸ an innocence that can only be betrayed.

Melvin's script fills both sides of his stationary. Once finished, he folded the paper four times with origami-like precision, terminating in a half-fold. The artful creases, the fastidious, leftward-leaning penmanship, the fact that he turned the stationary horizontally to accommodate the march of his long sentences, registers an unconventional sensibility. The kind of sensibility, in fact, that might carry a violin into war.

On November 4, 1918, one week before the Armistice, the Coeur d'Alene Evening Press carried this front-page headline, top-left: "Melvin Petersen Reported Dead."

Several soldiers in Melvin's sector had written home to their Coeur d'Alene families reporting the news.

One Captain Ed Powell wrote to his wife: "No doubt you have heard of the death of Melvin Petersen. He was killed by a shell splinter. It was certainly a sad event to me, Pete was a cheerful boy, full of courage."

The story noted Melvin's father, Joe Petersen, "a prominent real estate man in this city," held out hope. Months before he'd been notified his son had been seriously wounded, which proved false.

"Melvin Petersen was one of the two brothers, Melvin and Loren, who gave up their studies in the Coeur d'Alene high school to go overseas with company C. They were prominent in high school activities and popular in this city," the story continued.

On Saturday, November 9 edition, two days before the Armistice, the Evening Press carried this front-page headline: "The Death of Melvin Petersen." This time the paper ran a photo of Melvin: a dark-haired, square jawed image of All American young manhood in uniform.

From the newspaper: "The two brothers were more than brothers ⬚ they were talented musicians, athletes and foremost in all school activities, they gave up a promising future and entered the service of their country.

"In France, the boys were inseparable, being together as much as military orders would permit."

A few years after the war, Melvin's body was shipped home for reburial, as were the bodies of some 46,000 other American soldiers. He lies in Coeur d'Alene's Forest Cemetery beside his parents.

And Melvin's violin? A violin is not something blithely tossed on the trash heap.

I like to think it's passed through several generations of a French family, accompanied by the story of the nice American boy who left it behind for safekeeping. The pretty, dark-haired, young French woman, now dead, would likely be someone's well-remembered grandmother. Someone about my age ⬚ 67.

I also permit myself to dream a little. Or a lot. It's possible Melvin's violin is still played, bow lowering to strings to touch the present tense. The odds are not impossible.

I keep a framed copy of Vermeer's "View of Delft" on the wall of my study. Now and then I stop what I'm doing and gaze at the handful of people gathered there on the foreshore of the River Shie, the spired city and stained-glass sky beyond them, as they go about their business towards forgotten graves, unaware as sparrows.

The day is so transparent and clear Vermeer's painting seems a tender, posthumous vision, as if the artist had just been told he had three days to live. And so he gives us the world as it is, and all that it ever could be ⬚ the beautiful, shimmering world all of us must vacate.

I realize, now, when Melvin's letter passed between us, my dying mother and I glimpsed ourselves gazing down upon a story we just happened to be in ⬚ larger, more resonant than the story of our own mere lives. Life was there before us, clear and whole, as we see it in "View of Delft. For one brief moment, the dancers caught sight of the dance.

Melvin's letter will be handed over to my oldest son, now 34, when the time comes.

About the Author:

Mike Dillon lives in Indianola, Washington, a small town on Puget Sound northwest of Seattle. He is the author of four books of poetry and three books of haiku. Several of his haiku were included in "Haiku in English: The First Hundred Years," from W.W. Norton (2013). "Departures," a book of poetry and prose about the forced removal of Bainbridge Island's Japanese Americans after Pearl Harbor will be published by Unsolicited Press in April 2019.

LIVING IN AND BEYOND THE WORLD
by L. S. Hope

Truthfully, there are things I miss about living in the world.

If I lived in the world, I would go to natural history museums. I would visit art galleries. I would buy Stilton cheese and real, crisp rye pain de campagne with salted butter. I would drink thick Italian espresso and revel, still and silent, in the delightful anonymous solitude that a bustling city affords. I would do several things I have been meaning to do for a decade or so now; I would probably find a good psychiatrist.

Sometimes I even miss wearing clothes. In my youth I dressed myself decoratively and with such pleasure, from the marvellous piled emporiums of Goodwill and St Vincent de Paul – thick soft scarves and hats and a big blue leather trenchcoat; my tight brown slacks and that wispy white and green blouse that made me look like a tree. I wore miniskirts and checkered stockings and black eyeliner; I dyed my hair ebony. I was pretty in those days, and I liked to show off my long legs.

I miss the second-hand bookstores. There was a treasure cache near Lygon St, an Aladdin's cave of books that stretched on and on, around narrow corners and into deep grottos, every wall lined to the ceiling. I spent hours, and a good portion of my bartending wages here.

I remember my early youth in the city. I was emancipated and aflame with passion – for ideas, for books, for beautiful things. Although it was almost always overcast, most of my recollections are inexplicably lit by pale, warm shafts of gold as the sun set behind the dark granite bricks of Carlton's meandering back lanes. I was a social creature in those days – I had passionate affairs and deep, fervent friendships with kindred souls. I felt deeply connected and secure in my role as a human being, and the colourful bustle of the hive around me was pleasantly reassuring.

I am no longer certain, when I recall these poignant gold-hued days, if it is the world that I miss, or simply my own youth.

It was my partner C. who coined the term. Sometimes we look up from a distressing headline or an inane youtube comment upon which our glance has accidentally fallen and say: My god. I'm Glad I Don't Live In The World. We visit relatives out in the world every year, and ask them what has been happening. A friend thought it was hilarious recently that she had to explain to me what F.OM.O. stood for. Gluten free water? Selfie-sticks? Driverless cars? They chuckle at our surprise, and I laugh, too: *I guess I live under a rock.*

The truth is almost the opposite, really – we do not live under a rock, but on a sailboat. We bought her not long ago, after several years of living in the remote islands of the Indo Pacific, where we work. We plan to sail between our employment contracts now; we hope to idle about the extended Malay archipelago, mostly, when we are between contracts. We possess no television (although we are admittedly chronically addicted to the internet). The vast, distant realm of the world as we refer to it is a term which has sprung up in the private language of our intimacy, as such expressions do amongst all couples. It does not connote any implication that the remote islands of the Indo-Pacific where we live are not a valid portion of the planet. We simply refer to a world in which we no longer belong. The world of modern western culture in general; the world from which our families respectively hail, Canada and Australia; that wide, marvellous and frightening place that C. likes to call the Excited States Of America. It refers to the world of cable television, suburban strip malls and traffic on the freeway. It is also, of course, the world of art galleries, bookstores, espresso coffee and kindred communities. In any case, the world appears to be rolling on without me.

We live, much of the time, in simple solitude on our girl, our beautiful, second hand, paint-peeling tank of a sailboat. She is white, and rather chalky in some places, with a navy blue triangular stripe on her hulls. On a gentle tack, as the sun sets behind her broad canvas sails, the breeze rushes up through her creaking trampoline nets. I love to sprawl on these, my head resting on my folded forearms, watching the water roll and churn beneath me. On hot nights in sheltered anchorages, these nets are the perfect place to watch the stars, as cool air wafts up from the sea below.

 Our shower is a garden hose on the back deck; I like to bathe in the open air, watching the sea eagles swoop overhead as I soap myself, listening the tremor of the baitfish flashing across the surface. We neither possess nor require hot running water. The climate in this part of the world precludes the necessity for clothing, and we rarely bother with it when there are no other people around. I like to potter about the deck wearing only my sunhat, flecks of cool water drying on my skin in the breeze.

My figure is perhaps not quite so trim and gracile as it once was, when I revelled in adorning it with clothes; my hair is the mousy color I was born with, flecked with grey now and frizzled by the sun. I haven't worn make-up in years.

Our on board refrigerator is cavernous beyond our wildest dreams; all in all we probably have around two square feet of cold space which fluctuates between frozen solid and a dank, limp-vegetable temperature. We had assumed that we would forgo this luxury, having lived without refrigeration on a previous sailing odysseys, and the ice box the previous owner installed was an unexpected surprise. Regrettably, good European cheese is a rare

commodity in this part of the world; in any case it does not keep well in our temperamental marine chiller.

C. revels in the fact that we live so far away from the world – that brightly lit world of SUVs and daytime reality television and wide supermarket aisles lined with myriad superfluous variations of sugary cereal. He grew up on a farm, way out in the woods near the eastern coast of Canada; he spent his childhood romping through pine forests, building forts, and falling out of trees. I share his revulsions for the shopping malls and the traffic, but I cannot share his abhorrence for cities. I had a wonderful time, when I was young and lived in the world.

It is not my intention to preach our present lifestyle as superior, or suited to everyone. We use very few resources. We burn diesel when there is no wind to fill the sails but for the most part, our solar panels are more than sufficient for our needs. However, we are also contributing very little, in the long run – to people less fortunate than us, to the various contemporary social and global concerns that our treasured wifi connection remind us are rife, out there in the world. Neither of us are eligible to vote in the countries of our citizenship – we have held residence overseas for so long.

Of course we maintain some connection to the world, along the channels we most value. C., an enthusiastic amateur luthier, hunches eagerly over the instructional online videos of various violin makers and music teachers. I treasure my kindle beyond all other possessions. I carry a spare with me, still in its original box and packaging, wherever we go; in the unthinkable event that my current kindle fails, I know I can retrieve all my books, stored in my online account, in an instant. (It is perfectly true that we marvel and delight in the world that produced this splendid technology).

The close friends that remain to me are those who love to write; penpals might be a more accurate term, although this label scarcely does justice to the multipage tomes we send to each other. My friendships mostly exist through email, these days. I am a confirmed introvert and solitude is a difficult habit to break, the more one becomes accustomed to it. For the duration of our last island property contract, I was warily courteous to a fellow co-worker; I warmed to her, in my slow and undemonstrative fashion, more and more as I got to know her. After twenty four months, when our contract was up, I was quite sure that I liked and admired her very much. Fortunately, she too greatly enjoys the written word, and our friendship has flourished since I left, far deeper and more expressive than it ever was when we lived in the same place. I know more about her, and she knows far more about me, from the online letters we regularly write. Perhaps I ought to have seized upon the chance to get to know her better when we lived in the same place and saw each other every day, but I cannot help observing that I find it so very much easier to relate to people through the written word than to converse in person. Even if I were to return to the world, to become connected with a like-minded community, I will never be the vibrant life of the cocktail party. I have grown accustomed to solitude; I like it.

There are moments when I regret my absence from the world, and moments when I feel guilty at my lack of societal participation. There are a good many things and bookstores and people and cheeses that I love, out there in the world. My short, infrequent visits back there are a great pleasure to me.

But I harbour no fear of missing out. Deep down I know that I have finally found my place, for the time being, out here on the water. I was a reluctant, anxious convert to the sailing life; I remain anxious, much of the time. Sometimes I am downright terrified. I would never, ever have agreed to the purchase and our permanent residence on our sailboat if it had not been for C. It was he who persuaded me to undertake the seven month sailing odyssey, on a friends boat, through the Pacific and into Indonesia. It was the first time I had ever lived aboard a small water craft; it was a journey that decided my fate and ultimately changed my life.

And now, there is simply no question of turning back – it's too late. Life at sea simply gave me too many wonderful and beautiful things that I know I might never have encountered otherwise.

We saw stark islets, glittering in the sun like gems thrust up from the sea, a thousand miles from any other appreciative human witness. One night as we sailed across the Solomon Sea, a damp-feathered booby circled the boat before perching himself on the solar panel beside my seat in the cockpit. He lifted and shuffled his rubbery feet on the smooth glass; he blinked in companionable exhaustion. The boat lilted and soared on in the darkness, with sails set; he kept his balance, and stayed with me, for hours.

Off the coast of the Louisiades, a lone minke whale lingered with us for a time, lumbering in circles around the boat. I swam with him, or rather I allowed myself to become a spectacle for him; I floundered in the infinite cloudy blue chasm beneath the boat and he orbited me, gliding gracefully.

Once, here at a breezy island anchorage, I woke and looked up through the open hatch. The first sight my eyes drank in was a pair of russet colored sparrows, perched on the rails, framed in a square of pinkish blue pre dawn sky. Their twittering must have woken me.

I am far from the people with whom I have intimate friendships, but I have met people on our sailing travels whom I will never, ever forget.

On a tiny far flung atoll far north of Vanuatu, a tall man thrust his arms out to us, enraptured – Welcome! Welcome! He lined his wife and daughters up on the chicken scratched earth in front of their reed hut and sang us a song. He had written the song himself, he told me, in honour of this rare delight, a visitor. He hoped I didn't mind, but he did not know how to write music, so he used the tune of a song he already knew. Wel-come to iiiisland home, You are now our family now - his wife and girls, clad in ruffled mother hubbard dresses, chirruped along as the man held the pencilled lyrics on a crumpled piece of exercise paper in front of them. They sang to the tune of God Save The Queen. Later, he led us beyond the hut, around the point, to the thunderous cliff of falling water; thick wafts of mist rose from the falls and the constant spray had blanketed the surrounding cliffs with luxuriant damp green foliage. We bathed in our clothes, soaped and ecstatic, and the sound of our laughter was swallowed in the deafening thunder of the cascade; we pummelled ourselves clean beneath the magnificent torrent.

In the Solomon Islands, a handsome man with a sparse beard and broad muscular shoulders approached us in a tiny dugout canoe. He lingered at the bow, without speaking a word. A small boy sucking his finger, naked and wide eyed clung to his muscular knee. Hello. Hello. The man did not want anything from us, he explained gently, and he had nothing to trade; he had merely seen us and brought his young son out for a closer look. He hoisted the boy onto his knee affectionately. The boy brushed his fingers along the side of the smooth fiberlgass. The man politely ignored us now, and they lingered, silent and fascinated around our floating home, as though beholding an alien craft from another planet.

In Papua New Guinea, a wild man hollered down the open hatches as we lay slumbering at anchor early one morning – Ahoy! This wiry gray-haired eccentric Australian had lived out in the remote stretches of the Papuan coast for years; visitors were a rare treat. He took us officiously under his wing; this was the bus to take, and this the best place for canned provisions; we must check in with the harbourmaster by going here and then taking another bus – no matter, he would take us himself. We returned to his tug boat Barbarian and he took us scuba diving in the adjacent bay littered with war wrecks. We spent days, ecstatic and entranced, exploring the sunken remnants – overturned fighter airplanes and cavernous troop carriers, still and covered in silt. From the crevices of these rusting monuments skittish cardinal-fish regarded us with alarm and moray eels twisted indifferently along their way. The holds of the wrecks were riddled with ammunition shells and bottles and, here and there, human bones.

It was only by living on a sail boat, far away from the world that I learned to truly appreciate scarcity. After weeks of rice and canned food and the slapdash meals of long passages, the sight of fresh vegetables in a village market gripped me with a delight I had never felt

before, for food of any sort. Red, plump tomatoes piled in pyramids of five on a lime-green plastic soup plate; stacks of purple ubi potatoes in palm thatch woven baskets; a tray of green mangoes with the sacrificial sample baring its luscious orange flesh atop the pile; the ruffled bouquet of dark green spinach leaves – all of it gloriously fresh. After weeks since our last provisioning, I would fairly swoon upon such treasures.

Living on a sail boat has afforded me the chance to scuba dive some of the most

spectacular and untouched reefs on the planet, thousands of miles from anywhere; it has taken me to thick-vined jungle islands where I tripped and fumbled my way, binoculars thrust up at my face, in pursuit of some of the rarest and most beautiful birds in the world. It has introduced me to another world of stark, unforgiving natural beauty. It has introduced me to remote communities of island souls whose society cannot match the frenetic pace at which the world of my colloquial expression seems to be constantly accelerating, but who emanate an otherworldly charm and eccentricity born from their very isolation which I love, deeply. Such souls have shown me incomparable kindness and conveyed to me a sense of welcome which is scarcely translatable to the world from which I hailed.

Everywhere I turn, I behold the constant, endless line of the horizon, a vast plain of blue unmarred by human presence. It reminds me of all that I possess within myself; of the fact that I am capable of things that terrify me. Sailing at night, which still holds for a novice like myself a good deal of attendant terrors, reminds me of the words of the thirteenth century mystic Meister Eckhart that I read long ago, in a musty meandering bookstore:

What is this darkness?

What is its name?

Call it: an aptitude for sensitivity.

Call it: a rich sensitivity that will make you whole.

Call it: your potential for vulnerability.

I am vulnerable outside the protective hive of the world from which I hail in a manner that I'm not entirely sure C. is, or understands. I am vulnerable out here to the elements, to the wind and the waves. More than one occasion has found me hugging my knees to my chest and crying in the cockpit, an absurd childish tantrum of irrational fright, as the wind whistles through the boom, the waves crash on the hulls and the mast creaks. C., exuberant and delighted at the sporty sail turns to regard me and frowns, dumbstruck and baffled. Sometimes, in my furious terror, I feel the compulsion to slap his joyful, clueless, fearless face hard, or perhaps shake him by the shoulders; I'm scared, you idiot. But he just shrugs and chuckles, with affectionate exasperation. He makes me to the helm and internally I shake myself, hard. It turns out I can, in fact, do it.

Living far from the world has allowed me to discover what lies within me, bare and unfettered by the old refuges I sought - the noisy, thoughtless, well-meaning affirmations that my hyper-absorbent ego craved, the raucous solicitation to participate in a prescribed fashion that was well within the boundaries of my own comfort. It has allowed me to realise what I am capable of. It has been one of the most important and valuable lessons of my life.

It is not out of the question that I might return to the world, someday – I should not be sorry to find myself there. I will wrap myself in colourful shawls and idle through the corridors of high ceilinged galleries; I will languish amongst musty stacks of yellowing paper in the second-hand bookstores. But for now, I could not possibly feel that I am missing out. For the time being I remain enraptured, painfully stretched, overwhelmed and delighted by this wide sky and the empty horizon. I am quite sure the world can wait.

About the Author:

L.S. Hope lives and works on tropical islands in the remotest reaches of Asia Pacific, managing resorts. Her work allows her access to some of the most beautiful scenes of natural spectacle and some of the most eccentric, colourful characters one could ever hope to encounter in a lifetime. She is an ardent scuba diver, an appalling housekeeper, and – at the time of writing – still a rather middling sailor. L. S. Hope has published articles in Better Mental Health magazine, and photography in DiveLog Magazine.

THE LAST VISIT

by Debra Neumann

I'm driving up to see you one last time. Our years of daily communion will soon end. I should be thinking about this, finding words – the right ones, to express myself clearly and succinctly. I must not omit anything. This is my last chance.

Instead, I'm listening to the radio, to the market reports, although I never listen to them. Today I am absorbed with the types of steel and aluminum used in the production of beer kegs. I am also absorbed in the traffic, which threatens to delay my arrival, shortening our time together. An old dump truck, trailing branches and leaves, pulls out in front of me and slows me to a 15 mile per hour crawl. I curse – why couldn't the jerk wait until I drove past the intersection to pull out? I can't think about our last visit, yet I don't want to miss one second of it.

The truck, with me in its wake, is approaching the one-lane bridge. The bridge with the five-minute wait between signal changes. I easily would have made the green, but for Mr. Jerk trucker ahead. Here I sit at the signal, chafing at time lost from our visit. I could use this extra time to compose my thoughts, but they race around like gnats – the 'no-see-ums' that bite at exposed ankles in the summer time. My anxiety made palpable.

With a screeching and clanging of gears, the truck starts up, issuing a fart of soiled air. I hold my breath, but in time am forced to inhale. The radio is now reporting the latest in unpleasant and horrifying news about the games those in power over me are playing. I switch over to the jazz station. The lyrics and music of the current tune, "The Adams Family" theme, match my mood, actually elevating it in a kind of diabolical, and frantic way. "They're creepy and they're kooky. . . They're altogether ooky . . . Strange, deranged, the Adams Family." The lyrics bounce around in my mind. I cannot escape the buzz in my brain and body. I feel like it is toying with me and recall the time my colleague's seven-year-old kid tore the heads off my daughters' dolls – each and every head and tossed them in the pool. I vow to pull my thoughts together, to allow them to settle so the clarity of my feelings about our last visit might emerge.

The early morning March sun rays pierce through the gathering clouds into the eyes of the oncoming drivers. I give thanks that it's them struggling to see oncoming traffic, and not me. I think of a book that I just finished, "Shantung Compound." The memoirist, an American expat interned at the Weihsien camp in China during World War II, describes the profound disruption of his liberal and altruistic moral foundation when he observed the self-centered, corrupt behavior of his fellow prisoners. When an American Red Cross truck arrived in the camp with a large store of food and supplies for each prisoner, no matter their nationality, the American residents claimed sole ownership of the goods, even though that meant the Americans would have sufficient goods for almost two years, while their fellow prisoners would continue to live on a bare minimum. Homo homini lupus (man is wolf to man), I reflected. The author reflected on the fact that even in the most moral and up-right individuals, self-interest and cruelty to others prevails in desperate circumstances. This is something you and I have discussed at length -- the possibility for everyone's inner wolf to attack when sufficiently terrified.

Now turning into your neighborhood, I become wolf to myself, berating myself for not using my time on the drive wisely but rather scattering my thoughts like the proverbial seeds tossed upon shallow soil. I realize that I, too, teeter on the brink of terror at the thought of seeing you for the last time.

Then I look up. The barren towering elms lining your neighborhood streets are bedecked with rose red rays of early morning sun. They shimmer like alpenglow on Vogelsang Peak. They have donned quince blossom caps to greet us this morning. I pull into your driveway and inhale this heart-rending beauty as I walk to your office. I want to show it to you, but it has vanished before you appear.

Once together, I describe my scattered state of mind on the drive this morning, and we talk about how difficult it is to say good-bye, and the anxious and angry feelings that are stirred up in me under the buzz of thoughts. I share my recollection of the beauty I encountered on my drive, the glowing caps of the trees. We reflect on the beauty of nature that can encompass the losses of life and provide a respite from this terror-sodden world.

And then it's time to take my leave. When I walk outside, the sky has transformed. It is now leaden gray and dropping tears of snow, as my tears also drop. I am held by beauty today – the beauty of the rose red rays and the mirroring tree limbs, and now by the snow. My tongue seeks to lap up a delicate flake. Drinking in this magical beauty, I want to share it with you. I've only just left, and yet I miss you so already. I send a text, "look outside if you can, it's snowing, it's magical" and your quick response, "Yes, I see!" comforts me. Yes, I feel, no matter what, you will see it with me.

About the Author:

Debra Neumann is a psychologist and emerging writer who lives and writes in Bethesda, Maryland.

ON LOSING THINGS
by Serene Jansen

A three week break from a two year shit show

I met Drew when I was eighteen years old. I just finished my first semester of college and was home visiting from San Francisco. I was still under the spell of the new and complete freedom that college in a new city had offered me. My first semester had gone well. I lost my virginity--a drunk and effervescent threesome that took place on the second floor of our college dorm. I passed all my classes even Astronomy. I made some really amazing friends. Now that I was back home I tried to keep the momentum of newness and adventure, so as restless ladies of my time are wont to do, I logged into Tinder. After filtering through the many frogs and fuckboys, I met Drew. He showed up to my parent's house with a sultry glistening smile. I saw him just as he was entering the gate and told him to wait for me in his car. I said, "Never come to the door" and he obeyed. We drove off somewhere in the hills of Hollywood, I can't remember where I just remember him lighting his backwood the second he pulled off. I giggled and watched him with a steady gaze that I so often gave then. A gaze. One that beamed at myself and not any person in particular. My voice was slow, solid. And the things I said were fleeting and uncommitted. He fell in love with this. On our way back to my house he asked if he could see me again I said I would let him know. My hook was fastened tightly around the nape of his neck and only I knew this.

My next semester was quite dark. I suppose too much of the frivolity caught up to me. I was hospitalized twice, my grades were all fails and my friends felt farther and farther from reach although they weren't. Julie especially was always patiently waiting but at the time I couldn't see it. So I isolated myself, leaving my dorm room only to eat or walk around the lake. I went through a bunch of short-lived acquaintances that were not very good company but I would entertain them anyway. My anxiety grew, my depression worsened and a semester later I dropped out. I stayed in my SF apartment for a few months, not leaving except to get groceries or if Drew was visiting. I became agoraphobic and my depression was at its peak. During that time I only saw Julie a handful of times. Not because I didn't want to or because I didn't miss her but because I was ashamed of how far I felt from happiness and I didn't want it to show. So I kept it hidden, my hands and voice shook when I saw people I knew. My relationship with Drew became a possessive one. I would call while he was away at school. I called, and called, and called on him. Eventually my parents let me move back home. I returned weary and out of touch with myself. Tristitia.

But I did have some beautiful days. I clung to the familiar: the unchanging curves of my neighborhood, the sound of my family walking through the house. I was comforted. And for a few moments in the day, I found myself unburdened by the failures.

It was Drew's turn to come back. He finished his last year of college in New York and moved back home, fifteen minutes from me. I was overjoyed. I revelled in the fact that I could see him whenever I wished. I drove around the reservoir at every chance.. I would stay with him for days and cling to him to the person I loved, unable to see how much pain he was in. He saw me not as a whimsical living thing not the mischievous creature just freshly eighteen, but as a broken, timid, inhibited being that I became. He hated that he still loved me. It was plain to see. I saw it in the sighs he took right after lighting the spliff that always rests behind his ear. In the clouds that formed over his eyes when I screamed that he was disloyal. It was in his muscles that tensed as I approached him, each time I went near him. His eyes pinched shut as if he was fighting to awaken from a painful dream. And when his mother died I clung to him harder so he didn't think I would disappear like her. Although he hated me being there. He hated my eagerness to be with him. We would look at each other and say nothing and I knew he hated that I loved him. The hook was no longer in him it was latched to my last rib, it was in me so tight that even when his pressed lips said nothing I felt it reeling.

I haven't seen him for two weeks and I suppose in another week we should reconvene and come to terms-- we have to spare each other the burden. I know that time is coming so I've been removing the hook little by little and cleaning the waste I left myself. That stinging feeling from the last couple years is still there and I know it always will be, but through that ache I can feel something in me is opening up.

ACROSS MY BROW
by Thad Elmore

Beyond the fence

I keep a garden out back just beyond the fence
If you stand on a chair
you can see it without going there
The sun is just right
the soil is dark and rich
full of worms
I keep a garden outback just beyond the fence
There are stories behind everything I plant behind everything I harvest
what I let go to seed
There is so little work to do beyond the fence
I let the ghosts pick the weeds and turn the dark rich soil
I only plant what does not die with frost
When in the darkness I look out to see my plants
The ghosts and plants wave and call
opening the gate for me
ghosts talk of the garden as if it were theirs
I keep a garden out back beyond the fence
One can lose themselves in my garden
I rarely go there the path is far too long
far too steep
And I can see it just fine from here

Across My Brow

I have seen
warriors dance on hilltops
I have seen the dark mass
of dreams hide behind
sleeping flowers
I have let sleep soft maidens
run passion across my brow
And from lips came hidden words
and from green to gold
the value of flowers shine true
I have let crickets
gather around my doorstep
And given to chance
that passion has its warriors
sleeping on HILLTOPS

About the Author:

Thad D. Elmore lives in Washington State and has returned to writing after a thirty-year hiatus. Currently volunteers with the IFRC and American Red Cross in Disaster Assesment and is active in environmental issues worldwide. Any free time is occupied by sailing, hiking and traveling every and anywhere.

ILLUSION

by Don Thompson

Waning

The crescent moon flat on its back
Bleeds out, low in the West
With no stars nearby⬚ witnesses
Who didn't want to get involved.

Illusion

No wind, but sparrows like leaves
Scatter as if blown away,
Undoing a brief illusion.
The bare tree is bare again.

About the Author:

Remorse

Residual glow on a moonless night
Must be delusion⬚ or remorse:
The dark earth itself longing for
The light it used to have.

Don Thompson has been writing about the San Joaquin Valley for over fifty years, including a dozen or so books and chapbooks. For more info and links to publishers, visit his website at http://www.don-e-thompson.com.

FORGETFUL ME

by Ross Hardy

FORGETFUL ME

I remember on our first date.
We both had a list
of questions that we wanted
to know about each other.
Years from now,
I won't remember your favorite color
but I'll remember the way
it felt when our teeth
crashed into each other when we
kissed that first time.
Like it would be the last
time either of us
would ever kiss someone.
I won't remember where
you wanted to vacation next.
But I'll remember
every color pigment in your eyes
and how they had the perfect
balance of melanin in them.
Your favorite TV show
won't even register.
But the way you'd laugh
will be the laughter track
to every comedy I watch.
The story about you riding a bike?
It's a blur.
But I remember every outline
to every tattoo on your
flawless fucking body.
There's a good chance
I won't remember the day in May
that you hated every year
because it reminded you
of a dark past.

But the way our bodies
were like a tessellation
when we spooned at night
will never escape my mind.
Where you went to high school?
Not a clue.
But I'll remember every note in
the bouquet of your breath
when you first woke up
and I'd bury my tongue
in your mouth before
you brushed your teeth.
You hated that.
I won't recall the name
of your childhood best friend.
But I'll never forget the
mellifluous tone of your voice
when you said the words
"I love you"
And I swear to every God
I don't believe in
that I'll look for it
in every whispering wind that blows.
Because even the memories
just don't do it justice.

TICK OF TIME

The sun shining through the window
is burning my right leg
as I sit there staring into space.
Dust molecules float in the air,
suspended indefinitely, moving
purposefully to nowhere in particular.
The condensation drops cascade
down the side of a glass,
meandering as they do so
as if trying to avoid something
that I can't see from where I'm sitting.
The clock in the kitchen
ticks, and tocks,
and ticks, and tocks.
Outside I see the clouds moving.
For a second I contemplate if
the earth is moving
or the clouds are.
As if it even matters.
Birds sing their verses
as the neighbors car pulls off the drive.
And everything is just so
unremarkably remarkable.
Because today is my last day.
My cocktail of vodka and pills
feel like they are burning my body
and it feels like I'm floating in air,
suspended indefinitely, purposefully.
And as I slip away
my body gives one last jolt
as if trying to avoid something
I can't see from where I'm sitting.
The birds aren't singing any more
and the clouds slow down,
and I think about how remarkably
unremarkable my life has been.
The clock stops ticking
and tocking
and time
is up

SOME NIGHTS

Some nights I go to bed
and think about you all night long,
unable to sleep,
crushed by the unending pain
that I feel.
Other nights, I sit up
writing about you into the early hours
until I'm so tired and
emotionally drained
that I fall fast asleep
and I don't think of you at all.
I still don't know which is worse.

About the Author:

Ross Hardy moved to the US at the age of 25. His writing is intended for self-healing (I think) from relationships past and is less "thought out" and more "spilling words to survive". Divorcee, father, seeker of the soul. Ok kinda guy. Horrible picture taker. Always seeking perfection.

POLITICAL

by Peter Leight

Today I got up in the morning and started promising everything I could think of,
together with some things I've never even thought of,
it makes me feel political,
I'm looking in the mirror to see what I look like
when I'm making a point
I think it's a kind of screening, as when you watch a program to see what's going to happen.
Paving the way,
just listen to yourself.
It's still early,
I'm making myself some bacon and eggs, because they get along with each other in spite of their differences,
right next to each other
or on top of each other,
the yolk running into the sputtering bacon in spite of their different appearances and disparate origins,
bacon and eggs or eggs and bacon,
and as soon as I finish eating I'm going to spend what I don't have,
I'm not thinking about myself,
I mean I'm thinking about myself but honestly the main thing is the best for the greatest number
sometimes you can't afford to
but you can't afford not to.
I know it's political because it's the type of benefit that doesn't cost anything,
not right now.
When I'm political I like to walk around without looking in front of me or turning to the side,
or turning around,
like a tugboat that pushes the other boats around
without going anywhere itself,
it isn't a weakness,
not at all,
of course there are also times when you say I wish I could
when you don't actually want to,
it's a difference in emphasis,
which makes it political.
And my voice, I want you to like it,
I really do,
I'm telling you everything,
not everything but everything you need to know.
Looking for some content, it seems so basic although we often end up with process,
it makes me feel political.

Mutual

If you give me something I'm going to give you something,
you give me half the house
I give you the other half,
I'd like you to be the person I think you are,
when you don't pick up I'm leaving a voicemail that is the story of a man who is looking for
somebody to talk to
until he finds Isolde,
and then he is happy
until it all falls apart later on.
There's no need to push the mute button, or the stop button, like a mutual process of opening up
a wound
and waiting for it to close,
honestly I think we need to trust each other
before we trust ourselves.
Right now I'm holding onto your kneecaps⁇
holding onto part of something you hold onto what it's part of,
of course it's easier when everything about the body's shape
is a handle.
If you turn the wrong way
I'm going to turn you around
until we're turning together,
I don't want to stop⁇
I'd like to tell you how much I appreciate mouth to mouth and all the other forms of
resuscitation.
I'm not asking you to leave,
even when you're not here.
Right now I'm making a mixtape that is the story of a man who doesn't have anybody to talk to
until he finds Juliet,
and then he is happy
until it is too much to bear.
I'm not even taking
what you're not giving,
sometimes you say stay with me,
and I say where are you?
I'd like to be the person I think I am,
if you tell me to stop I'm going to tell you you're the one who needs to get started.

About the Author:

Peter Leight lives in Amherst, Massachusetts. He has previously published poems in Paris Review, AGNI, Antioch Review, Beloit Poetry Journal, FIELD, Raritan, and other magazines.

Private Investigation

When I look at myself in the mirror I think about how it worked out for Socrates who was
always looking at himself,
digging in
as if scooping out the tender part,
of course everybody needs to be examined from time to time, as in the kind of medical
examination
where you're not looking for anything in particular,
you often look more closely when you don't know what you're going to see,
giving it your full attention⬚
you don't want to mess with your attention.
In the mirror my mouth is open,
my eyes are moist, as if there's something I'm not responsible for,
not pointing fingers,
not at all,
there isn't any point.
I don't even notice my hands leaving me
and coming back to me
as if they're passing secret information, information I don't know anything about, even though
they don't need to.
In the mirror my mouth is a red hole full of information,
I'm trying to keep my eyes open, but it's not always possible,
not all the time,
there's no need to apologize,
no point,
okay you apologize what happens next?
We often watch ourselves, keeping an eye on ourselves as if we're looking at somebody we're
not sure we trust,
somebody who's not completely responsible⬚
it's the kind of camouflage where you know what you're seeing
but not what it is.
You tell yourself I didn't mean to,
didn't you?
Personally as long as it's a secret I'm going to forget it right away,
I've forgotten all about it,
I already have⬚
that way I won't be tempted.
When I look in the mirror I'm thinking about Socrates calmly sipping his soup, like an accident
nobody's responsible for,
I mean there are errors,
you get an error message⬚
you're not thinking it's your error,
not necessarily,
when there's an error you try a lot of different things to make sure nothing works,
sometimes you tell yourself I'll find something that does.
I think I'll blame myself this time.

TONIGHT

by John Horvath

WORRY ABOUT A LOVER WHO EAGERLY RUSHES TO WORK EACH MORNING

I feel she does not love me as she had so long ago;
It's not some thing she's said or done, but something that I know
Deep in my heart and soul. I feel she doesn't love me so
Delay to ask the question whose answer will make me go.

Every morning when I awake she is already gone
Greedily to work: it's not the pay nor respect she's won:
One lover is not enough for a woman who is blonde.
She does not love me; I will go. I shall go soon, be gone.

Love is a frightful thing to own; it mingles jealousy
Inside itself with unsaid thoughts to make false memory.
Before the sun is down at end of day, there is no WE
"In love"; for, love has turned to lust and sex revengefully.
"Damned Bear" she calls me when back home: so eagerly -
Oh, how she craves - my tearing off her clothes for sex, you see.

She makes me worry just to have me at the end of day.
What's left is right when we set right imagined wrongs.
As age enfolds, it is the only game we still will play.

TONIGHT

I am yours 'til earth crumbles
too soon, too soon it crumbles
dogs howling along the streets
bitches marking their discontent
too soon it crumbles, too soon
be mine 'til moonfall and daybreak

REVE

doctoring smallish parts,
color of tablecloth whose
frayed edges flag in mid-
day summer breeze when we
met alongside creek built
dams under trees despite
humming insects, ignoring
water giggling over slate
and bedrock, into evening
insect infested when we
hurried to your apartment
to disrobe to examine what
new marks might lay claim
to our having been together
that summer day at creek-
side by tables covered in
green clothe whose frayed
threads waved to us good-
bye because love doctors
memory so happily ever...

TOO YOUNG, TOO SHORT FOR LOVE

at night alone, though proud of his
accomplishment, he lay in bed and wondered
whether he'd been her first, a face and name,
a man forever set apart from other men or had
there been a someone else for whom
she moaned, for whom her arms were meant?
He'd never know, like other men before him
never knew as would those coming after
know where he had been among her list
of long forgotten names. I'd very like
to know, he said almost aloud (the faintest
echo upon his bedroom ceiling broke
and all its fragments were absorbed
by this or that apparel he had too often
promised he would clean and straighten
up). Weren't there more important things
that he should be about? And, what about
those thoughts that needed close attention
in his unmade bed at night? He rose from
failed sleep in the middle of the night
to phone. It rang and rang and rang quite
much; he figured that she wasn't home.

Where had she gone? To someone else's house?
No, he'd left her dead, there was nothing
He should fret about. She couldn't move.
A petit death, the angels must have lifted
her to heaven when he fell asleep upon
her naked flesh dark as almonds, sweet
as cane, roiling like a rapid river during flood.

And yet... There was no blood. Was that a sign?
He'd heard it was the mark of first fling
or something near to that. My god, sixteen's
a bitch of time for having sex! No. Hard
as he thought, there was no blood, nor even
a small sign of it. He called her once again.

The phone rang once. Her muffled voice
as if from deepest sleep was there. And,
when he told her his thoughts then asked
whether he'd been first, she'd said, "Don't
trouble your sad self all night with that;
you were the first and probably the last;
now don't call back." So there he sat.
Where he had thought. Alone at night.

What was the name she gave him amid
the rampage of his love and lust: did
she call out "Swarthy" or "Shorty"
(he didn't know; he likely never would).
He stayed awake all starry night.

ORIOS WITHOUT HIS CHOSEN LADY

Orios on the morning of the twelfth
pretends he is not alone in bed,
has never been; his large hands
reach across linen to a stuffed pillow
soft and round, encased in the scent
of secret perfume, the kind she wore
when they had met then been together
(lovers unexpectedly she'd thought,
although he knows the shape and bulk
and use of words, how one might
lead if wed correctly to the next
to this so soft block, his roomy bed
of soundless delights). He swore
at emptiness then closed his eyes
against the fact that she had left
long before dawn on cattish toes,
without a whisper of goodbye, no kiss
(Orios had pretended sleep; he knew
she'd rise and walk against growing old
with him, perhaps together until death).

She had moved nimble without a sound.
He'd heard her breath, as if she feared
that he might wake and strike her down
(oh, yes, he wished he had) or bar
her exit (that too he wished) to hold
her always at his side. Orios alone
again at morning shaves his crooked
jaw and looks upon an ugly face. Its
nose half flat against his cheeks, ears
too grand and pendular.

Squinty eyes too narrow and too dark,
like blackened peas; his hair unkempt.
But he was large and muscular so that
in dimlit places late at night he might
be taken for quite a catch. Soft-spoken
too. He knew words' shape and bulk
and use so used them well in order
to entice his chosen lady to his lair.
But once-- just this once-- he wished
the woman he had chosen would
remain despite the truth of ugliness
that had appeared near dawn. Why get
out and go about a normal day as if
he were a man and not a beast?
Or, perhaps, it is the beast in each
of us, Orios thought, that makes
us act instinctively toward work and
lust. She would be back. Or, another
would soon take her place. Each
morning he would make that bet.

About the Author:

Mississippian John Horváth Jr publishes internationally since the 1960s (recently in Munyori Review (Zimbabwe); Broad River Review (print). Pyrokinection, Pink Litter, and Olentangy Review). After Vanderbilt and Florida State universities, "Doc" Horváth taught at historically Black colleges. Since 1997, to promote contemporary international poetry, Horváth edits www.poetryrepairs.com.

MUSIC BEHIND THE MELODY
by Jean-Mark Sens

Music behind the melody

Leave the melody behind to hear the music
coming out of the sound, notes plucked
run quick over the sidewalk, shoes tapping and stiletto crescendo,
a rumbling of trains, pianograffity⬛ Mingus
A Chinese dynasty⬛ the clarity of vases
resounds Charlie⬛ Ivory smooth of fioriture's
like Don the see the stars in a glass⬛ Perignon
and the kids in Kansas---eyes erased to snow motions on and off
the screen and screams what's more real than the shadows
a challenge to Plato of phenomenological double bass.
Notice the Doctor said that summer your face asymmetrical
lumped on one side---silent stroke
a musical aphasia? Bell Palsy of a percussionist
and how not to buy it coming from a specialist,
hologram on his smock? Pictures won't even tell.
Check otorhinolaryngologist---as if something wrong in the music box of your face
tabbed your cheeks, the end nerves of your skin
and that evening⬛ all inconclusive⬛
listen to Mingus⬛ left the melody behind
for the music and nothing to find crooking your lips,
turned and smiling.

Lips

It is only recently I have noticed
the many lips women leave behind
seasonal and changing to circumstances
they color their lips
the classic red, the auburn hue, the young and trendy
silvery blush, and some others of more extreme glossiness
even a rebellious velvet blue of a teenager
as if to accentuate this mysterious aperture
the worlds come back and forth through us
transmuting words and air
the tongue lolls and longs inside▯
lips women leave behind
semi-moons on paper coffee cups
a red rim on a cigarette
as to give back something out of the evanescent smoke
or the strange imprint
pursed lips on a napkin that unfold an oval silence
opened almost like an eye.

Lips multiplied to the marks they leave,
floating out of the mouths that bore them▯ like butterflies
as in a dream escaping
sensual and ephemeral imprints
more than desires can read
and coming back to me
those lips of a new year revelry
quick and elusive among the throng
the tease of yours I found years later in a kiss.

At the hospital my brother directs an art therapy workshop.
Lips appear often on drawings red and out of proportions
wanting to say what the mind can't articulate,
voluble silent a hand traces
and the women especially smear moon circles.
Once a participant rounded an O mouth with lipstick over the window
and wrote in reverse inside "We're in/ You're out,"
a divide transparent and tangible,
A lost kiss floating in the air for all to read to red.

Today you belong to the rain

The eyes of needles through its curtain.
It murmurs its own eternity.
Realm of gutters, culverts
its flowing in echo of a few discrete songs.
It belongs to the city⬚ glazes it
gives yellow eyes to busses, tiptoes avenues
fast high-heel clatters of its run.
The rain weaves silent threads
wet drapes stepping out open and close in
a passage on the air waves
news recitations, currencies dipping,
rise on interest, rice field profits
rattling billions of grains bagged from chutes.
You belong to the rain which does not belong to you.
It polishes your face bent over the banister
a ship sails two dimensional against the mist
chartered shells of cargo containers
parts to parts UNLIMITED the whole puzzle of a factory
a present presence interloper of its own journey
it withdraws, migrates washing colors behind to a new brightness
insects, plants, a spell of freshness as through spontaneous creation
a clear horizon, rebirth over sidewalks and gangways, a few promeneurs
your face wet with a new rain from under your skin
the rain you belong to within/ without your body⬚ 80% humidity the air and you.

About the Author:

Born in France, **Jean-Mark Sens** has lived in the American South for over twenty years. He candidate for priesthood at Notre Dame Seminary in New Orleans. His work has been published in the U.S. and Canada, and he has a collection, Appetite, with Red Hen Press:

http://redhen.org/book/?uuid=26010B90-F50B-AE04-1A31-0B86BB199EA4

He is also working on culinary book Leafy Greens & Sundry Things

LUNCH WITH JESUS

by Belinda Subraman

Lunch With Jesus

We held hands around the table
at Applebee's and prayed before eating.
Fox Network was there and low self-esteem.
"The white cops were right," they chanted.
"More people need beating,
We need more guns.
Too many getting rich off welfare
too lazy to work."
"Christians have no rights," one claimed.
"What about the Christians?"
I kept quiet. Dogs were howling for meat.
Jesus turned his head away.
Bibles slept in their cars.

Memory Is a Woodpecker Tree

We snuggle down for the cold
joyous greed and mercy
in carols of nebulous infinite love
and slaughter
where Biblical Yin-Yang
produce branding codes
tethered to12 layers of selves
half of them lovers
half of them trees
unnaturally used for torture
and cartoon sweetness.

Zen
gelatinous cauliflower magic
constructs reality as a river,
illusion with no legs
where everything is wet
and not one drop matters more
than another.

Trees with holes
leak sap eaten
and recycled by birds
who nourish life underground,
life that eats our death
when the coffins rot
and what we thought we were becomes
feces from thousands of worms.

The Unlikely Professor

is a serious poet
playing at teaching
what he believes
cannot be taught.

He's a sexy sexagenarian,
keeps a centerfold layout
in his open book
as he teaches,
gets hot on the subject
(sizes up the girls
in class
imagines them
spread out,
stapled).
The students admire
his smile, his lines,
his enthusiasm
and his strong, tall
podium
which hides his firm
disbelief.

Date Rape

First date,
he swings the car off the road,
says he has something for her,
the movie can wait.

Like a bank
hoping to earn interest,
he offers her money.
She withdraws.

Then he tries inserting himself
like a coin
into a vending machine,
want to bang impatiently
for the candy.

In the end
he prises her open
like a plumber
unclogging his pipes...
then asks her
if she loves him.

BEYOND THE HEAVENS
by Edward Bonner

Radiant Flames

The shifting currents
shoulder the cerebral coast,
sending sediment
through your brain.
Instinctively the mind wakes
more quickly to agony,
than a star-shaped heart
radiant with flames.

Brushing silica
from your fingers...
Scars of persuasion
like a violent storm.
The darkened skies
behind your lidded eyes
wild with wind
and beautifully formed.

This field wields it's bouquet:
hypnotic, exotic and consuming.
Our bodies tossed on thick moss,
surrender in kudzu,
soaked with sweat.
Too late to understand,
fate was in our hands.

Thanks to co-author Jocelyn Vaughan

Hovering Beyond the Heavens

Hovering beyond the heavens
the verdant dawn,
awed by the auric benefaction
of a painted horizon
saturated by our Mother's
dulcet murmured benediction.

Perched high in an oak,
a magniloquent Martin
harmonized
melodies manifest
with grace and delight
and the caress of the
mourning dove's coo.

Westerly winds
entwined the land
where secrets behold
from her tender hand.

Rejoice with the blessing of
Divinity's voice.

Howling Echoes

Lonely is the wilderness blanketed with snow,
whose ember eyes reflect a most dazzling glow.

In the twilight sky she hunts alone,
scanning the forest upon her throne.

Brilliant stars covet the earth.
Rising thermals embrace the secret spells
of nature's mirth.

Her first howl echo's through the misty hollow.
The alpha male perks up his ears and follows.

Together they search for prey.
A series unfolding they hunt for days.

Intelligent, cunning and calculating.

Hunger drives their instincts to excel.
An inbred survival of hidden spells.

Rhythmic sound waves shatter the sky.
Eyes slowly adjust to pinpoint why.

A cry from an elk, it's life in despair.
Holding tight, the wolves run in pairs.

Their ecstasy is mastered through a paradox of existing.
Only in the end, life will be forgiving.

Salivating.
Licking.
Chomping.
This surging wrath becomes a prosperous ending.

God's chosen to thrive,
these beautiful animals will survive.

Intoxicating Passion

As the earth time changed in early spring.

Somewhere now he stands, steam pouring from his body.
Heat and humidity screaming, but no breeze.

Her pulsating heart crossed over with trembling hands.

This hysteria is an intoxicating passion wrapped around their delirious emotions.

To the lips of forgotten fruit,
let them pass between rivers,
moistened for thirst of a delicate star.

Their hidden grace 'neath lace unraveled by the rosebud's thorn.
And when they transcend, petals unveil in a storm.

Eclipsed by Eros's shadow.
A pervasive zephyr begins to burnish their flesh like pearls refracted through glass.

A love completely spontaneous and uninhabited absorption.
Followed by a perfumed fragrance,
life's consummation has been fulfilled.

Thanks to co-author Jocelyn Vaughan

Nature's Silhouette

Darkness will cover what is hidden by light.
It let's you caress the imagination
of unknown sight.

Distorted shades play a story
only the character can assemble.
Ethereal images are accented
with beauty or ghostly tremble.

Calm winds whisper a solemn song
and the young fiddlehead ferns
wake for their turn.

Fresh, hushed, mesmerized hues
glimmer against the trees,
lightly covered with dew.

And there she is.
Her sculptured limbs flowing with design.
Curves of luscious sweetness
enveloped our pulsating minds.

A peace that captured the eyes of grace
answered to nature's calling place.

About the Author:

Edward Bonner grew up in a small mill town in Pittsburgh Pennsylvania.Hazelwood, Pa. A very rough neighborhood. Raised by his mother and grandparents until he was 13 years old. That's when his mother remarried. He then moved to a suburb south of Pittsburgh. Growing up, he probably got into trouble like most kids. An avid outdoorsman. 5th degree black belt / 36 years in Shotokan karate. Author of "One Kiss" Just One Kiss. A collection of love poems and more. Author of Through The Eyes Of A Lost Boy. A collection of poetry about "Love, Loss, Trauma, Pain and Healing." A journey of life through writing.

A STUDIO DISTURBANCE
by John Grey

UNCLE RAY'S MEMORIES OF VIETNAM

In one battle
he saw a soldier
ripped to pieces
by barbed wire and shell,
and the guy pleaded with Uncle Ray
to put him out of his misery.

And he was in a club in Saigon
where a band was playing Latin music
and that combo was really fantastic
but only the whores were dancing.

A STUDIO DISTURBANCE

A large room
as studios go,
light from east window
and skylight –

I narrowed my eyes
so they completed the circuit
with hand and brush and canvas and model.

My subject sat
enclosed in fine skin,
firm flesh,
her head proud and erect.

She placed her feet
firmly on the floor
and her left hand
rested on her right knee,
arched her shoulders
to meet her tossed-back hair.

Were she just a woman
she would have
disturbed my thoughts
greatly.

But she was my model.
She disturbed my thoughts
abstractly, intellectually,
transcendently and hypothetically.
Oh yes, and greatly.

LAST I SAW OF THE BARNETTS

They were as bankrupt economically
as that so-called preacher on TV was morally
except he didn't have to leave his fancy mansion
and their modest cottage couldn't wait
to see the last of them.

The husband took all his clothes off
and was found wandering in the suburban mall
after closing hours.
His wife considered suicide
but settled for a job scrubbing hospital floors.
The kids took to booze and drugs,
both before the foreclosure and after.

That was when the stock market collapsed
and some folks pissed their savings away.
And everybody sued everybody else
to ensure the ascension of lawyers into heaven.

The husband promised to keep his clothes on
from that day forth.
The wife developed a herniated disc in her back.
One kid checked himself into a clinic to dry out.
The other didn't.

That was when lives
that weren't travelling so smooth anyhow
were side-swapped or smacked head on,
and some went crazy
and others hunkered down and started over.

The husband and wife are still together.
They see their kids once in a while.
Everyone somehow survives
though I don't know how.
But then it's like I'm viewing things
from something like Google Earth.
You never know when the picture was taken.

About the Author:

John Grey is an Australian poet, US resident. Recently published in Fall/Lines, the Coe Review and Columbia Review with work upcoming in Cape Rock, Poetry East and Midwest Quarterly.

SUNRISE

by George Korolog

Smelling as a Position

Now there is just the hard cement under your feet,
a foot path where birds might surprise you
with a suggestion to inhale deeply

and spindle downward, featherlike,

off the road,

rolling into the absolute certainty of dirt,

acrid and stinging, like you remembered,
before everything had all gone bad.

They are singing in the swells

of air that used to be nestled
around you,

like tendrils of mist rising from block ice,
a nose planted in a well oiled glove,

or a face, nestled in honeysuckle,
or something smelling blustery

if you only turned in the right direction.

The bouquet of tar bubbling on the street,

the perfume on her sweater,

inhaled so deeply that
you forgot how to breathe.

The scent of sweat panting.

Now the world is just clean lines

and competent design
pretending to provide a path,
even as you turned your back on it.

You didn't want to be noticed sniffing
or having someone steal

you away on the inhale.

You wanted to stay in it more than you knew.

Sunrise

The sun is adamant.
It traces the world with fiery fingers,

filaments intent on their own slow rising,

insinuating with a taunt,

teasing the underside of the nether world,

while blotting the new sky

with ribbons of fresh color,

like a new painter blossoming forth

with coming promise,

with the gradual reassurance

of time to settle

into the rhythm of change,

preparing us for the moment

when it reaches the other side

and begins, once again,

to take back the light.

The sun does not choose to spew

and splatter wildly.

It takes the fight out of us in silky measure

and soothes

the world into gradual change.

It knows that if it rose too quickly,

our eyes would melt through

the cracks in the hands that

were held up to cover our face.

The sun does not want a fight.

It beautifies and refuses

to leave us alone with the pain

in our terrified eyes.

It comes with the promise of return,

of slow transit, and the assurance

of an unbearable beauty

that we dare not face.

Twilight

I strode into your
raw fluttering,
your exhibitionism,
thinking of us,
both willing as moths.
I looked up and saw you,
tonguing the last of the sky
with your marble dreams,
rocking burnt amber
crescents
slowly across the wind,
your sad crimson bleeding
across a macaroon sky,
I reached out and
cupped the scent of your color
to my face and inhaled,
hoping to fathom
fathomless things.
Did you miss me
hiding in the far corners,
blushing myself,
waiting for you to arrive?
I am desperate to transform
you into the purest white
but I am consumed by
gobbets of recollection,
by the greyest blue,
seeping with me into the ground.

blood moon

The moon is hanging in there
with a big ego,
receding at one and a half inches per year.
It's not a trick.
10,000 years ago the Sahara desert
was wet with frogs
and the moon was four football fields
closer to earth,
reminding me again
that I become when I listen
to the growing distance
of my own round image,
embarrassingly red.

About the Author:

George Korolog is a San Francisco Bay Area poet and writer whose work has appeared in over 100 literary journals internationally, including The Los Angeles Review, The Southern Indiana Review, The Bookends Review, Tar River Review, Pithead Chapel and many others. He has twice been nominated for the Pushcart Prize and twice for Best of the Net. He can often be found backpacking alone in the mountains or forests, along the ocean or in the desert, and is sometimes known to write on bark and rocks with pine quills. His first book of poetry, "Collapsing Outside the Box," was published by Aldrich Press in November 2012, His second book of poems, "Raw String" was published in October, 2013 by Finishing Line Press. He is working on his third book of poems, "The Little Truth."

MISSING MESSAGES
by David Ryan Palmer

The White Letters

Dearest son,

I hope this letter finds   well. I have not seen   address since the accident, but my friends here have interesting ways of knowing things. I was not sure I would like the   but once I real-ized that I was not looking anymore, I became used to it. I have found that I can become used to anything.

I do miss   father, but my   here told me that   has his own friends, now.   tell me that   is still looking, and so is not used to his new color. I do not have much time to think about him, and   discourage me. Instead, I write to you, my own darling son.

Are   still seeing that man? Even as most mothers want to become grandmothers, and I know I harped on that so much in the past, my   have told me that more children are not always the answer.   discourage me here, too. Grandchildren without a grandmother are not grand-children, they say.   discourage everyone here from asking for grandchildren. My   do not think it is worth the effort, any longer.

Do   still have that calendar I gave to   ?   should mark December, any day in December. The day itself does not matter, only that   come. Bring   man - my new friends would like to meet him! They would like to meet everyone, even if when   meet them, they do not much like their color. Like with   father.

Oh, there I go again. It is a bad habit, dear, dwelling on the past. My   tell me about the future, about December. Remember, my son, and come to   in December. The end of the year was always my favorite time. I only regret that my   here are not overly fond of New Year parades.

     do not see the point. But for me, I do not see. I became used to it.

Love in eternity,

Mother

Hungry Moon

In school, they encouraged them to shoot for the moon.
The engineers, who never really worked in metaphor,
sent men atop redirected violence and hit lunar paydirt.

They found grey dust and craters full of void.
Three years later they stopped going,
left the lunar scape littered with metals and patriotism.

In school, they encouraged them to shoot for the moon.
The poets, whose skill at metaphor increased with age
sent words out into the negative between mother and child.

Curious, the moon drifted close to look,
and in looking found it wanted.
In wanting, it found hunger, too.

They found meaning in phases and cycles,
cause poets will find meaning in all places.
They didn't expect meaning to find them.

In school, they encouraged them to shoot for the moon.
And landing there, the poets and engineers did not guess
That the moon would come for them.

The moon found red movement and green silence,
it cast a metaphor about its marble blue neighborhood,
a mind woken by the feet of ants on its skin.

In school, they encouraged them to shoot for the moon.
The military opened up more constructed explosions,
this time in dense packages to the silver lunar soil.

And all the explosions of the engineers
and all the maneuvers of the military
may have scarred the lunar surface, still it came.

In school, they encouraged them to shoot for the moon.
But when the moon rose last the only thing left
were rust and wilt and young dead words.

Ink Heavy Dawn Clouds

It is ebony black.
If you ink heavy clouds
your other senses report in:
smooth and cool, soft, with
raised goose down as I explore.
Some would come to this land
seeking conquest.
A quickening wind, waves
which signal codes,
followed by a low tone
it escapes, rolls down
smooth and cool wonder
alights on waiting ears.
Conquest means different things.
This land responds to my touch.

It is red orange.
If you stay up all night
your sanity's reports will garble:
first, a crawling sky blushes,
renewed and flush as a lover.
Some would come to the sky
seeking answers.
A quick open panic
the deep sky
spreading through as a warm drug.
It overtakes, swells up
a crawling worried wonder.
Your hand covers mine.
Answers mean different things.
This sky awakens to our touch.

About the Author:

David Ryan Palmer is a graduate student pursuing his Masters of Arts at McNeese State University in Southwest Louisiana. He spends too much time on Youtube, and just enough time petting his two cats, Quinn and Foster, and not enough time petting his fiance, Michelle.

ARTISAN

by Anthony Lawrence

As Down is to Snow

We wake holding hands.
It is early, yet too late
to return to sleep.

I had surfaced to lines
by Robert Frost - one
where a horse stops

to shake the bells
of its harness, and one
that tells of how

promises are to keep
as down is to snow.
You had woken to

a detail in a painting
by Richard Diebenkorn
in which the ocean

meets the land head-on.
If anything had been
uncertain or withheld

during the night, it has gone
as a tram breaks
over the sound of rain.

Leonard Cohen

At a Jewish food stall, considering knaidlach,
shakshuka and falafel, Leonard Cohen took my
order. His apron was dusted with fingerprints.
His name badge flashed in the sun as he moved
along tables, describing ingredients. When I
asked about the origins of cochin coriander-
and-cumin chicken, he spoke of spices and the
shipwreck that saw his descendants settle in
Mumbai, in 175 BCE. He talked of eating fra-
grant strings of goat meat in the light of Sab-
bath oil lamps. I bought carrot halva and a bag-
ful of bagels and he wished me well, suggesting
I return to try his masala lamb stew -A tonic for
the heart and soul, he said, with loving attention to the weight and sound of each syllable.

Inheritance

Begin with a cast-iron pan, handed down
from a long line of kitchen magicians
on your father's side, men and women

who understood the word season
and its implications
for the way metal cultivates a sheen

like tannin from traces of earth
released over heat and time, yet now
it appears more expansive in style

and form, its handle like a stem of shadow
coaxed from a Dryden couplet
so prepare a meal

by shaving mangrove tapers
into the swim-bladder of a fish
whose name means atoll

and leave it to simmer in the brine
it was lifted from, along with the liquid
from peppers so red

you had bundled the rest
like pliable ampules of blood
tied with string dyed green from a nettling

and after the eyes of the fish go to cloud
and the gills close the way
bivalves rock shut when they're sick

shuffle the pan
until flame pours over the sides
then add slivers of kelp

with a flourish you learned
from watching your father in smoke and steam
and before serving what the sea and land

have conspired to make visceral, say a few words
in praise of the shoreline and reef
something that speaks to how

wading birds read the margins of the tide
then sit down with your loving
attention to detail, and rejoice.

Cleaning Trout

Spangled drongos were leaving the trees in theatrical collapse.
I'd cleaned a table of trout, my hands lit with scales.

Attempting the call of a bird with a long forked tail
I disturbed a Labrador, a breed whose bark I can tell

from collie, kelpie, mongrel. Then a man chimed in
with the kind of abuse I'd heard when playing rugby, lying

under a maul. A dog yelped. A man signed off on his vitriol
by slamming a door. Twice. Too late to consider

how fishing kills what I love in communal or pelagic form
I put the fish on ice and threw their gills to the gulls.

With a feeling like I'd lost or forgotten something
I drove home.

Artisan

A box of old-style drill bits and plane blades
like a pain monger's inventory.
A brass plumb machined by hand
in a stutter of lamplight, when Shakespeare
was sipping a wreath of smoke from a pipe
with a starling skull for a bowl.
And as for the theory
that if your old man could make a cabinet
from celery pine, the grains aligned
to give the impression of pale flames
and despite having never shown interest
in working with timber, you can still
craft a bookshelf with dovetailed joins
from offcuts and driftwood...
just saying the word carpentry
is enough to give me shingles.
So when I see, on the cover
of Hand-Made Homes, that someone
has raised the canopy of a rainforest
as a sky pavilion, or I take a virtual tour
of a cliff-top eyrie with a lift
from cinema to helipad through a shaft
in the limestone, I give thanks
for my two thumbs, a desk, lamp
and chair in a room someone else has made
so I can make this.

About the Author:

Anthony Lawrence has published fifteen books of poems. His most recent collection, 'Headwaters' won the 2017 Prime Minister's Award for Poetry. He teaches Creative Writing at Griffith University, Queensland.

THESE ARE THE OPEN ARMS

by Ralph Geeplay

These Are the Open Arms

You woke me up
when I was dead,
teaching the night
stars wantonly to obey
the Atlantic; then slashed
my arteries in flight
to Lake Piso, humbling
its boundaries, before fusing
them calmly to a gel.
When the elders speak
in parables, it is a mix of
pepper soup which the fufu
welcomes and surrounds.
As the deer is trapped
in the undergrowth,
so does it waits to be strapped.
---These are the open arms
to the farms, mucking the
deserted mansions decked
in chocolate nuts, covered
in honey; the lost spectacles
of yesterday now over.
Once gowned with cluttered
cow-webs and peppered
with shrubs, this, before
the revival of the
grimy walls, serenade
and greened with lilies
whose aroma calls
from a hundred miles
to the carpenter---the tool
man and his bride waiting to be
announced as the sun swell the
hilltops, smiling to the boats
sailing on smooth tides.

II

Moving quietly to fair waves,
the clouds crushed, hovers,
washing the mud away,
freeing her from the rocks,
bathing the earth
and taking away
the dust disguised as chaffs.
the yacht's inviting voice is
heard throttling along
---between hearty murmurs,
chuckling to the weaving
currents, curving the Atlantic surf,
dancing fervidly, where the fires
meet the pits of burning woods.
The hearth in a melody on the
placid shores of Sinkor, intimately
as Monrovia grins to the Atlantic.

III

Bewitched, racing to the beaches
is a sweetening of the surf stones.
The shells humbled under the rocks.
In trance, the turtles are running
with the whales, the currents,
silvery, the smell of salt water
overpowering, yet elegant. Your
slender sailing finger rubbing
my rough ankles brings comfort.
---You woke me up when
I was dead, teaching
the night stars wantonly
to obey the Atlantic bay,
like seashells humbled under the rocks.

Africa

Africa, this sun drenched bliss,
come to Botswana and see
the terrific translucent creeks
of Okavango Delta, as it blends
with the sun rays and glistened.
Let the unmistaken eyes
catch the stretched neck zebra,
graceful---game in the name
of Africa. Its beautiful furs
decorated in broad strokes,
rising in circular waves, from head,
to hind. Now feast your eyes
on the herd of elephants and
the desert radiant landscape
of the Savute --- Africa, oh Africa!
The motherland ever so enchanting;
the beautiful safari,
and her handsome subtropical
wasteland, home to the Kalahari.
Then the overstretched sandy, salient
Desert, as she greets the Tourag of Mali.
Supple as their camels, nomads
and traders of the Sahara.
The colossal evergreen forest,
wildlife, and plateaus of Liberia.
From palm to palm, crystal clear
beaches along the Atlantic, vista.
Thrilling oasis of waters from
the Congo to Lake Victoria.
The land of my Fathers and its
stunning rapture---Africa, oh Africa.
Let me glean with naked eyes the
loveliness of the Table Mountains
in Cape Town, and live in Soweto
for a day, a borough of feisty warriors.
To stomp my feet as they do when
they dance and protest unreservedly.
In the land of the quiet giant, who took
on and beat Robin Island with glee,
then crushed it to dust in one palm.
Spectacular chronicle for generations.
The land of the Pharos,
The beautiful---Africa oh, Africa!

Masekela!
I can touch the rhythm of your beats,
and sense the chirpy throb; the music
streams it currents to my pulse, the
hair on my skin rises, the trumpet
ricochets, filling the room, seizing the
passages in my veins! I am drifted,
to the swings of the melody, the
harmony synchronizes, its bliss is
on the hill which now fills my mind!
　A bass once stole my dancing feet,
　Whistling away on the veld in Witbank.
Oh, Masekela. With my snapping
fingers, the pulsating tempo is curving
my arteries, there is feasting in the
fields and a Grazing in the Grass, the
herds with nudged cadences can
barely hold their joy, feeding off the
Jazz, synchronized with Kuti, Makeba,
and the gifted Huddleston.
Your trumpet wore the piano, and a voice that
seduced the dancers, caressing to
melodic sway, rings the saxophone-man,
whose fervor tenor blasted, then won
against Apartheid, now drives away,
leaving me, to an empty room, to
which, sits a set of idle instruments.
　Who is going to stroke the trumpet?
　And beat the bass, and own the saxophone?
Where his shiny flutes once breathed,
now silence pervades to rust
laden winds. The gadgets left behind
glossed with silvery gleam beckoning
to be picked up from the stage that
once flung them to being in Soweto.
Is it true that Pepper birds live in
those hoary tubes, singing beautiful
strains, whistling to the moon?
Or that in your opus, love invites a
romantic ocean filled with golden surfs,
laced with cords of grooves? Which drifts
softly to the waiting night, to be picked up.
In the music I know, there is hope
flying on the horizon, with no brawls in the
way to hinder its flawless trail,
　now lost on the stage that once
　flung them to being in Soweto
[in tribute to Huge Masekela:]
---1939-2018/January

Farewell to Ellen

It rains so much in Monrovia
that a day is like the bloated dough
on a grey earthly May, washing
over October. My love, the sun, hides
in her bright den refusing to be seen.
Life comes to a slow twiggy motion;
   the forest is breathing with moisture,
   like a hut puffing smoke as a pipe.
While the creeks bridged their ledges, 09
there is a seismic run-down Waterside!
Enough, no more, the sewage can take!
She is in my arms, listening to the music
pounding the roof. Still, calm, reading
Ebony Dust, though, with lightning bolts
   yelling to be heard. The clatter is like
   a rumble---tumbling falling rockets.
The sorry corrugated zinc holds her seams,
the bed is dry, but the room is a puddle. 18
The city is cramp and damp, like a soaked
sponge dripping with water.
The hustling contested old city in
an evening fog, the Mesurado in
   a bulge, taking Fanti fishermen
   to and fro, to the edge of Westpoint.
To love in the midst of mists,
of raging thunder under your ears
and an air filled with blithering 26
vermin, is to drink a linctus in
anger, cooped in wretched penury.
So when the wait, cannot wait
   to be over, you my love must endure,
   waiting to part with the wrath the rains
imposed, much needed however,
to calm the California wildfires,
gifted on these shores, for free. Now:
you understand, then,
the irony of nature! 36

About the Author:

Ralph Cherbo Geeplay was born in Pleebo, Southeastern Liberia, West Africa. He is among the younger Liberian youth who were forced to attend college during the brutal Liberian civil war. Geeplay, studied at the University of Liberia, majoring in Journalism, and while still a student worked in the media during the 1990s, starting in radio broadcasting at the Liberia Broadcasting System (LBS), the national radio, and later worked with Radio Liberty before freelancing with Radio Monrovia where he worked as a producer and reporter. He later transitioned to the print media, particularly, with the Monrovia Inquirer Newspaper, where he worked as a senior staff reporter. Geeplay published his first set of poems in 2009 in the Liberian Sea Breeze Journal, edited by Stephanie Horton. His themes include: Africa, the Liberian civil war and its tragedy, his Grebo heritage, and everything in between. He is the editor of an online journal, The Liberian Listener, and lives in Edmonton Alberta, Canada, with his family.

GHOST GUMS

by Jan Napier

Eqalussaq
(Greenland Shark)

far
far
below
Inuits skimming skin kayaks   uncertain bergs   foghorn's mourning
d
o
w
n
where the world is dark and fluid   there giants swim
fin slow   slow   kilometres   seek and feed
where ship bones broken by pack ice snap and crack
men's soft pink bodies
m
o
t
i
n
g
into silt
sliding beyond kraken's haunt   sharks hear nothing but skreek
of floe   faint scrape of walrus tusking molluscs

    observe short sighted scientists in habitats of tin
goggling at depths netted to empty   metal tick ticking
limits   as caught in flash's actinic shock   tasting
only tainted water   monsters cruise deeper

    pursue the surety of obscurity
become mythic   and not yet extinct
s
i
n
k
into shamanic vision

PINK QUARTZ PEBBLE

Who knows how to speak the philosophy of stone?
Each pebble dust humble but not easily formed for all that.

Born of heat lacking in pain and expectation,
skin rough and lightly pink, crystalline meld of silica
and oxygen warms in the hand after a moment spent

in touch, and is relevant, always relevant, as a red
feather dropped, or tadpole ponded in a universe
as mysterious and necessary as any.

No sin splits its existence. So if frost and fire and soil
conspire to alter place or structure, unbuild it to some
new symmetry, then nothing is lost, that too being strange

and perfect and marvellous as sunlight on lemons,
or the brownian motion of tea in a cup.

Landscaped as part of matrix, this small god, translucent
and ever as the rest, was there at the beginning, but
who knows how endings go?

GHOST GUMS

Ghost gums, signage etched in desert
tells nomads where water rests far below
limestone; eroded caverns smashed, Devonian,

home to beetles and mites, echidna,
numbat, lizard, mummified, dried; cave fish
flickering like tapers lit to defend

against darkness; deeper lithography
alive with myths, glyphs, sea creatures seared
into dreaming, ciphers to pools secreted

before stories. Roots of these eucalypts crack rock,
suck softness far from parch. Women filling
emu eggs from seepage, glance at wagyl

on boulder; white ochre trees, yodelling
dingoes, smoke of birds, each easy to read
as spoor of explorer and horse drooping exhausted
further into the dry.

About the Author:

Jan Napier is a Western Australian poet whose work has been showcased in anthologies and journals both at home and overseas. Jan's first poetry collection Thylacine, was launched in 2015.

VELIMIR KHLEBNIKOV'S POETRY

translated by Boris Kokotov

I don't know whether the Earth is spinning or not...

I don't know whether the Earth is spinning or not,
It depends on whether the word fits the line.
I don't know whether apes were my grandparents,
Because I don't know what I want, sweet or sour.
But I do know that I want to seethe, I want the Sun
And the sinew of my hand to tremble together.
I want the ray of a star to kiss the ray of my eye,
As one deer kisses another (oh, their beautiful eyes!).
I want to believe there is something that remains
When a maiden's braids are replaced with, say, time.
I want to find the factor that is common to myself,
To the Sun, to the sky, to the pearl dust.

Я не знаю, Земля кружится или нет...

Я не знаю, Земля кружится или нет,
Это зависит, уложится ли в строчку слово.
Я не знаю, были ли моими бабушкой и дедом
Обезьяны, так как я не знаю, хочется ли мне сладкого или кислого.
Но я знаю, что я хочу кипеть и хочу, чтобы солнце
И жилу моей руки соединила общая дрожь.
Но я хочу, чтобы луч звезды целовал луч моего глаза,
Как олень оленя (о, их прекрасные глаза!).
Но я хочу верить, что есть что-то, что остается,
Когда косу любимой девушки заменить, например, временем.
Я хочу вынести за скобки общего множителя, соединяющего меня,
Солнце, небо, жемчужную пыль.

1909

Numbers

I'm peering at you, oh, numbers,
And you emerge clothed in animals, in their skins,
Leaning calmly on uprooted oaks.
You bestow unity between the snake-like movement
Of the universe's spine and the dance of a rocker.
You reveal centuries as teeth of a rapid laugh.
My eyes have opened, prophetically,
To learn what would be I when its numerator is one.

Числа

Я всматриваюсь в вас, о, числа,
И вы мне видитесь одетыми в звери, в их шкурах,
Рукой опирающимися на вырванные дубы.
Вы даруете единство между змееобразным движением
Хребта вселенной и пляской коромысла,
Вы позволяете понимать века, как быстрого хохота зубы.
Мои сейчас вещеобразно разверзлися зеницы
Узнать, что будет Я, когда делимое его -- единица.

1912

Neither fragile Japanese shadows...

Neither fragile Japanese shadows
Nor mellifluous Indian daughters
Sound as sorrowful
As the last supper orations.
On the verge of death all that has happened
Repeats itself quickly but differently.
And that is the basis
For the dance of death and its achievement.

Ни хрупкие тени Японии...

Ни хрупкие тени Японии,
Ни вы, сладкозвучные Индии дщери,
Не могут звучать похороннее,
Чем речи последней вечери.
Пред смертью жизнь мелькает снова,
Но очень скоро и иначе.
И это правило -- основа
Для пляски смерти и удачи.

1915

Oh Asia! You are my torment...

Oh Asia! You are my torment.
I fancy thunderclouds like maiden's brows,
And lengthy gatherings at night
Like the bloom of tender shoulders.
Where is the prophet of a new day?
Oh, If only Asia would cover my knees
With the hair of blue rivers,
And whisper her cryptic pleas,
And softly weep for joy
Drying her eyes with the tip of her braid --
She loved! She suffered! --
The vague soul of the universe.
And my heart would respond
To the struggles of Mahavira, and Zoroaster,
And Shivaji. I would be a contemporary
To those fallen fighters,
Asking questions and giving answers.
And you would cover my feet with your hair
Like a pile of blond money,
Whispering "Oh, Master,
Shouldn't we seek out
The ways to freedom
Today, together?"

О Азия! тобой себя я мучу...

О Азия! тобой себя я мучу.
Как девы брови, я постигаю тучу.
Как шею нежного здоровья.
Твои ночные вечеровья.
Где тот, кто день иной предрек?
О, если б волосами синих рек
Мне Азия покрыла бы колени
И дева прошептала таинственные пени,
И тихая, счастливая, рыдала,
Концом косы глаза суша.
Она любила! Она страдала!
Вселенной смутная душа.
И вновь прошли бы снова чувства,
И зазвенел бы в сердце бой:
И Мохавиры, и Заратустры,
И Саваджи, объятого борьбой.
Умерших их я был бы современник,
Творил ответы и вопросы.
А ты бы грудой светлых денег
Мне на ноги рассыпала бы косы.
«Учитель, -- мне шепча, --
Не правда ли, сегодня
Мы будем сообща
Искать путей свободней?»

1921

The lonely actor

While Achmatova's tears and songs
Were raining over Tsarskoe Selo,
I, unwinding the enchantress' ball of thread,
Dragged myself through the wilderness
Where impossibility was dying,
A tired actor
Striding forward.
Meanwhile the curly head
Of the subterranean bull was chomping people
In the dark caves
Amid impudent threats.
So wandering under the lunar crescent's spell
I was jumping canyons
And moved from one cliff to another
In the cloak of dreams,
Moved blindly
As winds of freedom
Propelled me and hit me with heavy rain.
And then I chopped the bull's head off from mighty shoulders
And put it against the wall.
A warrior of truth, I shook it and shouted to the world:
Look, here it is!
The curly head that crowds idolized!
And then, with horror,
I recognized -- no one could see me:
Eyes should be sown first,
A sower of eyes must come

Одинокий лицедей

И пока над Царским Селом
Лилось пенье и слезы Ахматовой,
Я, моток волшебницы
разматывая,
Как сонный труп, влачился по
пустыне,
Где умирала невозможность,
Усталый лицедей,
Шагая напролом.
А между тем курчавое чело
Подземного быка в пещерах темных
Кроваво чавкало и кушало людей

Как в сонный плащ, вечерний странник
Во сне над пропастями прыгал
И шел с утеса на утес.
Слепой, я шел, пока
Меня свободы ветер двигал
И бил косым дождем.
И бычью голову я снял с могучих мяс и кости
И у стены поставил.
Как воин истины я ею потрясал над миром:
Смотрите, вот она!
Вот то курчавое чело, которому пылали раньше толпы!
И с ужасом
Я понял, что я никем не видим,
Что нужно сеять очи,
Что должен сеятель очей идти!

1921 - 1922

If I turn humankind into a clock...

If I turn humankind into a clock
And show how the century hand moves
Wouldn't war disappear from our age
Like an obsolete letter from the alphabet?
Our kind got itself piles
From the springy chairs of war,
But I tell you what I learned about the future
Through my preterhuman dreams.
I know you are faithful wolves,
To your five shots I respond with a handshake.
Still, don't you hear the rustle of Fate's needle --
That wonderful seamstress?
I will flood existing government formations
With the deluge of my powerful thought,
I will reveal fabulous Kitezh
To acolytes of the old fatuity.
When the gang of globe's chairmen
Is offered to the hungry like a moldy bread crust,
Every existing government's nut
Will become obedient to our wrench.
And when a bearded girl
Throws the promised stone
You'll say: "This is exactly what
We were awaiting for centuries."
Ticking clock of humanity,
Turn my thought into your moving hand!
Some will grow as governments fail, others -- through the book.
Let the Earth be domineerless.
Chairglobegreatest!
This song must be like a dodder:
I tell you, the universe is the strike of a match
On the face of numbers,
And my thought is the master key
For a door behind which -- a suicide...

About the Author:

Velimir Khlebnikov (1885-1922) -- one of the great Russian poets of the 20-th century. His work was translated nearly into all European languages and many others. Perhaps the most comprehensive translation to English is The Selected Poems / Ed. R. Vroon, trans. P. Schmidt. – Harvard UP: Cambridge, 1997. Still, as you know, there is always a room for another try. Khlebnikov was called sometimes the poet for poets, meaning that his poetry isn't quite accessible for a common reader. To remedy that some translations are a bit more explanatory than the original text. My approach is different: I attempted to present his poems "as is", with their exotic semantics and twisted logic. It's up to critics, of course, to decide whether this attempt was successful.

Если я обращу человечество в часы...

Если я обращу человечество в часы
И покажу, как стрелка столетия движется,
Неужели из нашей времен полосы
Не вылетит война, как ненужная ижица?
Там, где род людей себе нажил почечуй,
Сидя тысячелетьями в креслах пружинной войны,
Я вам расскажу, что я из будущего чую
Мои зачеловеческие сны.
Я знаю, что вы -- правоверные волки,
Пятеркой ваших выстрелов пожимаю свои,
Но неужели вы не слышите шорох судьбы иголки,
Этой чудесной швеи?
Я затоплю моей силой, мысли потопом
Постройки существующих правительств,
Сказочно выросший Китеж
Открою глупости старой холопам.
И, когда председателей земного шара шайка
Будет брошена страшному голоду зеленою коркой,
Каждого правительства существующего гайка
Будет послушна нашей отвертке.
И, когда девушка с бородой
Бросит обещанный камень,
Вы скажете: "Это то,
Что мы ждали веками".
Часы человечества, тикая,
Стрелкой моей мысли двигайте!
Пусть эти вырастут самоубийством правительств и книгой -- те.
Будет земля бесповеликая!
Предземшарвеликая!
Будь ей песнь повеликою:
Я расскажу, что вселенная -- с копотью спичка
На лице счета.
И моя мысль -- точно отмычка
Для двери, за ней застрелившийся кто-то...

1922

About the Translator:

Boris Kokotov was born in Moscow, Russia. Currently he lives in Baltimore. He writes poems and short stories in both Russian and English languages. His translations from German Romantics were published in the anthology "Vek Perevoda" (The Century of Translation) in Moscow. His translation of Louise Glück's "The Wild Iris" was nominated for the best translation of the year 2012 in Russia.

NAILS

by Jennifer Lauren Collins

Nests in Corners

Gripping three fingers of my left hand,
my son drags me forward to a corner of our yard.

He moves aside dry brush, leaves, dirt that's been
fueling his little-boy musings for weeks, I'd bet,
and he gestures gently with a stick
to a now unhidden nest of snakes' eggs,
excited and unafraid.

His eyes are as wide and oval as the moist ovals
in front of us, almost hissing
with possibility
and with what another mother
(so different from myself)
has hidden away for our quiet findings.

His chatter, my fear, our sight:
how to tell him that we can't tell whether
these eggs will bring on little devils or god-sends
for the garden, for guarding--
how to tell him that what we see and what he wants
is not something to return to⬚
how to tell him that I am frightened and⬚
that, upon hatching,
the young are far more dangerous
than the grown.

Nails

You used to paint your nails,
fluttering them in the air
around us as if they were mosquitos
to dart and sting
their color along clothing
or my cheek,
threatening feminine touch
while drying on makeshift wind.

I'd be watching, waiting
for the tell-tale tap of your nails
along each other and then
elsewhere, proving dryness by virtue
of the fact that no color ran⬜
as if the test would disappear
from fabric or skin
if you were wrong.

You used to paint your nails
as if to draw my attention to your ends,
to your tips and lines and the
colors of your wants,
red or brick, solid or shining...
metallic or built
to withstand a conservative gaze.

You used to paint your nails
as if my gaze mattered,
as if you wanted my eyes on you
in moments of coloring,
the flirtation of adornment
something you played with and plied
over our afternoons,
every so often,
as if I couldn't watch.

I'd be watching, waiting,
when you used to paint your nails,
as I watch now in case you begin
again to play my attentions
along your lines, along your colors to be
so that I might stay my gaze
on yours, and lead elsewhere.

Until now, when I say you used to paint your nails
and I wonder where those colors went,
where your brushes lie now,
and whether I could ever turn away
again if you began again
to paint yourself while I watched,

flirting in my gaze with fluttering hands
and teasing darts of fingers
that never stayed my gaze for long,
though my mind won't turn from them now
as I'm watching, waiting,
for used-to-be colors to come
calling, intentions fluttering
and flirting with want, to stay my gaze,
wanting and waiting
on your painted nails
to dry.

Muscle Dreams

The muscle memory of the dream pulls,
stretching and stratifying
my thoughts to find acceptance
for what it is, to find its place
and hold my mind
still, occupied
in its thrall and waiting
for the next show.

Malignant, such a dream
as it is tears away at my present
until again my heart is held
open and wanting
for what it offers, unreal,
as tempting as marijuana
to a fourteen year old who's never
tasted smoke
and has no one
watching.

Back again, felt again,
the dream sloths my eyelids
shut against any other
potential and cries its own ending,
wanting my want
and waiting
to be held as it holds me
against it,
breathing heavy
and untested,
its skin the very particles
of mine,
and salivating
for the same
control.

After Time

The proof had once been
heavy and deep in her bones.
More glistening than any jewel,
more clear than arithmetic
made simple for children.
The proof had once been
there, ruling and real.

Was there a stage where
it faded from the foreground,
where the math grew more complex,
the jewel tarnished,
the bones more brittle,
the proof fading, but there?
Or had there been a moment missed?
Like that point in a Physics class
where students realize:
what we thought was real
is wrong,
what was simple
is something else
we only didn't know enough
to see.

Or perhaps there was no epiphany to be seen,
to be recognized as damning
anything at all.
Maybe it all had simply suddenly been gone,
charred beyond recognition into doubt,
its memory blurred
and ashen, its shadow
circling her finger
as she searched for what one lay
beneath the ring, in her bones,
proving love in more
than sight,
more than society,
where it could be felt
once upon a
time.

Cold Hands

We shut the windows, but our hands are still cold.
This is one of those nights where comfort can't be easily found⬚
not with the winds screaming along the street
and such a chill in the air that I'm not so sure we shouldn't
turn on the heat, July or otherwise.

Electricity bill be damned, blankets be damned,
what should be happening be damned.
It's hard to get warm tonight,
and harder to remember that this will pass.

In sweatshirts and frayed jeans,
we spill ourselves into wine and television,
creature comforts piled onto cold air and tired eyes
as if to numb our minds from complaint.

I feel the window, the cold against my skin,
and wonder at how spoiled we've become,
hiding from even this weather
in the middle of the summer,
stilled into luxury and poisoning our blood
as if it means nothing,
or everything.

We've shut the windows, locked the doors,
and offered kisses and flirtations,
our hands still cold,
and now we turn off the lights, room by room,
before burrowing beneath chilled blankets
and pretending our way toward sleep.
This is our luxury, with our large bed and our cold hands
and our locked windows and our bodies set apart
while together, as if safe.

This is our luxury, and perhaps it's not the electronic heat
that matters now, but the warmth that still
isn't felt, or even dreamed.

About the Author:

Jennifer Collins is a tattooed poet and animal lover who grew up in Virginia and has recently relocated to Cape Coral, FL., where she and her husband have four rescues – one neurotic hound, and three very spoiled cats. Her poetry has been published in various journals and nominated for a Pushcart by Puerto Del Sol, and she spends her summers as an instructor of creative writing and drama at the Cardigan Mountain School. Her first chapbook, Oil Slick Dreams, is available for sale from Finishing Line Press.

FLOWERS SCENES FOR THE PRIE-DIEU
by Anna Evas

1   Wisteria

How is it, being real,
you evoke the unreal?
In Tuam,

your aerial lavenders
suggest a soiree of elves.
In Tokyo,

the paintbrush of Hiroshige
turns you into a drape
for a shrine.

2   Mimosa

Your soft brooms
sweep the sky.
Nimbus pinks,

the kilim-rug texture
of your leaves
tickle the breeze.

What magic
changes my rags
to feathers?

3   Black-eyed Susan

I wear you like a jaapi hat⬚
the dome on top
brown as a clove.

Your sunup petals
shade my vision.
It's a secret

how fields open,
the dark sweats spice,
my green eye wanders.

4   Dying Prairie Rose

Candelabra
on a sharp green stem,

I ritualize
my own disappearance.

First petals drop,
then sepals shrivel

like thirsty tongues⬚
divested on an altar.

5   Violettes Cristallisees

Tyrian purple,
your candied petals

flavor my humiliations
with a hint

of French soap.
Freshened,

I straighten like a tree
roosting with martins.

About the Author:

Anna Evas poems and essays have appeared in literary and medical journals, including Michigan Quarterly Review and Irises. She makes her living as a pianist, composer and lyricist.

GNOMON AND GLASS

by Robert René Galván

Gnomon and Glass *

Time's wing casts a shadow
on the spun world;

The pendulous moon
beats the shore into
grains of sand;

We fill the glass
and watch them drop
through the elegant waist
so that we don't forget,

Read in the shades
the time we have left.

RRG
1.22.18

A gnomon is the part of a sundial that casts a shadow.

Cheney's Heart

Lifted gently from the cage,
Deprived of the final light,
I continue to sing beyond the body:

A cold cell for the journey,
A last act of kindness for another's breath.

Bathed and caressed, finely stitched
To a plexus of streams and tributaries –
A jolt from the coil, the vena cava floods
And I awaken in a strange room.

This was once unthinkable.

What if I had relieved
Mahler's fading metronome?
He may have lived longer,
But would I have spoiled his muse?

And this fellow, whose own heart
So often failed him,
Will he become a better man?

Robert René Galván
9.5.16

Laniakea *

There was a time when ships fell off the edge of the world,
Sails blown by the puffed cheeks of the West Wind,
The open jaws of Leviathan waiting in the abyss.

An upended fish bowl contained the firmament:
The clouds, the sun and moon, and all the stars –
The only escape through death's door.

Scurrying about with crude instruments
We etched elaborate maps, now obsolete,
The face of the globe morphed as nations
Rose and fell, as even the gods dropped
From the sky when heretics breached the outer shell.

The spyglass gave way to vast arrays of electric ears
That sprang up in the desert like grey mushrooms;
On the highest peaks, stewards of the glass
Map the cosmos, a great eye beyond the clouds
Peers toward the beginning of time,

Gives shape to the chartless, a plexus of storms
That appears as a delicate eyelash, the Milky Way
Like a mote on a feather.

We cross the field of stars back to the body,
Drawn with irresistible force,
Into its inner filaments, its colony of cells,
Beyond the orbits in its base minerals
Where we retreat to an immeasurable heaven.

Robert René Galván 1.11.18

Hawaiian for "immeasurable heaven"

Hibaku Jumoku (Survivor Trees)

In the umbra of the skeletal Domū
A bough of yellow butterflies,
A swarm of gingko leaves,
Belies a wasteland wrought
By a malevolent windfall
On that August morning.

Toxic spores still linger
In the resilient earth,
But stubborn roots push back
With green shoots and burnished petals;

The stewards vanished without warning
In a cataclysm of light,
Their shadows fixed on the sidewalks
In mid-stride without a chance for astonishment;
In the distance, a lingering death.

Embraced by the shade of an ash oceans away,
I cast a threnody upon these leaves,
Begin to fathom my vulnerability
To things I cannot sense, or foresee.

I mourn and lament,
But find solace in the persistent persimmon
And its healing flesh.

Robert René Galván
7.6.17

Yggdrasil*

Tree of Life:

Guardian of the two worlds,
Its roots penetrate the abyss,
Its branches the heavens.

Giver of wisdom:

Odin once lashed himself to its trunk,
Lost an eye to the ravens,
But gained the secret of the runes,
And with a single bolt begat us from its wood.

Diviners stole their staves from the shoots,
Moved between worlds, serpents fled its shadow,
The gods held council beneath its span.

Sentinel from a narrow portal of poured stone,
The arms stir with the approach of the North wind,
Begin to molt their myriad sails.

It has known the changing faces of the moon,
Been a sieve of rain and sun,
Stood naked in the snow,
And voiced my morning thoughts
With its many tongues.

The old woman next door sweeps vehemently:
"Too much leaves!"

Robert René Galván
9.21.16

*The Viking word for Ash

About the Author:

Robert René Galván, born in San Antonio, resides in New York City where he works as a professional musician and poet. He has taught at Manhattan College, The College of Mount Saint Vincent and the Brooklyn Conservatory of Music. His last collection of poems is entitled, Meteors, published by Lux Nova Press. His poetry will be featured in upcoming issues of the Hawaii Review and Right Hand Pointing.

CANTICLE

by Riley Bounds

Canticle.

At the tail end of the earth
there's some landfill
of songs and screams
that were
all carried
in the jaws
of strays
and buried where
our relative
inclinations,
ennui,
meet the cosmic
and sift into
the aurora
ebb,
and it's still lost
on me
whether I'll
remember
from the pirouetting
particles
the glass
I've crushed
underfoot
or the futility
of every
levity,
cadenza,
but I doubt
I'll mind
since all strays
die alone
anyway.

Altar Call.

God pulls over
on the roadside
to dump her
in the bar ditch.
She lies
wilted,
the outer
rot,
the inner
lie,
she was elect for
a night; He
illumined her
only for
a time,
all the just
forsaken.
Satan crosses
from the cornfield
and absence,
and he hands God
a twenty,
and sacrifice burns
dim in taillights
as God
goes
to get gas
while the
Negative One
crouches over her,
working at
her belt.

About the Author:

Riley Bounds was raised in Alex, Oklahoma. He earned a BA in Creative Writing from the University of Central Oklahoma and is currently pursuing an MA in Philosophy from Talbot School of Theology. He plans to do doctoral work in theology. He resides in La Mirada, California.

SONG CHANGES

by Emily Brummett

They would go to the bar
every week after work,
to "Karaoke Thursday".
Together.

After graduating,
she moved in with him:
each drowning in eight years
of student loans,
ready to start their lives.

She knew he started going more,
"a regular" status
while she was only invited
on Thursdays

She was fed up
with his excuses and
the way he'd come back–
fingers and mouth
stained Marlboro
and jeans acid-washed Bud Light.

So now,
on Karaoke Thursdays,
she's in the apartment watching Late Night,
while he's swaying left to right,
singing "Don't Stop Believing,"
a beer in hand,
gulping whiskey neats
between song changes and bathroom breaks.

She envisioned their lives together:
Marriage, kids, white-picket-fences
Prolonging her decision to leave, but

she walks out without any argument
on his hangover,
because he was running late
to his daily five-dollar bottomless drafts
and spark of an unfiltered open-mic.

About the Author:

Emily Brummett is in her last year as an undergrad student, studying International Business. In her spare time she enjoys writing poetry, journaling and traveling.

REDTOP, MO

by Robert Eastwood

Concord Airport, CA.

She sits, restored, on tarmac,
blunt-nose-twin-barrels erect—
a squat, ponderous bird in California sun.

Old men, the stooped gray,
waver into line, peer up into her bay.
Aboard, they balance & crouch.
They mull dark interiors.
  Oppresive night, with cramps,
climb to buckle in radial thunder,
blood-red lights, throttled fire,
 taxi into wet wind.
They thread the old bird,
a docile brood, touch once more her skin.
They tune to chirruped frequencies.
  Blood-spray over yellow tanks, breeches'
rain, plink of casings.
For others flak torments air, the wings.
Some know shrieks, pissed thighs, blue ice whistling by.

She proffers decaled cups, an old wife,
tee-shirts emblazoned Liberator.
Liberator watercolors in shiny slip-covers.
Liberator wares spread on a folding table
beneath a sheltering wing,
No one buys. A wizened captain
collects a toll, remembering
how he counted missions.
and missing crews.

Griffith Observatory, L.A.

Ask Stephen King or R. L. Stine,
a ghost story begins with sun
through a window, & lilt
of friendly voices. No Ravens. No dread.
That rises gradual as smoke from the light.
In '44, Dad worked for Lockheed,
& each evening he drove home smelling
of machine oil, his '36 Buick's muffler
bellowing at the climb up North Verdugo Road.
One Sunday, a man knocked at our door
with a woman, & a boy—a boy a bit older than me.
A childhood buddy of Dad's, the man seemed older.
He'd driven his family from Kansas,
hoped for a job at Dad's aircraft plant.
Mom had been ready for them.
We crammed in the Buick
& drove to Griffith Park for a picnic.
After egg salad sandwiches & iced tea,
Dad took us up the hill to the observatory.
On the parapet, the Kansas family gaped
at L. A.'s city hall & Hollywood below us.
The Kansas boy owned a telescope,
shiny silver, sliding out & in of itself,
& we picked out Grauman's,
& corridors of famous boulevards.
I looked through the magical scope
at the larger world, so clear that afternoon
in warm breath of Santa Anas.
I could see webs of blue veins
on the boy's hands, as though his skin
had been scoured. His eyes sparkled
like earrings mom wore some Sundays,
& he wore a corduroy jacket, even in the sun.
Before they drove off that evening,
the boy handed me his telescope.
Dad says he'll get me a bigger one,
one that will reach the moon.
I thought, how lucky can a guy get!
Too soon I spied a far country
dividing the moving & the forever still.
Farther yet, as far as Kansas, a white, wasted body.

Diablo Lodge, Danville, CA

What will they do when we can't stand
staring to the flag, when dogs ignore us?
(They bring dogs to lick fingers, dogs
with joyous eyes sense the strange
murk & don't turn from our smell.
It clears with their tails. They cadge
hands that search for warmth, lift
boredom, a stew of Lysol & piss.)
Glossy doors sense me as I come,
they slip into shadows. Will it be years
flat screens flicker everywhere?
We circle like battered Conestogas,
all of us arrived to a barren place. Dreads
chatter in echoes, in deepening canyons.

Redtop, MO

Uncle followed, knee-deep, past gnarled elms,
splay-rooted sycamores, rocks like slabs
from torn graves.
We sloshed on testy feet,
our pants rolled to the groin.
He'd hardly noticed me,
but now, at twelve, I felt chosen,
taken for a wade in Redtop creek.

Perhaps he'd open up his mysteries,
his time on Leyte, the malarial shakes,
his ringed, turtle eyes.
He went ahead, energetically, calves balled
as fists, stone to stone.
I dragged through water toward shore.

"Hey general," he called
from a canted rock, "no cameras there."
Where he thought we were
that humid afternoon I couldn't say.
Shadows concealed his face.
I've forgotten how it ended.
The puzzlement I do remember,
my standing mute as he drifted off upstream.

Long after, I opened a tattered Life
in an old book store. There, the photo
taken one October day in '44: MacArthur,
shades like locusts' eyes, strides knee-deep—
the resolute old egotist's ample khakis
cling to his knees,
his cold cob pipe.
Soldiers perch above on a grounded barge,
watching as he & his brood of officers
clamor through shallows toward shore,
past sycophants, the Graflex wielders,
& a placid audience of palms.

Santa Monica Cancer Center, CA

"...and in this moment, like a swift intake of breath,
the rain came."
—Truman Capote: Other Voices Other Rooms

He enters smiling, though the room is frigid.
Invasive creatures detest the cold.
Somewhere inside his body are monsters
that repulse a caress, a warm hand.

Attitude is an oily sop for recovery.
Just one of several he's been slathered with.
A pixilated screen lulls the seated,
on and on: a soft susurrus on tropical sands,

a pristine sky's royal blues, boundlessly
smothering a teal-feathered sea.
Recurring murmurs, faint cloudlets of breath,
sighs out of faces that have an open stare,

and yet, other sounds—palm fronds'
dry rustle, froth's liquid fret as it slips to the sea.
Or are they rain's persistent pelt at the windows,
hopeful trills of the runnels?

About the Author:

Robert Eastwood's work has appeared widely, most recently in The Bird's Thumb, Up The Staircase Quarterly, The Peacock Journal, Steel Toe Review, Halfway Down The Stairs, Spry Literary Journal, Naugatuck River Review, 3Elements Review, Poet Lore, and Triggerfish Critical Review. His chapbooks are The Welkin Gate, Over Plainsong, and Night of the Moth, by Small Poetry Press. His book Snare: was published in 2016 by Broadstone Books. His second book, Romer, is forthcoming in August from Etruscan Press. He is Vice-President of the Ina Coolbrith Circle, a nearly century-old group fostering poetry founded by the first Poet Laureate of California.

DAMN THIS DAY

by Andrew Spence

Damn This Day

I will go for a walk. Today I will go to the coffee shop.
Elevated, to see the next town. Elevated to see where the kids play in the streets.
I am here to drink black dark liquid made with poor labor and signed waivers.

I get the spiced roast, because I deserve the kick in the mouth.
Behind me, in line, there is a man in dark clothing.

He is made of dirt and creepy crawlies. He drinks mud with a grin.
He is made of mold and candy corn dropped last Halloween under your bed.
He steals my coffee and throws it at the Red Head behind to counter.

She turns to me, her burnt bad braces spring. He ran before she saw. She only sees me.

I just want to show her it all doesn't matter.
I just want to show her that we are made of mud and hateful things.
I just want to show her that we are made of moldy candy corn,

but she points to the street out the fogged up coffee shop window.
The kids outside on the street shuffle past snowboards in hand with hateful stares.
I turn to leave and with no drink

Think I might just dehydrate before autumn ever comes again.
Soon the kids will pound the pavement
Soon the kids will prey on the weak.

Tin Foil From Fukushima

No Rain
Not often // Government Conspiracy Theory #1

the Tin Foil is made
in Fukushima now
The Believers are contaminated
rain could wash it away
they know
they sent their weather changers,
those weird orbs,
to stop it to keep it
contaminated
we might
die
here.

I send in workers to stop the leak
one by one they come back
green
glow worms burrow
out their ears

broken larceny plans at rebuilding
buildings of some many lost blue prints

nobody is in the mansion of my childhood
only the old man who told me
ALIENS ARE REAL
is hiding in the basement bunker he made himself
instead of having children

children
they told me I have those
somewhere
they are not contaminated because they are so far away
they are in pure space
like a mountain that kept going up and up and up
and up
where nothing could breath
and nothing was happy not to breath
because it was nothing
That is where the children are
they are happy because
they want nothing and have nothing
and see the nothing

I see nothing and wonder
how much longer
I can keep the satellites pointed
away
keep the non-believers
from believing
I am afraid
if they find it
if they believe
I am scared
because
then
I am not special
I am just a man
with space children
and radiation poisoning
and friends with glow worms
burrowed out their ears

We all our helpful hints
from the alt-news sources
they gave out the secret signal
the secret signal for government take over
everyone who was a believer knew about the signal
an article about always telling the truth
then we knew it was all over
we the truth seekers
abandoned
to lies once again
even if it still sounded real
it was not
the signal proved it

About the Author:

Andrew Spence is a broken hurricane of non-sense waiting to crash onto the beach of your boredom. 25 years old and currently residing in Denver, Colorado, Spence first grew up in Midwestern Ohio suburbia before he fell in love with mountain hikes. Recently graduated in the fields of Asian Studies and English Education, Andrew's poems often reflect his experiences abroad intermingled between the beautiful and sometimes disturbing images of being a lifelong learner in a world so quick to teach him a lesson. Andrew makes a hobby out of poetry, skateboards, alcohol and book collecting. He knows very well that he wouldn't be anywhere without his monthly calendar with pictures of basset hounds and late night long-board rides full of self-loathing.

The Philosopher and the Golem traces a very rootless man's journey from obscurity to literary hero and back to obscurity again, and from love with a human to love with a mythological creature, a golem. Karl Pringle, a PhD student in Philosophy, seemed to have a burgeoning career in academia until he punches out his academic supervisor. Haunted by his actions, he roams aimlessly about the city until he receives a phone call that changes his life. That call leads him to a treasure trove of literary works that, in a quest to rid himself of the black cloud that plagues him, he passes off as his own. Literary success follows but his now perfect life, which includes a girlfriend, slowly begins to unravel. His downward spiral leads him to dabble in the paranormal, and he soon replaces his human girlfriend with a female golem, a creature brought forth by a rogue rabbi from the mud and clay of a river. The two embark on a life of debauchery, which includes robbing a bank. Karl continues to take greater risks until his sanity starts to slip terrifyingly out of control.

Originally from Montreal, Jerry Levy now resides in Toronto, Canada. His short stories have appeared in many literary magazines such as The Nashwaak Review, Parchment, Lowestoft Chronicle, and in 2013, a collection of 14 stories - Urban Legend - was published by Thistledown Press (the lead story in the collection - Urban Legend - was given honorable mention in the well-known Canadian Authors Association contest 'Ten Stories High'). He is also the author of 4 children's books. He is a regular judge for the Writer's Union of Canada's annual Short Prose Contest and occasionally does a similar task for an organization called Vea'havta, judging short stories from people who are marginalized and who have experienced homelessness at some point. He has a B.Comm. degree from Concordia University in Montreal and a teaching certificate (Teaching English as a Second Language) from CCLCS in Toronto. The Philosopher and the Golem is his first published novel. His website can be accessed at: http://jerrylevy.weebly.com

THE PHILOSOPHER AND THE GOLEM

A novel

By Jerry Levy

Paperback: 340 pages

Publisher: Adelaide Books (July 2018)

Language: English

ISBN-10: 1-949180-09-3

ISBN-13: 978-1-949180-09-1

Product Dimensions:
6 x 1 x 9 inches

DANCE UPON THE FORREST FLOOR

Poems

By Donny Barilla

Paperback: 150 pages

Publisher: Adelaide Books
(July 2018)

Language: English

ISBN-10: 1-949180-10-7

ISBN-13: 978-1-949180-10-7

Product Dimensions:
6 x 1 x 9 inches

Donny Barilla, a poet covering the realms: human intimacy, nature, mythology, theology, and man's relationship with death and the departed, has been writing for over three decades. He writes daily and strives to renew himself as an artist from page to page and body of work to body of work. Very seldom does he take a break from writing as he views it as a full-time job. He lives a reclusive lifestyle and finds himself clinging close to nature and all her elements. His home state of Pennsylvania strikes chords of poetic depth about him as he finds loveliness from cornfield to meadow.

Whether it's feelings of love, intimacy, or a special closeness, he maintains the feeling that death does not take these with him/her to the grave. Emotions and feeling outlast the flesh of the human body. Human intimacy draws near an enigmatic spiritual passion which conquers all on the prismatic scale of experience. When speaking of mythology Donny says, "myths were created to make sense of feelings which are complicated by very nature. They are perhaps more easily understood through persons greater than oneself. As for theology, a disciplined aspect, incorporates quite finely with passions and secured poetic comforts.

In one of Donny's poems, he states, "Geese flood northern skies, mushrooms crop a blooming glade, her scent lingers slow." Here reads a wonderful example of how Donny incorporates sex and intimacy with nature. In truth he has always felt there is no real difference. There rests a comfort in nature which clearly exists on the same parallel as sex and sexuality.

Donny lives calmly and mostly to himself as he draws inspiration for Asian poets, such as: Yasano Akiko, Basho, Issa, Tu Fu, and Ryokon. Finding beautiful contrast as well as condensed, packed, short lines which fulfill the reader takes Donny on a spiritual journey. This, in turn, brings him to a enlightenment of a strong poetic nurture which he strives to duplicate with each poem. As a general rule, but not always, Donny writes poems no more than a page. He feels the piece should be found, read, digested, and understood as a single experience. He also believes the sounds of the words chosen create the images, not the definition of the words. Therefore, clear images resonate through the palate of the reader. These ideas have the reader enjoying the poem in a more mysterious sense rather than a chore to probe one's way through.

Donny has written eleven books of poetry, nine of which were self-published. He has dozens of poems in journals and magazines, as well as twenty books in libraries (public and academic). He placed in a contest, the Adelaide Voices Literary Award, as top finalist. He has hosted six poetry readings and two book signings.

Lush Life is a collection of short stories that range from the adventures and creative play of girls dreaming in 1970s Brooklyn to the wanderings and aspirations of a poet in the fairylike forests of Finland. These stories will appeal to adult readers of all ages and gender that enjoy New York City stories as well as stories that capture the adventures and aspirations of dreamers and drifters, poets, artists, and near-do-wells wandering or at play in Brooklyn, Spain and Italy, and even as far away as the foggy forests of Finland.

Tinka Harvard is a writer and theologian with a gift for interweaving insightful ideas for inspired living with theology, philosophy, and the arts. She shares internationally beautiful concepts and tools that help to usher in more peace, joy, and well being in our every day lives. A graduate of Union Theological Seminary at Columbia University in New York City with a Master's in Divinity, she offers her intellectual talents in preaching, inspirational speaking, workshops and retreats.

Tinka's writing has appeared most recently in publications including StepAway Magazine, The Independent Literary Magazine, Adelaide Voices Anthology 2018, and Polychrome Ink.

http://www.tinkaharvard.com

LUSH LIFE

Short stories

By Tinka Harvard

Paperback: 150 pages

Publisher: Adelaide Books
(July 2018)

Language: English

ISBN-10: 1-949180-11-5

ISBN-13: 978-1-949180-11-4

Product Dimensions:
6 x 1 x 9 inches

THE THREE
OF US

Short stories

By Mike Cohen

Paperback: 210 pages

Publisher: Adelaide Books (July 2018)

Language: English

ISBN-10: 1-949180-14-X

ISBN-13: 978-1-949180-14-5

Product Dimensions: 6 x 1 x 9 inches

"In choosing the short stories gathered here I couldn't help but be reminded of Aristotle's prescriptive elements for drama: a protagonist, an antagonist, and a complicator. The reader of these stories might also note that Aristotle could have been writing as well about a three person family: mother, father, and one child.

This, of course, was the underpinning of my family's drama where Aristotelian lessons played out, lessons reinforced for me later in literature and on the proper stage in the plays of Ibsen, O'Neil, and Miller featuring conflicted families.

Our drama emerged when my family abruptly left Minnesota to resettle on the west coast during the middle of my fifth-grade school year. Nothing compelled my family to move: no new job, no newly purchased home, none of the myriad events that might trigger a dramatic relocation.

However, that sudden departure from the Midwest foreshadowed three decades of deepening discord between my parents. As I grew older I realized that whatever the stated reasons for relocating, a deeper desire on my mother's part had been hidden. She wanted to leave my father. This accounted for her anxiousness to depart even if we as a family were utterly unprepared for what lay ahead.

While I was hardly surprised that my parents separated, the timing – late into their senior years - felt as bizarre and awkward as the abruptness of our hejira west so many decades earlier. My mother informed me thereafter that her life with Dad had been "A Greek tragedy." Aristotle again.

The disintegration of my parent's marriage taught me not to ignore the daily opportunity to experience some personal truth. Though invisible, wounds left by unspoken longings and unsatisfied needs can be lethal.

By exploring moments in which hidden personal yearnings are exposed and blind spots are illuminated (sometimes with discomfort but not without humor) perhaps we may see ourselves with humility and those about us with greater empathy and compassion. If one or more of my tales strikes you as having been successful in illuminating one of those moments I will be gratified." (Prolog - The Three of Us)

Mike Cohen practiced law for over four decades and now specializes in estates, trusts, and related litigation. He attended the Portland State Haystack Summer Workshop Conference from 1992-96 and the University of Washington Extension Writing Workshop from 1995-98. He had studied with Craig Lesley, Tom Spanbauer, Whitney Otto, and the late Robert Gordon. He recently self-published his first novel, Rivertown Heroes. He holds a JD from Georgetown Law and a BA in Zoology from the University of Washington. His short stories have been published in Streetlight Magazine, Adelaide Literary Magazine and others. He lives with his family in the Pacific Northwest.

THE UPROOTED AND OTHER STORIES

by Michael Washburn

Paperback: 180 pages

Publisher: Adelaide Books
(July 2018)

Language: English

ISBN-10: 1-949180-13-1

ISBN-13: 978-1-949180-13-8

Product Dimensions:
6 x 1 x 9 inches

Headlines about displacement, identity, and alienation are in the news every day, but little real insight into these issues is available from Twitter feeds and short news items. The role of a fiction writer at the present juncture is not just to be always observing, as Henry James had it, but also to explore and analyze issues of global concern in all their richness and complexity.

Michael Washburn's short stories, some of which have appeared in national and small-circulation periodicals, are reflections of a fractured world. They depict the adventures and trials of people unsure of their place in the world and desperate for a sense of belonging. Here are just a few highlights:

In "The Hunting Party," a fatal confrontation in rural Wisconsin throws tensions between newcomers and longtime residents into sharp relief. This powerful, suspenseful, and timely story has eerie and haunting overtones of Norse mythology.

In "Dissonance," a journalist undergoing specialized therapy at a resort finds his bourgeois world increasingly fragmented as memories of trauma assume a new, frightening immediacy.

In "The Convict's Tale," the administrators of a prison on a remote island find ways to turn sociologist Erving Goffman's theory of the "total institution" into a reality, with terrifying results for the inmates and ultimately for themselves.

In "The Detour," a naïve young American finds himself lost in the wilds of Romania at a time of heightened global tensions, but the people he encounters do not conform at all to his blinkered expectations.

In "Voyeur," a lonely man in a hotel comes face to face with the real social beliefs and attitudes of townspeople who have reluctantly sent their young generations out into the cities, and the truth is more shocking than any nightmare.

These tales about the theme of "uprootedness" have riveted and captivated readers, and now they are available for publication as a book.

Michael Washburn is a Brooklyn-based writer and journalist. His short stories have appeared in numerous journals and magazines including Green Hills Literary Lantern, Rosebud, Adelaide, Weird Fiction Review, New Orphic Review, Stand, Still Point Arts Quarterly, Lakeview Journal, Black Fox Literary Magazine, Bryant Literary Journal, Meat for Tea, Marathon Literary Review, Prick of the Spindle, and other publications. Michael is the author of an acclaimed cover story in the Philadelphia City Paper, entitled "Home and Abroad." He is the author of a previous short fiction collection, Scenes from the Catastrophe (2016).

THE SONS AND DAUGHTERS OF TOUSSAINT

A novel

by Keith Madsen

Paperback: 340 pages

Publisher: Adelaide Books
(June 2018)

Language: English

ISBN-10: 1-949180-02-6

ISBN-13: 978-1-949180-02-2

Product Dimensions:
6 x 0,9 x 9 inches

In this commercial fiction novel with an historical backdrop, The Sons and Daughters of Toussaint, Isaac Breda seeks to renew the revolution of his famous forefather, Toussaint Louverture. He is depressed that a revolution which had so much potential, and which had cost so much, seemed to have so little to show for it. He resolves to start a non-violent revolution to make their freedom real. In the first half of the novel, the story is told by alternating chapters between historical sections, telling the story of Toussaint and his compatriots, and contemporary sections, where Isaac seeks to renew Toussaint's spirit in his people.

Isaac's story intersects with that of his best friend's beautiful sister, Marie-Noëlle. At first she is mainly focused on moving to the United States and making her fame and fortune in modeling. But her character develops into a powerful agent of change herself. When Isaac dies at the hands of entrenched interests in Haiti, the revolution falls on her shoulders. The immense challenge transforms both her and her country.

Keith Madsen is a retired minister who is using his retirement to pursue a lifelong interest in writing fiction. In addition to writing, he has also acted in community theater, having particularly enjoyed playing the roles of Jack (C.S.) Lewis in Shadowlands, Atticus Finch in To Kill a Mockingbird, and Porfiry in Crime and Punishment. This background in drama has helped him both with character development and his dramatic touch in writing. Keith finds that being part of helping characters come alive is one of his greatest life pleasures. He has visited Haiti four times, while helping to build a grade school there. In the process he has become fascinated by Haitian culture and history, a fascination which inspired the writing of this novel. Keith has published short stories in Mobius: A Journal of Social Change, Talking River, Short Story America and Adelaide. He is a member of the Pacific Northwest Writers' Association. Keith lives in East Wenatchee, Washington with his wife Cathy, where he enjoys teaching chess to grade school children.

Adelaide Literary Magazine
OUR FIRST THREE YEARS

adelaidemagazine.org